Poor Labouring Men

History Workshop Series

General Editor

Raphael Samuel, *Ruskin College, Oxford*

Already published

Village Life and Labour
Miners, Quarrymen and Salt Workers
Rothschild Buildings
East End Underworld
People's History and Socialist Theory
Culture, Ideology and Politics
Sex and Class in Women's History
Living the Fishing
Fenwomen
Late Marx and the Russian Road
Theatres of the Left 1880–1935

Routledge & Kegan Paul
London, Boston, Melbourne and Henley

Alun Howkins

Lecturer in History,
School of Cultural and Community Studies,
University of Sussex

Poor Labouring Men Rural Radicalism in Norfolk 1872-1923

First published in 1985
by Routledge & Kegan Paul plc

14 Leicester Square, London, WC2H 7PH, England

9 Park Street, Boston, Mass. 02108, USA

464 St Kilda Road, Melbourne,
Victoria 3004, Australia and

Broadway House, Newtown Road,
Henley-on-Thames, Oxon RG9 1EN, England

Set in Bembo, 10 on 12pt
by Columns of Reading
and printed in Great Britain
by T.J. Press (Padstow) Ltd, Cornwall

Library of Congress Cataloging in Publication Data

Howkins, Alun.
Poor labouring men.
(History workshop series)
Includes index.
1. Agricultural laborers—England—Norfolk—History.
2. Trade-unions—Agricultural laborers—England—
Norfolk—History.   3. Radicalism—England—Norfolk—
History.   4. Rural poor—England—Norfolk—History.
5. Norfolk—Rural conditions.   I. Title.   II. Series.
HD1535.N67H69 1985   322'.2   84-15941

British Library CIP data available

ISBN 0-7102-0295-4 (pbk.)

Contents

This book is dedicated to
the past of my family
and to its future.

Jack Howkins 1886–1917
Lillian Howkins 1914–1980
Harold Howkins 1913–

and the kids
Simon, Ben, Jonathan and Benedict

There's some do say the farmer's best, but I must needs say no,
If it weren't for we poor labouring men, what would the farmers
  do
They would beat up all their old stuff until some new come in;
For there's never a trade in all England like we poor labouring
  men.

Illustrations

Plates

Figures

Tables

Introduction

The history of the rural poor

This study began from a paradox. The English, a predominantly urban nation are to a remarkable degree obsessed with the 'rural'. One only has to look at the Country Book Club and the continuing large sale of books of rural memoirs and country life to see this in literary terms. This phenomenon has been analysed to some extent by Raymond Williams, and more recently, Wiener.[1] Less obvious, but probably more important, is the extent to which cultural images of the rural predominate in areas like advertising. In these the recent (up to about 80 years ago) past becomes a symbol for stability, continuity and purity (especially in food and drink) which is contrasted implicitly with the problems of late twentieth-century Britain.[2]

Yet, given this cultural dominance, when I began this work, the rural was remarkably unstudied, especially in the area of labour history. The great advances made in the 1960s by Marxist and socialist historians like E.P. Thompson and Eric Hobsbawm had, by and large, left the rural areas alone. This was not surprising. Coming from a labour movement tradition which was overwhelmingly urban, and distrusting the rural as either 'backward' or, at best, 'utopian', they set out to write the history of that movement on its terms. Hence Thompson's great study of the early nineteenth century is, by his own admission 'inadequate to its theme', in relation to the rural poor.[3]

There were then, and are now, obvious exceptions to this rule. These concern two relatively brief periods – that of the 'Swing' riots, and that of Arch's union in the 1870s and early 1880s. The twenty or so years around the Swing period has attracted a good deal of attention, especially since the publication of Hobsbawm and Rude's Study in 1969.[4] Similarly Pamela Horn and J.P.D. Dunbabin's work on Arch's union, although this has problems, has covered some aspects of that period.[5]

What is lacking is both a general 'labour' history of the nineteenth-century countryside and specific studies of the different groups within the rural poor. For instance we have to go back to Hasbach's work in the 1890s for a study of the English labourer which even begins to comprehend the totality of labouring life.[6] Perhaps more surprising is the lack of detailed academic studies of the various problems of rural life. There is, for instance, no study of the rural poor with anything like the authority of Gareth Stedman Jones's study of London,[7] no studies of the artisans and tradesmen to compare with those of Gray and Crossick,[8] and most surprising of all no studies of agricultural trades unionism outside the articles already referred to. The exception here is Reg Grove's excellent history of the National Union of Agricultural and Allied Workers, but this is now 35 years old and has many problems.[9]

What we are left with, in terms of the history of the rural poor, are a number of beacons, standing above the surrounding darkness, lighting a small area with no obvious route from one to the other.

The other source of light one might look to is even less revealing – that of the academic discipline of agricultural history. A journal and a learned society has existed in this field since the 1940s but has concentrated ever more on legitimating agricultural history as a branch of economic history. This is not to deny the importance of this approach. An understanding of problems of the land market, of cropping and so on, are a vital part of the study of rural areas. However, there is little room within this approach for the human inhabitants of the countryside.

The main area in which there are a number of exceptions to these strictures is the area in which the present study lies, that of local studies of various kinds. These vary enormously in quality from the locally produced pamphlet to the full-scale academic study. Many of them have been influential to the writing of this study and where that is the case they figure either in the text or the footnotes. However, one or two of them should be singled out. First, James Obelkevich's study of religion in north Lincolnshire, which is in fact so much more than that, was influential on the writing of Chapters 1 and 3 of this study.[10] Similarly the single most important historical study of the farm worker yet published, Ian Carter's *Farm Life in North East Scotland*, although about an area very different from Norfolk, had a profound influence on the whole of this work.[11] Finally the essays in Raphael Samuel's *Village Life and Labour*, as well as the people involved in that project, mark this study throughout.[12]

Norfolk and history

When I began work on the history of the rural poor some twelve years ago I began in Oxfordshire. This was simply on the premise of 'dig where you stand' – I was a student at Ruskin College, I was born in Oxfordshire and had been involved in the countryside all my life. In 1973 I went as a graduate student to Essex University and decided to work on Norfolk. Here my choice of subject was perhaps more rational. As an ex-member of the NUAAW I wanted to work on that union's history, and as the union had been founded in Norfolk, that seemed a logical place to begin at least.

I went from a very conventional history 'school' at Oxford to a thoroughly different one within the Department of Sociology at Essex. The shock was enormous. Sociologists, then at least, had scant regard for history which they saw as little better than antiquarianism and the student was pushed in quite different directions involving all the classic concepts of 1970s sociological theory. This was both stimulating and frustrating at the same time and some of that argument is here, especially in Chapter 2. However, the main reason for going to Essex was nothing to do with sociology, it was to do with oral history. I had begun using a tape recorder myself in 1969 in connection with a study (still unpublished) on poaching and had found it enormously stimulating, not only in what people could tell but also in the nuance they gave to historical material. Tone, accent, ways of speech transformed my historical understanding. More important was the way in which the questions asked by the historian of a particular period were changed.[13]

For instance much of the emphasis in this study on conflict at farm level and on the localism of much political and union activity came directly from interviews. Similarly the emphasis on work and the interpretation of the seasonal pattern of labour as a determinate of conflict also came virtually exclusively from interviews. Most importantly of all, talking to the old men and women who had worked the land of Norfolk in the latter part of the period of which I was writing, permeated the whole texture of my work in a way which altered my approach to the subject from being a 'labour historian' to being, I hope, a historian of the Norfolk labourer.

In this change, which is perhaps not as total as it ought to have been, the radicalism and trades unionism of the Norfolk labourer remained central but not as a history of organisation. Instead, what I have tried to do is to set up a relationship between different kinds of organisation, chapels, unions, political parties, and labouring life in a local context. This context is not prescribed by academic considerations but by the reality of experience.

The phrase 'Norfolk do different' is perhaps not as meaningless as it seems, and nor is it as specific. Central to this study is the notion that for most of the period up to the early 1920s the culture and consciousness of the rural poor was local as opposed to national. This is not to propose some notion of the stupid countryman cut off from the nineteenth or twentieth century, but rather to argue that the concerns of the labourer were increasingly not those of national politics and policy. For instance, government economic and social policy, and thus the concerns of the major parties were, from the mid-nineteenth century, effectively dominated by urban and industrial matters. When party allegiances became a matter of class the classes involved were urban ones, at least theoretically. The labourer, and indeed the farmer, became increasingly marginalised. It was not until the 1890s, and then for 'urban' reasons, that any real interest was shown either in the condition of the rural poor or in their political behaviour.[14]

This is not to argue that the great issues of nineteenth-century politics passed the labourer by – quite the opposite. The Norfolk labourer, especially after 1874, was open to all kinds of national influences, especially those coming from the radical wing of the Liberal Party. It is important to stress that these national issues were mediated through a local leadership and a local political culture which was not, as yet, 'subordinated and integrated into a single national political arena'.[15]

But politics was a reflection of the economic, social and cultural sufficiency of the local world. By the 1880s a man or woman could find most things they needed within 10 or 12 miles of their home in most rural areas. This is a period of balance when the market towns had moved sufficiently into the 'modern' world to provide, for instance, clubs, dance halls, public houses, shops etc., but not far enough into that world to see their clientele drawn to Norwich or even London for these things. At this time, as is argued below, there was a real provincial culture in rural England which, while it was not perhaps that different, perceived itself to be different and expressed that difference in many ways.

What follows, then, is essentially a study of that culture in relation to radicalism and trades unionism. As such it neglects many aspects. For instance there is little on leisure or popular culture in a direct way, though both appear. More seriously, it will be argued, there is practically nothing on those labourers, and there were many, who were not radical. For instance the Primrose League and the various societies for rewarding 'good' labourers hardly appear at all in the following pages. To this I can only reply that in Norfolk at least these seem to have had only a marginal influence. If and when the labouring poor were organised, and they often were, it was more usually under the banner of radicalism in some form. The country gentry of Norfolk in as far as they maintained control seem to have done it informally through charity and deference. Both these subjects are discussed to some extent below.

At the beginning of this brief introduction I complained, as is usual in such pieces, of all previous writing. To an extent my own could fall on at least some of those judgments. However, in what follows I hope I have answered at least my own demand for detailed study of one group within rural society over a period of change. I also hope that through the work the voice of the labourer is heard, and that a real sense of his or her hopes, fears and aspirations comes through. If it does not then I will have failed. If, on the other hand, something of the mythology of the rural past, whether it be the inherent stupidity of the rural poor or the harmonious, organic and lost past is dispelled, then at least room will be cleared to analyse and understand the history of the farm labourer.

This work has taken a long time out of my life and I have incurred many debts. I should like to thank all those who have helped.

First are all the men and women who I interviewed for this study. Most are now dead and never saw this work finished.

However, without them it would literally have been impossible. To single out a few is perhaps invidious but I owe a great deal to some. To Arthur Amis of Trunch, Norfolk, thanks for wisdom and guidance; to the late Jack Leeder of Knapton, Norfolk, thanks for help with understanding work; to Jack Sadler of Titchwell, Norfolk, for showing me I was not the only rural communist in the world, and finally Taddy Wright, of Knapton in Norfolk, for liking a pint and the old music.

Second, I owe a debt to many friends and colleagues over the years who, perhaps unknowingly, contributed thoughts and support. Thanks to the *History Workshop Journal* collective, who despite an urban bias have put up with me. Thanks to the Department of Sociology at Essex and the School of Cultural and Community Studies at Sussex for the same. Again to single out individuals is wrong and here I will avoid doing this. However, there are many outside those groups who I would wish to thank. Thanks then to Sue Himmelweit, Eve Hostettler, Thea Thompson, John Walsh, Vic Gammon, Mick Reed, Nobby Duncan, John Archer and George Ewart Evans.

Third, the many people and organisations who provided material for the book and helped in its production: the British Library and its staff at Bloomsbury and Colindale; the libraries of Essex and Sussex Universities; the Museum of English Rural Life, Reading; the National Union of Agricultural and Allied Workers (I prefer the old name); Norwich and Norfolk Record Office, Norwich; Mr Cyril Jolly. In this group some people deserve special mention. Thanks then to Sadie Ward at Reading; to Nick Mansfield and Bridget Yates at the Norfolk Rural Life Museum for help over the years; and last but far from least Caroline Mulford and Liz Fidlon at Routledge for help and patience in getting the book through the press.

Finally there is a group of people who have helped in very specific ways. Thanks to Paul Thompson for being a good supervisor and a mate for ten years; to Geoff Hemstedt for reading the manuscript and correcting my appalling spelling; to Celia Twining for typing the thing and correcting the mistakes both I and Geoff Hemstedt missed. Finally and overwhelmingly, thanks to Linda Merricks who, with many a well timed kick up the backside, as well as much moral and physical support, has made sure this work was finished.

1   The land and the people

Norfolk is celebrated for the diversity and the high cultivation
of its soil; for the abundance and excellence of its agricultural
productions . . . and for its numerous antiquities and historical
associations. . . . It is divided from Suffolk by the Waveney and
the Little Ouse; from Cambridgeshire chiefly by the Great
Ouse, Welney and Nene, and from Lincolnshire by the Wash.
Thus surrounded by marine and river boundaries, Norfolk is in
fact an island.

White's History, Gazetteer and Directory of Norfolk, 1890

If we are to explain and understand the rural radicalism and trades
unionism which was such a marked feature of Norfolk in the
period 1870–1923 we must begin with some consideration, no
matter how brief, of the social and economic structure of Norfolk
rural society and of the systems of farming which predominated
in the country.

In this discussion the onset of the agricultural depression in
1874–5 is of the utmost importance and an event which
dominated, to a greater or lesser extent, all the thinking of
contemporaries. As Perry has written,[1]

It is . . . indisputable that the last quarter of the nineteenth
century was a period of agricultural crisis . . . more numerous
bankruptcies, lower rents and untenanted farms. These were the
facts which left contemporary farmers, landowners and agricultural pundits in no doubt as to the reality of their problems –
problems which were to continue with only one brief respite
until the 1940s.

The agricultural depression and after: Farming

The depression, as historians since Ernle have argued, hit the eastern counties particularly badly,[2] but Norfolk was not one of the worst affected. According to P.J. Perry, Norfolk 'escaped comparatively lightly',[3] and this is born out by Druce's comment on the number of unlet farms in the 1881 Royal Commission.[4] Although less affected than other areas, Norfolk did suffer. In common with most southern and eastern counties Norfolk had unlet farms, rent reductions, a decline in farming standards and the putting of arable land down to permanent grass. Within the county there were regional variations. C.S. Read wrote in 1883 that those on 'very light and very heavy soils have fared worst', that is those in the Breckland and the south-east; but there were obviously problems elsewhere.[5] For all involved, history compounded real economic problems. Norfolk farming had been prosperous for two generations which made many feel that the depression was temporary and discouraged innovation until the late 1890s, and then on a limited scale.

The depression affected the different classes of the agricultural community differently. At the top of the rural hierarchy the landlords suffered from reduced rents, especially in the areas of poor soil. The Earl of Leicester, whose estates contained a good deal of light sandy land, estimated that between 1878 and 1894 he reduced his rents by about 45 per cent. Other decreases mentioned by the Royal Commission range between 26 and 60 per cent. Even this was not enough in some cases. On Leicester's estate (which had a justifiably good reputation for treating its tenants well) eight farms coming up for renewal in 1895–6 were stated as 'not going to be renewed' despite rent reductions of between 40 and 60 per cent.[6]

Unlet farms and rent reductions meant a reduced income for landowners. On the largest estates this probably had little effect: as Rew noted, 'it does not involve the positive distress which may be brought upon the owner of a small estate and his family'.[7] At worst it involved the cutting of expenditure or the selling of land. F.M.L. Thompson shows how the Earl of Verulam cut his annual expenditure by about £4,000 a year between the early 1870s and 1889.[8] Cutting expenditure was relatively simple, selling land was less so. As agricultural prices fell investment in land became less attractive, even a great house and estate in the relatively prosperous corn lands of west Norfolk, Houghton Hall could not find a buyer.[9] As Thompson notes,[10] the evidence of the figures and the annual reports points unmistakably to a great drop in the amount of land sold; land was a drug on the market, unsaleable, the market was flat and dull and little business was done.

The effect of these kinds of financial problems on village society varied enormously. At the simplest level they meant the loss of jobs and perks for household staff and hangers on.[11] More complex were the adjustments necessary as a result of letting the hall to 'strangers'. Little Hockham for instance acquired a new 'squire' in this manner. As Michael Home writes of his boyhood,[12]

the early Victorian house known to us as Little Hockham Hall, was given the courtesy title only because Squire Finch was living in it . . . it was only when the estate was running at a dangerous loss that our Squire Finch left the handsome Early Georgian Hall and [went] to live [in] Little Hockham.

In Hockham, as elsewhere in Norfolk, the Hall proper was let to a stranger, a wealthy banker called Green who was begrudgingly given the title 'squire' along with Finch.[13]

Yet we should beware of putting too much emphasis on such changes. *Nouveaux riches* did not necessarily mean that the social relations and roles within the community altered. John Lowerson has argued for Sussex that the influx of new money and names was dealt with, by and large, very smoothly:[14]

The transition overall seemed smooth enough, if the older families resented being swamped they allowed few of their feelings public expression, whilst developing more sophisticated mechanisms, not so much for expressing social ostracism as for filtering aspirants.

Also, 'Squire Green' kept the Hall in style. This provided a good deal of employment for the village, especially village women, which Finch could never have done even if he was a real gentleman rather than an upstart; 'the village prospered under Green's tenancy of the Hall and shooting rights'.[15]

Elsewhere, where the Hall stood empty and unlet, not only did work opportunities decline but charities and doles, the great unknown of village incomes, would probably vanish. Colonel Pedder, one of the most vitriolic critics the English landed class has ever had, wrote of[16]

> the withdrawal of many of the smaller country gentry who left their duties behind them to be looked after by anyone who chose, much as the ordinary London householder leaves his cats when he goes down for a month to the seaside.

Between the large estate owners and the tenant farmers were intermediate strata of owner occupiers. The effect of the depression on this group varied greatly depending on the size of holding. There were 10,096 landowners in Norfolk in 1873 holding a million and a quarter acres of land.[17] Of this heterogeneous group those who suffered worst were probably the large owners who had mortgaged land, as it is likely a fair number had by the early 1890s. Perry's work on farming bankruptcies is interesting here but inconclusive as far as Norfolk goes.[18] What does seem to emerge is a pattern of bankruptcy concentrated in the central and southern areas of the country, with relatively few failures in the western areas and only a few more in the eastern.[19] This latter group may be accounted for by the fact that farms were smaller in the east; therefore the 'dot map' used by Perry may overestimate the effect in the eastern part of the country.[20]

Where land was mortgaged but bankruptcy did not result there was a definite decline in farming standards. On occasion the land was 'sucked'. Some did this deliberately; more were driven to it:[21]

> the land will be run with its labour bill brought down to an irreducible minimum; the hay and straw will be sold off it instead of going back to the soil as manure, weeds will be left to seed, drains to choke and 'holls' left uncleared.

The larger owner occupiers farmed on much the same four-course shift as the larger tenant farmers and so the effect of the depression on farming practice can be left to the discussion below. The very small owner occupiers were, however, different. Relying largely on family labour, their own hard work and sometimes wage labour as well, they often weathered the depression better than the larger owners, unless their income was so reduced as to lead to eviction.[22]

As far as it is possible to generalise, the most remarkable thing about the farmers' reaction to the depression, despite a fairly general drop in standards, was the lack of effect it had on farming practice, at least in the medium term. That farmers as a class were hard hit by the depression there can be little doubt, even if the experience was differential. The system of 'farming up to wheat' was particularly vulnerable to the sharp drop in wheat prices after 1874, especially on marginal lands. However, what should be borne in mind is that Norfolk is good wheat country, with the possible exception of the Brecklands and parts of the south-east. Yield per acre was significantly higher in Norfolk on all cereal crops from the mid-1880s to the mid-1890s, wheat for instance averaging 31.4 bushels per acre as against a national figure of 28.94 bushels. Given the large farms of west Norfolk this represents a considerable margin.

Even so the fall in prices was serious. It often meant, despite remission of rent, living on capital. One Norfolk farmer told the Royal Commission, 'Men who have capital are wasting it; those who have none are being ruined.'[23]

The first onset of the depression brought little reaction, Perry has noted:[24]

It is scarcely a matter for surprise that those most directly caught up in the events and changes of the depression, tenant farmers in particular, were ready to adopt explanations of their misfortune which were imperfect, subjective, individual, and almost invariably neglectful of their own shortcomings.

The first factor blamed was the weather, especially in the evidence given to the 1881 Commission. This belief that it was the 'bad season' was made worse in Norfolk by the long period of prosperity before the depression, and the blind faith this created in the four-course shift and farming up to wheat. As we noted above, this meant that change took place largely within the bounds of the four-course shift. First there was the possibility of inserting an extra 'catch crop', sown in the autumn for spring feed, although this could make little difference.[25] More serious was in some sense abandoning the shift more or less completely.

For instance, in reply to Rew's questions about alterations to the shift since 1881, the Swaffam Board replied 'Four course shift broken, oats and barley taking the place of wheat'. Similarly the Freebridge Lynn Guardians noted that barley was being substituted for wheat and that 'artificial grasses are occasionally kept for two years instead of being ploughed up after the first year.'[26]

As well as breaking or modifying the shift there was the simple, and common, remedy of simply lowering farming standards. The standards demanded by the Norfolk system had always been high, perhaps artificially high, with its emphasis on weeding, stone-picking, and 'clean' crops in general. All this seems to have been substantially reduced during the depression. Six out of the seven area meetings called by Rew in 1895 were of the opinion that farming had deteriorated. For instance, Freebridge Lynn's representatives wrote, 'The land has deteriorated in cleanliness and condition',[27] while Rew himself said, 'as regards cleanliness certainly, and as regards condition probably, there has been some deterioration within the last few years.'[28]

The ultimate response in an arable area like Norfolk was laying down to permanent grass. This was certainly a major national trend. There were 11.1m acres of permanent grass in Britain in 1866, 14.4m in 1880 and 16.7m in 1900.[29] In the same period the acreage under wheat dropped from 3.36m acres to 1.8m acres; under barley from 2.25m acres to 1.9m acres and other corn crops from 907,000 acres to 474,000. Only oats, never a major Norfolk crop, showed any increase and that was not large, from 2.75m acres in 1867 to 3m acres in 1900.[30] The Norfolk figures are less spectacular but still significant. Between 1881 and 1894, 53,452 acres of land went out of cultivation which had formerly grown wheat, although this had been matched, in part, by an increase in the acreage under barley and oats. Nevertheless, there was a real drop, and if all stages of the rotation are taken into account there was an increase in the period up to 1895 of about 30,000 acres under permanent grass.[31]

Recovery from the depression was slow in coming, and indeed it could be argued that the whole of the period 1870–1925 (with the exception of the war years) was one of economic difficulties for the landowners and the farmers. However, from the early 1900s onwards things did improve in the wheat growing areas. Lord Ernle in the classic account wrote in 1912, 'Conditions slowly mended. More favourable seasons, rigid economy in expenses, attention to neglected branches of the industry have combined to lessen the financial strain.'[32] The year 1894–5 was the nadir of British wheat prices with wheat at 22s 10d a quarter. By 1898 it reached a temporary high of 38s, and indeed in the April of that year Sir Henry Rider Haggard's bailiff refused 48s a quarter at Bungay.[33] If 1898 was a temporary and artificial high point there was genuine, though slow, improvement, so that the *Estates Magazine* could write in 1905 of wheat growing 'there are probably few crops which will work out so satisfactory a result with proportionate risk'.[34]

More important in the long-term recovery was, 'the substantial reduction in the rents of agricultural land'.[35] For instance, Haggard, in his *Rural England*, written in 1902, quotes Mr Sapwell of Felmingham as saying that although 'things' were 'no better', 'he advised the buying of the best land in good positions at the present low values, as this could not be done to pay the purchaser five per cent on his outlay.'[36] There was also a demand for rented farms in the North Walsham area according to one of Haggard's informants, although he claimed there was an underlying change as 'nearly all the landholders had another trade which they combined with farming'.[37]

Within the four-course shift which continued, albeit in a modified form, to dominate Norfolk farming, the most serious change was the introduction of sugar beet. Through the late nineteenth and early twentieth centuries there had been various attempts to grow sugar beet commercially in Norfolk, but it was not until the opening of the Anglo-Netherland Sugar Corporations factory at Cantley on the eastern marshes in 1912 that any headway was made. The scheme, which was government supported, met with limited success, and considerable opposition from the labourers since imported Dutch labour was used.[38] It was the war which gave sugar beet its much-needed boost and Norfolk was central to these developments. Up until 1920 Norfolk had half of England's sugar beet acreage and even after 1925 when production nationally had reached over 52,000 acres, Norfolk still contained 15,515 of these.[39]

By the early 1900s Norfolk farming was out of the worst of the depression. Farming patterns had changed, and were to change more fundamentally after the early 1920s, but the four-course shift was still the main way in which the arable land was worked. However, the changes in the period 1870–1920, which appeared to have relatively little effect on the farming pattern, and the personnel of the farming and landowning classes, had a fundamental effect on the labourer.

The agricultural depression and after: The labourer

The effects of the agricultural depression on the labourer have to be seen in the context of long-term changes, some of which predate the depression period. Perhaps most basic were long-term demographic changes.

TABLE 1 Numbers of agricultural workers in Norfolk, 1841–1921[40]

	Male	Female	Total
1841	39,757	890	40,647
1851	47,693	2,157	49,850
1861	49,533	3,234	52,767
1871	41,263	3,935	45,198
1881	40,453	1,736	42,189
1891	37,249	590	37,839
1901	34,738	351	35,089
1911	32,740	351	33,091
1921	34,058	1,267	35,325

Up until 1861, as can be seen from Table 1, the number of labourers in Norfolk was growing, but they formed an increasingly casual workforce, fully employed only at harvest times. Additionally, and not usually shown in the census, there were large numbers of women and children employed, especially in the west of the county, as casual workers. This casual workforce was essential if the increased acreage under wheat, which characterised Norfolk agriculture in the first half of the nineteenth century, was to be harvested and kept clean.[41]

The most extreme form of casualisation was the agricultural gang. The gang was simply a form of sub-contracting whereby a gangmaster hired a number of workers and then sub-contracted specific tasks from the farmer. Thomas Parkins, a gangmaster from Swaffam, told the Children's Employment Commission[42]

> I take my gang to work on the land of any farmer that engages me, and he pays me according to the number of workers which I bring, at so much a head, with a certain sum for myself; or else it is taking work, i.e. I contract to do certain work for him by the piece.

The other essential feature of gang work was that it was overwhelmingly performed by women and children.

Casual and gang work created a situation in Norfolk where the number of 'true' full-time farmworkers was extremely low. Estimates are difficult to make but some indication can be gauged from contemporary estimates on the numbers employed per acre, etc. This gives, in 1841, a regular workforce of about 17,000 out of 40,647 who are described as labourers in the census. However, this figure does not include women and girls who formed the majority of the gangs. Thus a ratio of 2 regular to 3 casual workers at nominal times of the year could alter to 3 casuals to 1 regular at harvest.[43]

The structure of the labour force before the 1870s added to the settlement pattern, especially in west Norfolk with its 'open and closed' parishes, and the large size of Norfolk farms produced an agricultural workforce which was, up until the 1870s at least, very different from the classic model of 'Hodge'. Many Norfolk labourers of the period 1840–70 in west Norfolk especially were employed as part of a working unit that was bigger than many factories of the time, in that it probably employed 16 full-time workers, 24 semi-casual workers and 48 true casual workers. Unlike the classic model the labourer did not live on the farm but probably as much as five miles from it in a village large enough to be described as a small town in other areas, and he was therefore often well outside the control of master, squire and parson. He was likely to face long periods of unemployment as well as low wages, and precisely because of the farming structure was unlikely to have these supplemented by doles and charities. He was in short a proletarian, with nothing to sell but his labour power in a free market which was overstocked, and which valued him at nought.[44]

However, from the late 1860s this situation began to change. The first major factor (or set of factors) was the decline in the number of casual and migrant harvest workers. Hand in hand with this went the wholesale depopulation of rural areas. Thirdly, partly as a result of this, and partly as a result of the depression and the desire to cut costs, we see the introduction of machinery, especially into the harvest field. The result was the gradual establishment of a smaller and more regularly employed workforce.

This process is a complex one and will probably never be charted with any real precision. However, it is necessary to outline it at least. First comes the decline in supply of casual and migrant labour. As migrant, especially Irish and Scots, labour had never played a major part in Norfolk agriculture, more important here was the drift to the towns and even the colonies of native workers.[45]

From the 1830s there is evidence of movement away from the rural areas of Norfolk and a number of schemes to settle the able-bodied poor in industrial areas.[46] But it was more normal voluntary migration that, by the 1860s, was beginning to bite. In 1867 Mr Hudson, who farmed 500 acres in west Norfolk, voiced a complaint that was to become more common as the century went on, when he said, 'A great many of our best labourers and boys have been leaving the neighbourhood; their only commodity is their labour, so one cannot wonder at their disposing of it to their advantage.'[47] After the decade 1851–61 the rural population of Norfolk was never again to see absolute decline. However from 1861 onwards, as a result of continuous migration the numbers employed in agriculture went into permanent decline.

In the 1870s two institutional factors intervened to reduce the casual labour supply still further – the legal control of agricultural gangs and the introduction of compulsory education. The direct effects of both these measures remains essentially unassessed at local level, but it is clear that coupled with the lowering of farming standards and the laying down to grass of arable land after 1875, they substantially reduced both the demand and opportunities for the employment of casual workers, especially women and children, in Norfolk agriculture. Added to this was the greatly increased demand for women domestic servants in the latter half of the nineteenth century.[48] By 1894 Wilson Fox could write that although there was still a good deal of women's work in Norfolk it was 'only at odd intervals'. He went on,[49]

> There is no doubt that both in the Northern and Eastern counties women are less inclined to work in the fields than formerly. As a rule they now prefer to obtain situations in domestic service or in shops. . . . Under these circumstances it looks as if the employment of women in agriculture is, at no distant date, likely to become a thing of the past.

As to children, although a glance through school attendance records quickly shows that child labour was not a thing of the past, even in the 1920s, there can be little doubt that after the 1870 Education Act the majority of village children ceased regular work on the land. As Thomas Parkins, the Swaffam gangmaster said, 'After the Compulsory Education Act the children had to leave off working in the fields.'[50]

Another factor which reduced the number of casual workers during the depression period was the introduction of machinery. British agriculture was, for most of the nineteenth century, incredibly labour-intensive. The work of Collins and Morgan has shown how changes within hand-tool technology accounted for the harvesting of the hugely increased wheat production of the period 1790-1850, while capital investment remained low.[51] By the late 1860s, however, this situation had changed: as Collins writes 'the chief problem being no longer to absorb a labour surplus but to obtain sufficient labour for key summer operations'.[52] This shortage coupled with the depression led to the slow introduction of machinery, especially reapers, worked by a regular workforce.[53] Nevertheless the extent of mechanisation should not be overestimated. According to Collins only about a quarter of all farms had a reaper in 1871 and this figure may not have increased substantially by 1900.[54] Even where a reaper was introduced, shooking and binding still had to be done by hand and oral evidence suggests that the reaper binder was by no means common in many areas of Norfolk even in 1914.

Finally the depression directly contributed to the reduction in casual workers by the lowering of farming standards and putting arable land down to permanent grass. Lowering farming standards not only meant the end of much of the weeding, dock-pulling and stone-picking which were so much a part of the casual work pattern, but also less hedging and ditching, clearing of drains, 'out hollin" as it was called, and so on. Putting down to grass considerably reduced the workforce required. The 1895 Royal Commission showed many such changes in Norfolk:[55]

> The first great cause of the reduction of labour is the diminution of arable land. . . . In many instances farmers themselves informed me that they had reduced their staff of men, and were still reducing it. As an instance, a farm of 700 acres in South Norfolk is worked with 12 labourers whereas a few years ago a similar farm half the size, would have employed as many.

As a result of these changes, the Norfolk labourer found his situation, at the end of the worst of the depression in the early 1900s, much altered. For the first time he found himself with the upper hand in the labour market. First, the huge casual reserve army had disappeared. In the late 1840s, as we saw above, there were a minimum of 3 casual workers to every 2 regularly employed and at times this could move to 3:1. By the 1900s this balance had shifted decisively to 3:1 or even 4:1 in favour of the regularly employed. By the 1920s it was to reach 5:1.[56]

It was not only the disappearance of the casual workers but wholesale depopulation. By the early 1900s labour shortages began to be a regular part of the seasonal round. Wilson Fox wrote in 1905, 'Generally speaking, since about the year 1896 ordinary farm labourers have been regularly employed. During this period farmers in all parts of the country had complained of a scarcity of labour.'[57] This scarcity was particularly noticeable among skilled men and those who worked with animals. All observers saw an unwillingness on the part of the young to remain on the land. Henry Rider Haggard wrote in 1898,[58]

> of the four ploughmen whom I employ, not one is under 50, and two must be between 60 and 70. . . . For more than a year I have been looking for a young skilled labourer to whom I could offer the advantage of a good cottage, but have been unable to find one.

This was continued by the outbreak of the war. Nationally

between August 1914 and July 1915 about 150,000 young men left agriculture for the services, the vast majority of them farm labourers.[59] By April 1915 Norfolk County Council heard Sir Alwyn Fellowes, a Norfolk landowner, demand that boys be released from school early as, 'not only was labour now very short in most parts of the country, but in the next three weeks or a month it would get even shorter.'[60] Despite opposition from the Labour side his request was granted and by mid-summer 1915 over 600 boys had been granted exemption certificates to leave school early and work on the land.[61]

As the war continued, not only were boys used in ever larger numbers, but soldiers were also used from haysel 1915 onwards.[62] Women also reappeared in the fields, both the middle-class volunteers of the Women's Land Army and the wives and daughters of labourers.

The other great change brought about by the war was the introduction of the Agricultural Wages Board which regulated the hours and wages in agriculture and set a minimum price for main crops. This long-fought-for demand stabilised wages and conditions for most workers during the war period and up to its abolition in 1921. Its effects, in a more detailed sense, are dealt with below.

Apart from decasualisation and the creation of a regular workforce, other, less tangible, changes took place as a result of the depression. The decreasing size of the workforce created closer bonds between master and man, as did the growth in the number of tied cottages. There also appear to have been, from the 1850s, conscious attempts to create the notion of a 'community of interest' in agriculture whose common concerns crossed class barriers. The most obvious of these were Lord Winchelsea's National Agricultural Union of the 1890s. However, apart from these institutional forms, there seems to have been a distinct attempt to reestablish some sort of 'idyllic' notion of rural England in the last quarter of the century. Systematic work on this remains to be done but the impression, and it can be no more, is there. For instance there appears to be a great increase in private charity at Christmas (that quintessentially Victorian invention) from the 1870s and an increase in the celebration of harvest by 'horkeys' and, especially, harvest festivals in the Church of England during the same period.[63]

Looking back from 1925 a long-lived Norfolk farmer or farm labourer would probably have stressed the changes in his lifetime. Apart from the recent war, the Brecklands were again barren and the great crops of corn on the Fens had been replaced by fruit. He would have pointed to unlet farms and unemployment as well as much reduced profits compared with his young days. The farmer would certainly have complained of the quality of labour and the labourer of unemployment. Some of these thoughts would have been true, others a product of looking at the past as a golden age. What neither would have expressed were the real continuities – crucially, even in the early 1920s the pattern of agriculture was, as yet, substantially unchanged. The four-course shift as laid down in the eighteenth century, though battered, still held sway in the cereal areas, and cereal farming still dominated Norfolk. Norwich Market Hill was still black with 'Irish Stores' in the autumn. Many of the great names of Norfolk society in the early 1920s would have been recognisable to a Norfolk farmer of the 1850s. The farms were still large in the west and small in the east. Even farm work itself had changed less than many economic historians would imagine. The steam threshing drum, the sail reaper and the elevator were now common, but men with scythes still cut round the edges of the fields as well as cutting 'laid' crops, especially barley. On some small farms a gang of mowers still took the whole harvest, by hand for a price, as their grandfathers had done.

If we had got our imaginary labourer on his own, away from the master, he would have added another dimension to that story. Born in the late 1840s he would have spent a childhood in dire poverty, starting work at six years old in a gang pulling docks. He could have seen the gradual rise of the first union and the Liberal Party, and their collapse and betrayal. He might have then talked about the second union and labour. It is to his version of the story that the rest of this book is addressed.

2 Structural conflict and the farmworker

Structural conflict I: The workplace

Relationships between master and man on the farms of Norfolk in the period 1870–1925 were exploitative. This currently unfashionable notion means simply that in pre-mechanised but capitalist agriculture, labour is the main source of value, and that the labourers were consistently underpaid for the production of that value. Thus the workplace was the scene of constant potential conflict. Again, put simply, it was in the interest of the master to get as much work done for as little as possible; in the interest of the labourer to do as little work for as much as possible. As Lord Ernle recognised in an age less worried by the hypocrisies of modern management jargon, 'The interests of agricultural labourers . . . conflict with those of their employers. They want high wages and low prices: their employers want high prices and low wages.'[1] Of course there were many qualifications to this crude picture but they do not alter this basic antagonism. Whatever strategies of 'management' were adopted to obscure this must be seen as no more than that.

Perhaps the preceding paragraph is unnecessarily crude but it is essential if we are even to begin looking at labour relations as they *are*, outside behaviour in an institutional sense. If we ignore the *fact* of exploitation what is, as Howard Newby points out, the delicate balance of a deferential relationship[2] is elevated to a permanent and harmonious reality.

The area of potential conflict was defined by the farming year and by the different demands for labour generated at different points. Additionally hours and wages were subject to traditional definitions and these were open to constant disagreement. For instance, Jack Leeder of Knapton in Norfolk said that you stopped work in winter 'when you could see two stars with one eye'.[3] Indeed time was a constant source of dispute. In 1911 the union

supported a man who stopped work at threshing at 3 o'clock in
the afternoon, 'that being the usual time'. The farmer disagreed
and sacked him.[4] At Plumstead also in 1911 the men on the farm
of Mr March were instructed to start work at 6.30 in the morning
from 13 February. They refused and turned up at 7.00, 'the
traditional time', and were all sacked.[5] On the farm of Womack
William Ringer in north-west Norfolk the introduction of the
Saturday half day caused problems when the 'traditional' clashed
with the modern institutional. Ringer insisted,[6]

> they couldn't stop for dinner. They had to go seven or six, or
> whatever it was, 'til three without any food, although they
> stopped for breakfast then, that's right, and the foreman was set
> up there to see that they didn't stop. At twelve o'clock my
> father said, 'Well Davie I don't know whether you got any grub
> but I have, and I'm a-going to eat it!', and they stopped. And
> the foreman went to Ringer and he said, 'If you want anybody
> to go up there and see about them chaps on a Saturday, you'll
> have to go yourself, I shan't go no more' . . . and course they
> stopped for dinner ever after that.

These disputes could though take on a more personal nature,
when an individual refused to do something which he or she
regarded as offensive even if their predecessors had done it, and
their master and family considered it quite normal:[7]

> When I turned the cows out the first morning, I went, and
> when I turned them out, I sat down and I ate me breakfast, and
> the old boy [in charge] he went on to me, 'Where had I bin.' I
> said 'Turning out the cows, and I had me breakfast.' 'Did you
> sit down and eat your breakfast?' he said. I said 'Yes.' Well he
> told the missis, 'cos she wanted to know where I was. So she
> come to me, and she said 'They tell me you sat down to your
> breakfast.' I said 'Yes mam.' She said, 'Well, there's no need,
> you can walk slowly, the cows can feed on the bank.' I said,
> 'How would you like to eat your breakfast walking behind
> these cows, all the flies and stink,' I said, 'and I'm not going to.'
> [Anyway, I said I'd leave but] 'I'll come in on Sunday', cos I
> took a boy's place. . . . 'Oh' she said, 'we want you to stop',
> but I said, 'I don't want to stop.' She said, 'Well, we like you

very much', and I said, 'Well I don't think much of you mam.'
I didn't ought to have said that. [laughs]

Personal conflict of this kind was endemic in a work situation
which was often marked by close personal contact between master
and man, and whose ideology elevated this relationship to a
position of prime importance. When relationships did break it was
often violent. In April 1911 the union was asked to support a man
'who had got wrong with his master' who had sacked him after
calling him a thief and saying he stole some corn bags.[8] In 1906
Thomas Chestney of Runton burnt two barley stacks in his village
out of 'feelings of revenge' after he had been dismissed by his
employer.[9] Seven years earlier William Mansell told Norfolk
Assizes:[10]

I was upset when I left Gooch's having been turned out my
house, having nowhere to go. I went across Drakes Field to Mr
Murfet's wheat stack and set fire to that, and across the fields to
the back of Kenny's and fired his stacks as I had a bit of a
grudge against him as he owed me 15s. to 17s. and would not
pay it.

More extreme was resort to personal violence. In 1913 Isaac Vann
and his two sons contracted to finish a harvest field for 6d an acre.
When Isaac turned up late and was dismissed his two sons walked
out with him. Vann, and his sons, after having threatened 'to
knock the farmer to h____l' went to the pub. They returned at
5.30 to ask for largesse and when this was refused, carried out
their earlier threat. All received 14 days with hard labour.[11] One
imagines something similar might lie behind the case the union
investigated in July 1911 of a man dismissed because 'he got
wrong' with his master at the Royal Show.[12]

Job definition was a less serious but recurrent problem. In
November 1900 Marshall Townsend was summoned for assault
on Mr Gray, an estate steward,[13]

On 17th November defendant was sent out with a horse and
cart, and on returning complainant complained that he had been
too long on the job, and that the horse looked over-driven.
Defendant thereupon took hold of the complainant and hit him
in the face and threw him down.

A number of similar cases occur in the union's books, for instance a man named Taylor from Carbrooke who had been dismissed by his employer, Mr Harvey, after a disagreement over the amount of muck laid on a field, or 'some men' from Weasenham 'who were discharged for refusing to commence threshing because the engine stood on the wrong side of the stack'.[14]

Perks, though few enough, also caused problems. In general terms most of the men interviewed for this study agreed that perks were the exception rather than the rule and in this they are supported by the reports by Wilson Fox in the 1900s.[15] Nevertheless they did exist and there were often disagreements over them which ended up in court. For instance James and Arthur Eagling who appeared before the bench in 1900 charged with stealing eggs defended themselves by saying that they were taking them to the farmer's wife as 'it was the duty of the groom to collect eggs, but the labourers, if they found any were given them'. They were found guilty.[16] A more serious offence was that of Dennis Gray of Northrepps who was sent to the Assizes for embezzling money collected for milk and stealing milk. He defended himself on the latter charge by saying that 'Miss King had allowed him to take two pints of milk every day'. He was ultimately imprisoned.[17]

This kind of conflict, which was present on most farms, points to the ways in which an apparently 'stable' work relationship concealed antagonisms of various kinds. It was created by the very 'closeness' and informality of the workplace relations which, because of the notion of agricultural work being special and different, dispensed with formal contracts, time sheets, even regularly agreed wages. All these were subsumed under the 'human nexus' of master and man. More regular, more serious and on a much larger scale was the conflict which sprang from the nature of farmwork itself, from its essentially seasonal nature, and from ways in which the farm functioned.

Howard Newby has argued that the farmworker is the 'archetypal hired man', subject to the vagaries of the labour market.[18] Thus many rural areas are 'definitely a buyer's market for labour',[19] the only exception being 'the small part . . . of the labour force that consists of highly skilled specialists, particularly in stockbreeding.'[20] Again while this may be true of the post-

Second World War situation it would have to be modified, both in the short and long term, for the pre-wages board labourer.

First, there was the workforce itself. Decasualisation and rural depopulation left, by the 1890s, a rigidly structured farm workforce. Rural workers were not an undifferentiated mass of 'hired men', any more than factory workers were an undifferentiated mass of proletarians. At the top of the farm workforce in Norfolk stood the man who worked the horses, the team-man. These accounted for 20 per cent of the labour force in 1901 and were the most skilled of the arable farm workforce. Under horse culture even a relatively small farm of 100–150 acres employed two or three team-men. Bert Hazell, who started work on a farm near Wymondham in 1919 said,[21]

> you had five horsemen, five adults and a boy, [and] we all had six horses each, and then there would be another two or three looked after by someone else. They would be sub-divided so that we would run ten plough teams.

Within this structure the teams were rigidly organised. At the top was the head team-man, who was the most skilled, had the best horses, was aided more and occasionally had a free cottage. His position was reflected in the morning ritual of 'leading out':[22]

> When we were working in the plough teams [the head team-man] would take the lead, and nobody would dare to leave the yard until he'd got onto his horse, and he'd got in front. He'd be followed by the second team-man and then subsequently down the line.

Once at work, the head team-man usually 'cut the field out'. Every 40 yards across the field he would cut one furrow and then turn it back. He was then followed by a less skilled man with a three-horse, doubled-furrowed plough, who took his 'line' from the furrow cut out.[23]

Equal, in theory, to the team-man were those men who looked after animals. The 'in theory' is important. In the arable system of Norfolk most animal husbandry was 'subservient' to the cereal crops. This is especially true of store cattle. Hence few farms had true stockmen. At most a labourer with some skills was employed full-time in the winter, when the cattle were in the yards, to feed and tend the bullocks. This more lowly status accorded to men who looked after cattle is made clear by the use of language. Nobody I interviewed used the word 'stockman', about the period before the Second World War. Instead they used 'yardman', 'cowkeeper', or perhaps lowest of all, 'bullock feeder'. The situation was of course different in those few Norfolk farms where dairying dominated. Twelve per cent of the labour force in 1901 were described as 'labourers who work mainly with cattle'.

The position of the shepherd was different again. Shepherding is a solitary occupation which meant that status was very much a matter between master and man. Again though, the number of shepherds in Norfolk was relatively small as the number of sheep per acre was well below the national average. Further, they tended, though there were exceptions, to be in the south of the county. Like cattle, sheep tended to be fitted into the rotation and so while many farms kept a few sheep, few kept a lot. In these cases there was seldom need for a full shepherd. Rider Haggard, for instance, had about 40 ewes, and he commented, 'With so small a flock on a mixed farm like mine, where there are many things to attend to, I have no shepherd'.[24] Only about 4 per cent of the Norfolk farm labour force were full-time shepherds in 1901.

Finally, there were the labourers. These come nearest to Newby's 'archetypal hired man', but as F.E. Green wrote, 'He who is so glibly dubbed an ordinary agricultural labourer, understands as a rule the skilled work which if sub-divided, would require a gardener to do one part and a navvy to do the other.'[25] They were by far the largest group, 64 per cent in 1901. Even labourers were sub-divided. Although 'casual' as a category had all but disappeared by the 1900s, there was a subtle distinction based on age, skill and 'reliability' which divided the workforce. Further, within the regular workforce there was a recognized 'leader', the head labourer or 'lord'.[26]

The position of women in the Norfolk agricultural workforce should also be mentioned. In 1901 all categories of farmworker, and indeed the separate category of farmer included women. However, by that date the numbers were minute. Even the largest group, 'female labourers (general)' number only 279, about 1 per cent of the 64 per cent of the agricultural workforce described as labourers.[27] However, this ignores the crucial question of casual work. There were, and indeed are, many reasons why a woman should not tell a census enumerator that she was a casual worker, and indeed many who did do such work probably did not consider themselves workers at all.

Nevertheless at various points in the seasonal round women's work was important, and on some farms, widespread. Labour books from Norfolk farms show women (and children) regularly employed at stone-picking and at harvest, especially where this was still carried out by hand. Information here is scant but generally these seem to have been women who were wives or daughters of men already employed on the farm.[28] Weeding cereal crops and, after the Great War, hoeing of beet was often carried out by women, as was potato lifting in those areas where they were grown.

The important thing for this study is that such work remained rare and was, until the war, declining. As with casual work in general women's labour became less and less the norm during the depression and even in the 1900s hardly reappeared. After the war, when there was a more widespread acceptance of women's work on the land as elsewhere, the economic problems of agriculture meant that few women workers could find part-time work let alone a full-time career.

The work situation into which this rigidly divided group fitted was essentially seasonal, but was not, and indeed is not, a 'lengthy production cycle' with 'only two periods of the year – sowing and harvesting – [in which] the withdrawal of hired labour' is a 'serious embarrassment to the farmer', as Newby suggests.[29] While seedtime and harvest certainly were the most crucial points in the agricultural year, there were many other points when withdrawal of labour could cause serious problems. Additionally, these were often precisely those points when, particularly because of the use of piece work, 'traditional' bargains as to wages and conditions were made. Finally, there were longer-term movements in the demand for labour created by a much more voluble demand for farm products and a population more ready to move in search of work, both of which characterise the pre-Second World War situation.

First, consider the medium- and short-term changes in the

employment situation created by the nature of Norfolk farming. These are summarised in Figure 1. In the medium term there were two points in the farming year (which ran from Michaelmas to Michaelmas) when the farmworker went from winter to summer and then summer to winter money and hours. In winter the amount of work done on the farm was greatly reduced. Once the cereal harvest was in, there was a rush to get any winter ploughing done before the frost set in:[30]

> You'd start after harvest what we called 'scaling', that's ploughing very fleet, which cuts all the stubble and weeds. [Then you'd] harrow it . . . so it all pulls out, you'd walk behind and lift the harrows, and of course that all had to be shook by hand, by fork, and then ploughed in.

Ploughing was team-man's work. For the labourer, apart from forking behind, the main work of the early winter was the root harvest. In late autumn the work, though hard, was not unpleasant:[31]

> The method employed was this: you grasped the leaves of the mangold with the left hand. . . . You pulled the mangold out of the ground, swung it upwards, and at the right moment slipped your knife blade through the leaves where they joined the root. Then, if you had judged it correctly, the mangold flew into the cart and you were left with the leaves in your hand. You dropped them, and stopped to pull another. The whole process took the labourer one second.

As the winter progressed the whole process got less and less pleasant. Once the frost set in the mangolds froze in the ground, and getting them out became freezing, backbreaking work, in which a misplaced knife swing could take a thumb or finger off. Along with potato harvest in mid-winter the root harvest was the most disliked of all farm work.

During this period of early winter conflict created by the structure of farm work emerged in two ways. First, it was the point in the year when those who were going to change masters did so:[32]

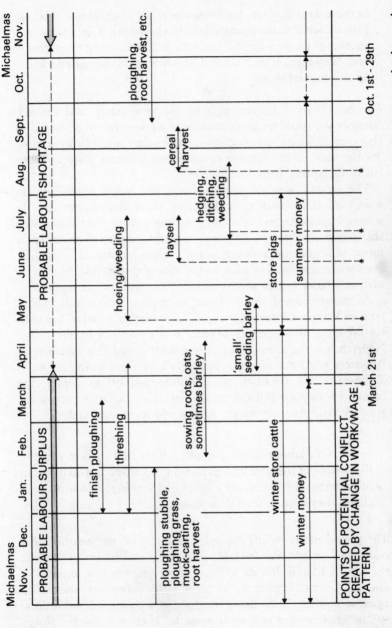

Figure 1   The yearly round on the four/five-course shift (c. 1890–1930) (wheat → oats → roots → barley → hay)

In those days you see, farm workmen [at] Michaelmas, that was 11th October in the country [old Michaelmas], if they wanted another place they left the one they had and moved to another one. Well then, if they wanted to move again they just packed up and moved again.

Moving involved bargaining with the new master and the old. Another job could mean an increase of a few pence over the old. It also created longer-term tensions since many seem to have hired 'by the year' in the autumn to guarantee a winter place and then left in the spring for better money.

The second area of conflict concerned wage reductions. In winter all farm workers traditionally worked a shorter day. In winter wages dropped by about a shilling a week and the hours by about two or three.[33] This was seldom accepted without some form of argument and occasionally more organised resistance, even if the date was at issue rather than the principle. However, such resistance nearly always failed, even with union support.[34]

As winter closed in the situation became worse still. Those farmers known contemptuously as 'dry weather masters' began to lay off men, although this practice was dying out by the 1900s. Nevertheless the *Labour Gazette* regularly noted that numbers of labourers were out of work in Norfolk parishes in the winter.[35] Team-men and yardmen were seldom laid off in winter, the former because his skills were too valuable, the latter because his was essentially winter work. As one old team-man said,[36]

some of the labourers was laid off, but see that's where you got the benefit of it if you was team-man or yardman, you got your full time in. But if you got a lot of bad weather, labouring chaps, they used to send them home.

The period of laying off depended crucially on the weather. In a really bad winter, like 1911-12, men could still be out of work at the end of March, having suffered three or even four months of unemployment. However, in most years farmwork started up again soon after Christmas. Ploughing was continued and drilling spring wheat started as soon as possible. There was also threshing, although most of the work here was done by travelling gangs hired by the threshing contractor who owned the tackle.

The men who worked the threshing tackle were a separate breed. They were often men who for various reasons could not get, or did not want, a regular job. It was often the resort of a man dismissed for union activity, like Billy Dixon who was sacked after leading a strike in a wood yard. He spent a year as 'second corn' on Bullimore's 'chining' crew from Bacton.[37] Another group who went were fishermen, especially those who had experience with steam engines from the drifters, and many ordinary crewmen 'did a couple of days threshing' in January and February when there was no fishing.[38] Finally there were those true casuals who simply did not like the idea of being beholden to one man. As a farmer, Harold Hicks, said,[39]

> Well, they used to go about with threshing machines you
> know, that time of year, and do all sorts of odd jobs, perhaps
> they'd go cleaning up ditches for somebody, or they would
> probably lay fences for somebody else, all that sort of
> thing . . . there was some liked to do that rather than be tied up
> to one place.

From November to February was the hardest time of the year for the labourer. Work was scarce and the labour market worked against him. In this situation of conflict thrown up by the seasonal round he was at a distinct disadvantage – he might get a good hiring, but then he might not, and any strike or walk-off over reduction in wages was almost bound to end up with the loss of a job and possible blacklisting. The only real chances he had for gaining any advantage from the season were carting muck by the piece and the root harvest. Since the former was scarcely urgent, only in root harvest did time, so often the labourers' ally, work for him:[40]

> So any rate I saw Miss Wenn [and] I said, 'That ain't enough
> what you're paying us for pulling them mangolds.' She said,
> 'What do them others say?' I said, 'Never you mind what them
> others say, *I'm* a talking to you.' She said, 'What do you
> want?', I say, 'Another shilling.' 'Well,' she said, 'we'll see how
> much you do.' So we went next day and I told them 'We
> mustn't work too hard today, otherwise we shan't get that

shilling.' So we went; we done a fair think like, but not so much, and she did give us this other shilling.

At the end of February or beginning of March, as the weather improved and the days grew longer the farm workforce went on to summer time. Now the situation began to change. In farm work the entire workforce is constantly working against the weather. Before the widespread use of artificial weedkillers, the combine harvester and crucially the grain dryer, the weather dominated most labour processes. A lot of work had to be done quickly, partly to fit in with the carefully planned rhythm of summer work, which often meant that if a job was not done at the right time it was not done at all, but mainly because a crop could easily be ruined if left too long, or if it was not sown at the right time.

The onset of summer time marked the beginning of the period when time moved in the labourer's favour. For this reason the change to summer money went much more smoothly than the change to winter. Although there were still arguments, particularly about the timing of the change and the exact length of the 'summer day' and the wages, these were generally resolved in the men's favour.[41]

A good deal of the urgent work on the farm was done by the piece. The 1919 Commission on the Economic Prospects of Agriculture listed hoeing turnips and mangolds, drilling, turnip-pulling, muck-spreading, threshing, haysel (hay harvest), corn harvest, rick-thatching and sheep-washing, as all being done by the piece in Norfolk.[42] To this list we can add weeding corn and roots, harvesting potatoes and sugar-beet pulling. All these jobs were bargained for – the price was set between master and man – and this is where conflict arose.

To the farmer the urgency of getting the job done was paramount, especially in the cases of haysel and harvest. To the labourer the money was all-important as piece-work earnings, even if he did not necessarily like the situation that produced them, were a vital supplement to a meagre weekly wage. Harvest earnings in particular paid the half year's rent, bought boots and paid for the one day out most workers got in a year. These considerations, working from both sides, created a series of situations of tension (see Figure 1) which could easily erupt into an argument, a walk-off or a strike.

Some examples can serve to illustrate this kind of conflict. The first concerns a dispute about hoeing turnips. This was done in late spring and was vital if the young plants were not to be choked with weeds at a time when artificial weedkillers were little used:[43]

> I had another run in with the farmer there about the price . . . hoeing that was. A chap come to me, one of the men (I wasn't Lord there), he said, 'Jack, we shall have to ask for more money . . . they're going to ask on another farm.' I said, 'All right, when he come *you* ask him and I'll back you up.' 'I aren't going to ask him,' he said. 'What you mean,' I said, 'is *me* ask him don't you. Well I aren't going to ask him.' Though I intended to that's what I told him. Then he [the farmer] came along, he came and spoke to all of us, and he started to go away . . . I thought I'd give them a chance, see if they'd speak, but they wouldn't. I said, 'We aren't satisfied quite with what you're offering for the hoeing.' 'Oh,' he said. 'what's the matter?' I said, 'We want another 6*d* an acre,' . . . and he said, 'All right I'll give it to you.' And when he was going away he said, 'Just because Jack was the only one what spoke, don't you think I don't know you others were dissatisfied.' . . . They were afraid you know, that was understandable.

The second example comes from a court case under the 'master and servants' Act. Henry Gunton, a labourer of Mattishall, near East Dereham, was charged with leaving his employer in July 1900:[44]

> On the 3rd, inst. the morning was wet and the afternoon was fine, and the defendant and five other men came to his [plaintiffs] yard. Plaintiff asked one of the men named Pitcher what was the matter, and he replied 'We are not satisfied.' Plaintiff told him he could do without him. Pitcher replied, 'We are all as one', and they all marched out of the yard . . . in consequence his hay had been lying about, and he had sustained damage to the amount of £20. He had set some tramps on in the place of men who had left, but they had been threatened in the village and called blacklegs.

The third example comes from perhaps the most tense time of year, cereal harvest. The date is the early 1900s:[45]

> We struck for harvest wages . . . we was getting six pound, and of course we were supposed to be the first to start in the parish. We used to meet you know, see if we could make a proper bargain, like some in them used to give a shilling hire money. He was the first to start and we reckoned we wanted six pound ten that year. . . . So I asked him if he was going to give us that six pound ten. 'No', he said, he'd give the same as other people, he shouldn't give no more. And I said, 'That ain't an answer',but he wouldn't tell us no different. Anyway, he wanted us to start the next morning. I was team-man then, and I had to go away and have a job done on the self binder, [the rest] was going up there, mowing round this bit of wheat ready for me, when I got there with the binder. So I said to my brother, 'Don't you start unless he say he's going to give you that six pound ten cos', I said, 'you know we're going to set the price for other people 'cos we're the first to start.' When I got up there they were having their breakfast and I say, 'Have you made a proper bargain?' 'No,' they said, 'Well,' I said, 'don't lets start then . . . that ain't no good starting like that,' I said, 'we set the price for other people, and they can give you what they like.'

Stoppages of this kind were endemic at harvest from at least the 1870s onwards. Records are incomplete and we are forced to rely on the coverage in the local press, which only noted such stoppages when they had reached a certain stage of seriousness. Even so there is at least one harvest strike mentioned in the paper every year from 1870 to 1895. Even when there was no union in existence, as in 1900, there were a number of stoppages at harvest. Indeed the brief attempt to start a Norfolk union in the summer of 1900 seems to have been a response to strikes which were already taking place.[46]

Such strikes and walk-offs were not inevitably successful. Charlie Barber, who gave the account of the harvest strike quoted above, found himself blacklisted largely because of lack of support from the other men on the farm:[47]

We heard of a man at Bradenham wanted some men, so we
went to see him. Course he wanted to know where we come
from. I told him, 'Mr Crane's at Fransham.' 'Oh well,' he said,
'I musn't take you on', he say, 'you'll hat to go back to Mr
Crane.' Then we went from there to Newton, near Castleacre.
There was a Mr Smith there, he was advertising for harvest
men . . . we went there and he was just the same. So of course
we didn't get one [a harvest]. Coming home that afternoon we
heard of a man in Dunham wanted one man, and my brother
went up there to see him, and he set him on that same night. I
went down to Little Fransham and see a chap. He didn't want a
full man, he only wanted somebody to help him get his little
harvest and I didn't mind that. I thought to myself, well, I'll
earn what I can, then I'll go about threshing.

If you were lucky, time and the state of the harvest would bring
the farmer to your door:[48]

So of course we had orders to start the harvest, and we said,
'What about the money?', we wanted £7 . . . so he said
'£6.10s,' we said, 'We want £7', and he said, 'No, £6.10s,
that all I'll give.' So I said, 'All right,' I said, 'we shan't start.'
So that was the Saturday morning, so course we walked
back down to the Hill, we leaned [sic] about the village, we
met ourselves like. On the Tuesday night the farmer's son-in-
law come round and said, 'You can start tomorrow morning,
£7.'

If you were unlucky there was little to do except set off, like
Charlie Barber, to an area where you were unknown, or hope that
there was some farmer outside the network who would employ
you.
   This seasonal structural conflict functioned within long-term
movements of the labour market. When the market was full the
likelihood of a successful strike was much reduced. The period
1897 to 1906, for instance, saw a fairly severe labour shortage for
most of Norfolk, as farming recovered from the depression and it
became clear that rural migration had done more than remove a
labour surplus.
   After 1906 the situation began to deteriorate, largely because of

increased use of machinery, especially the reaper binder at harvest time. As early as 1900 the *Eastern Weekly Press* wrote, 'Where there is a deficiency [of labour] the aid of machinery has been called in'[49] and in 1906 the *Gazette* noted the low level of harvest wages.[50] During the war the situation again improved, only to drop off badly after 1919. In the winters of 1919–20, and especially 1920–1, unemployment became acute in some rural parishes. The parish pits were opened in some unions for the first time in five years. In others, like Forehoe and St Faiths, the Rural District Councils made applications to the government for special funds.

Within these fluctuations the 'skilled' man was in a slightly stronger position than the 'unskilled'. As I said above, the men, especially good ones, could usually find some sort of work, but in winter, especially a hard winter, even good men often had to take severe wage reductions to get a job. Nor should the power of skill be overestimated. After the 1923 strike all the team-men on the Paston Hall estate found themselves blacklisted and three of them left the land for ever because it was impossible to find work in the neighbourhood.[51] If the employers were determined or the labour market was against you, no amount of skill could guarantee a job; there was always somebody 'looking over the gate'.

Structural conflict II: Crime and the village

Although structural conflict was, I believe, most common in the workplace, because late nineteenth-century Norfolk was a class society antagonisms and conflicts were potentially present within the wider social structure. It is difficult to see how this could have been otherwise, given that the inequalities of wealth, housing and general standard of life were so great and so obvious even in an 'open' village. Many may well have accepted the lines of the nineteenth-century hymn,

> The rich man in his castle,
> The poor man at his gate,
> God made them high or lowly,
> And appointed their estate,

but many did not. Even those that did would find at certain times of the year, especially in winter, the laws and social structure that reinforced this view of the world unpalatable at the least. Additionally, the social conventions of village life were, like those of the farm, often close and a 'bad' squire or parson could disrupt the carefully achieved harmony and balance which the rich and the townsman at least believed to be the ideal of village society.

Again here, we must return to the question of village types. It has been common to talk of the 'open-closed continuum' and draw from this predictive notions about social relations. My own feeling here is that this simply remains unproved. Any detailed examination of, say, village politics reveal all kinds of problems. Michael Home's account of Hockham, a 'closed' village, reveals a powerful rural underworld of Liberal radicalism and antagonism in a situation where extrapolation from a model would lead one to expect deference.[52] Nor was the social situation in any village stable. As we shall see later the firmly controlled and closed village of Titchwell in north-west Norfolk could explode into a bitter and even violent six-month strike in certain situations. Finally to different social groupings within the class structure the same village and even the same person within the ruling group could be quite different. The Rector of Gimmingham for instance, a High Church paternalist, was remembered with great affection by one man as a giver of charity who looked after the poor.[53] Yet to another man this same vicar was remembered as a tyrant whose paternalism found a corollary in violent opposition to trades unions, allotments and smallholdings.[54]

It seems more useful to think therefore in terms of a class structure which possessed the permanent possibility of antagonism between the classes and over which, as in the case of the workplaces, was laid a cycle of change determined by agricultural production and the demands of the market. This is perhaps clearest in relation to crime.

Crime, especially crimes of 'subsistence', broke through the outward shows of deference and revealed a quite different morality. Crimes of subsistence – stealing food, clothing or firing – as well as offences against the game laws have, as I have argued elsewhere, a clear seasonal pattern,[55] increasing in the winter and dropping off in the summer. More speculatively, crimes associated with drunkenness increase in the late summer to vanish almost entirely in the winter months. This is only to be expected. Even if game, for instance, was not regarded by the village poor as 'property', theft of any kind was not easily resorted to.[56] If for no other reason than that being caught often meant prison for the offender and the workhouse for his family, followed by blacklisting by the respectable of the village.[57] Thus it was only in times of hardship that the poor, by and large, took to poaching or theft. In January 1890 Walter Barnard was accused at Rollesby Petty Sessions of breaking and entering another labourer's house. He pleaded guilty but said that he was out of work and that 'the only thing he stole was a loaf of bread and ³⁄₄lb of red cheese . . . [and] he was very hungry and having nothing to eat he had done it'.[58] Similarly John Hicks of Hockwold, who was charged in February of the same year with stealing two partridges, got off as 'the prosecution asked permission to withdraw the case as the defendant was out of work, and Prince Frederick [the landowner] was unwilling to press the case'.[59] Not so fortunate was William Hall, a labourer charged with poaching before the East Harling Petty Sessions in January 1922. Hall 'told the Bench he had to do something to get food. He had been out of work five months and had a wife and five children.' Hall had been a soldier and wore his medals, including the 1914 Star, in court. He was fined 10s and committed for seven days in default:[60] a neat demonstration of the reality of paternalism and the profound hypocrisy of the ruling class of rural England.

If winter set one group of villagers at odds with their betters and disturbed the rural idyll, age did the same for others. The problem of village youth was a constant one. Whether through drunkenness, violence or just bloody-mindedness, the relative freedom accorded to those who had no families to support brought them into conflict with their elders and, crucially, 'betters'. Michael Home's village, as evening fell and the cover of dark offered itself, passed into the hands of 'them chaps' – the young men who had started work but not yet married.[61] This group, who met 'on the mound', the village green, and played rounders, fought each other and at certain times of the year disrupted village festivals, can be found in most Norfolk villages. It was such a group which was remembered by Harold Hicks as terrorising him and the other respectable youth of the parish of Trunch on their way to chapel on Sundays.[62] Frequently these groups ended up in court. Richard Sparks of Swanton Morley was sentenced to one month's imprisonment in 1900 for assault and the magistrate said, 'the defendant appeared to be the leader of a disorderly gang of young men who abused people without provocation and even went to the lengths of assaulting them.'[63] Similarly, two brothers, Fred and John Plummer, and Henry Blyth, all of Ringland, were fined in 1900 for assault and using obscene language. The policeman who gave evidence told the court that 'he was determined to put down the rowdyism that for a long time had been going on in the parish of Ringland.'[64]

As they got older this group fed naturally into the public house. In the 'low public' a whole alternative culture frequently existed which was well out of the control of the village ruling class. In a village beer shop poached game could be sold or hidden, radical opinions expressed, and rumours about the qualities of different employers handed on. It was in the beer shops that many of the early friendly societies met, and later the room upstairs was the union meeting place. It was also a stronghold of the rough culture. Dancing, singing and perhaps above all fighting constituted a world outside the view of the farmers and the squire, who seldom if ever went into the village pub. But it was also outside the view of the 'Methodys', who made up so many of the respectable working class. As a man who ran such a pub said,[65]

> I didn't take no notice of fighting years ago, you never took no notice. Yet latter years . . . [if] two of them got wrong you nearly be frightened out of your life about it. But in them days, if two of them got wrong, the pub would go out, nearly the whole lot of the pub would go out, and stand round in a ring, and see them fight it out, but latter years that faded out.

But it could extend much further than that. On occasions there were faction fights between whole villages on neutral ground. Fairs, especially Stalham Fair, were favourite places for them. Sometimes, though, a rival village would invade, then the fights were nearer home.

Attempts to intervene in this world met with a conspiracy of silence:[66]

> They wouldn't give you away. People wouldn't, oh no. They wouldn't give nobody away. *You* didn't give nobody away if

you knew . . . not in little things, they hadn't murdered anybody, and you kept quiet and let them get away with it.

This solidarity led part of the village at least to see the representatives of law as the enemy, 'Course the police were against the population then in them days . . . the police was sort of a bit of an enemy, you put him down. Them days they used what they could, whether that was a fair deal or not.'[67]

Not all antagonisms within the village were of this informal and unstructured kind. The classic division between church and chapel which we shall look at later split the villages of Norfolk into two opposed groups for much of the nineteenth century, as did membership of trades unions, friendly societies, and, crucially, political affiliation. We shall return to these but it is important to realise that village conflict of this kind was local. Its focus, like structural conflict in the workplace, was a small social unit and it was effective largely in those terms. Thus, as we shall see, trades unionism in Norfolk was a local phenomenon, the effective unit of organisation of the chapel was local, or at best regional, and politics was couched in local terms. This conflict could be generalised in theory but it seldom was. Class and class consciousness remained a matter of the local world.

Controlling and mediating conflict

Even given all that has gone before it is clear that the kind of workplace and local conflicts talked about operated within a general system in which control was effective at most times. While we cannot simply talk of unbroken industrial peace and rural harmony of classes the simple fact that this kind of conflict was not generalised suggests that it was controlled in some way or ways.

First it was controlled by the rural ruling classes themselves. Crime was ever more effectively dealt with by the growth in organisation and efficiency of the rural police. In addition, and this can only be a suggestion, the increasing self-control of the poor, so marked in relation to rural sports and leisure, probably made various kinds of crime less and less acceptable to the community.[68] Further, a perceptible, if slight, rise in the general

1.1   The farming year: early morning, the horses getting ready to leave the yard. The team-men left in strict order, the head team-man first, then the second down to the boy. See page 19. (Norfolk Rural Life Museum, Gressenhall, Norfolk)

1.2   The farming year: late winter/spring, ploughing, North Norfolk *c.* 1900. A three-horse team pulling a two-furrow plough. It is probably early in the season as a rick is still unthreshed in the background. (Norfolk Rural Life Museum, Gressenhall, Norfolk)

1.3 The farming year: early/mid summer, haymaking. Turning the hay by hand and then stooking it was almost universally disliked. It was seldom paid by the piece and was hard, tedious work in very hot weather. North Norfolk c. 1900. (Norfolk Rural Life Museum, Gressenhall, Norfolk)

1.4 The farming year: harvest. About 1900, north-west Norfolk, on an advanced farm three reaper binders pause for the photographer. A graphic illustration of the reduction in manpower caused by even this most basic innovation. Compare this with plate 1.6 which shows a group at the end of a more 'traditional' harvest. (Norfolk Rural Life Museum, Gressenhall, Norfolk)

1.5   The farming year: harvest, loading the wagon. 'We've reaped, we've
mowed, we've carried our last load, hip-hip-hooray' they shouted as the
last wagon left the field. Notice the boy riding 'holdya'. Every year one or
two died and many were injured when a horse bolted and the child fell
under the wheels. (Norfolk Rural Life Museum, Gressenhall, Norfolk)

1.6   The farming year: harvest.
    'Now harvest's done and ended, the corn secure from harm,
    All for to go to market boys we must thresh in the barn.
    Here's a health to all you farmers, likewise to all you men
    I wish you health and happiness till harvest comes again.'
So the song has it. Here we see the harvest workers, men, women and
children of Vale Farm, Stibbard, near Fakenham gathered at the end of
the most important event of the farming year, the successful completion of
the cereal harvest. (Norfolk Rural Life Museum, Gressenhall, Norfolk)

1.7   The farming year: winter, threshing. 'In the agricultural world but
not of it,' says Hardy of the threshing machine driver, and that was often
literally so, sometimes fishermen or townsmen, even ex-railwaymen,
worked the 'chines. Others were more agricultural. Labourers out of work
in the wet months of winter, or blacklisted for union activity found a few
days' work with a threshing crew. This is a set of tackle owned by
Andrews of Brisley, near North Elmham, photographed in the early 1920s.
(Norfolk Rural Life Museum, Gressenhall, Norfolk)

standard of living after 1870 with the end of casualisation and increasing regular employment, meant that crimes of subsistence became less necessary, more unusual and therefore were marginalised to a rough group.[69] More important was private charity. This is not the place to discuss the gift and its social function as this is well done elsewhere by Newby and by Stedman Jones.[70] However, its centrality must be pointed out as it is an essential part of the ideology of idyllicism which dominates the relationship between the classes in large sections of rural Norfolk, and indeed of much of rural England.[71] By the 1900s private charity, especially in winter, was the living proof of the 'special' nature of rural society. Its giving and receipt created a bond of dependence, its refusal or rejection was a permanent threat:[72]

> At Christmas we went to the big house in the park and there, in the huge Servant's Hall we had a sumptuous tea and we were each given, for the girls, a length of dress material, and for the boys, shirt material.

But if your father was branch secretary of the labourers' union the vision was not so idyllic.[73]

> I was in the choir when I was thirteen or fourteen . . . well it was Christmas morning, and the parson told the choir to stay after service. He gave all the men five bob, he give the boys half a crown, and he give me sixpence.

It may, or may not, be useful to characterise this spectrum of class relationships as deferential. Certainly it contains some of those elements. What is vital to stress, though, is that those relationships were created and maintained, they were not easy or natural, and if the gift and charity played a vital part so did their withdrawal and the blacklisting and eviction from a tied house which often followed. In the end I remain unconvinced by the usefulness of the concept. Certainly relationships between master and man on the farm were different from those in the factory, but they are different not in kind but in the representation. They remain, at least in the period 1875–1920, exploitative and contradictory and it is that fact, and the political and cultural forms it produces, which must be central to any analysis.

The second main form by which conflict was controlled was the bargaining system which developed around structural conflict in the workplace. As well as the short-, medium- and long-term movements of the seasons and the labour market the way in which the price was agreed, and the rate fixed, had within it a strong element of control which centres around the figures of the head team-man and the 'lord' or head labourer.

The lord was elected by the men, according to some accounts, or simply emerged as the occasion demanded according to others. He was not always especially skilled or even senior, in fact he seems quite often to have been young, as the young and unmarried were likely to be less affected by blacklisting or victimisation if that were to follow. As one worker said, 'There'd be a spokesman wouldn't there. He'd be a natural product if you like . . . he'd just fall into place, people do.'[74] His role was to bargain for the men, keep accounts of how much they did and set the pace and speed of work:[75]

> In regard to the hoeing, you'd always have what was called a
> Lord, he'd do all the talking . . . he'd look after the books,
> keep account of everything you earned if you were on piece
> work, and he'd draw all the money and pay you.

The lord himself sometimes received a little extra from the farmer for his job, but he remained firmly the men's representative.

The position of the head team-man was more ambiguous. He was appointed by the farmer (although he was not usually paid extra) and as his work was with horses this gave him a greater pride in, and closeness to, his work, than the ordinary labourers. Finally, he often lived in a tied house, frequently well away from the rest of the community. His work, as we have seen, put him at the top of the labour hierarchy. He had the best horses and the best equipment and would do the most difficult and demanding of the horse work. Like the lord he set the speed of work and kept accounts, but more than that, on most farms, even big ones, he was a kind of foreman:[76]

> he was more particular about things than the boss himself. If
> you run down the corn after a rabbit he'd stop the cutters and

play hell . . . my old man. He was very strict on time
especially. There was seven of them that he had charge of, and
they's do just as many rounds of ploughing as he did, and not
one more or less, they'd have to do as much as he did, and he
wouldn't stop a minute before time and he wouldn't be there a
minute after half past.

These two figures, the lord and the team-man, played a vital
role in regulating the conflict of the work situation. They spoke
for the men and what they took the men would take. But their
position could be isolated and difficult. If you inclined too much
to the men no amount of skill could save your job:[77]

you had to be very careful, you see [the team-man] had to be
fair to both sides, and let it be seen he was fair or he would have
got the sack. A lot of people did, whether they was fair or not,
that's why there was so many roadmen secretaries of the union.

But if inclining too much to the men meant the sack, inclining too
much to the farmer meant loss of respect and social isolation.
Arthur Amis of Trunch said, when I asked him if the team-man
on his first job was in the union, 'No,' and then added 'I never
had any respect for that man, even though he was a team-man.'[78]
This brings us to a final source of control on this kind of
conflict, and probably the most effective one of all, the union. I
shall look in detail below at ways in which the union movement
developed in Norfolk but sufficient here is to note that from about
1910 it had a real presence in Norfolk, though not elsewhere. It is
clear that the union disliked structural conflict: it was expensive;
the cases, because they involved so few men, were difficult to
fight and it conflicted with the union's long-term view of labour
relations in agriculture. This view was that the long-term problem
of low wages could only be solved through a trades board for
agriculture setting and enforcing a national minimum wage and
would eventually end piece work altogether. However, the union
could not ignore structural conflict, and indeed the very existence
of the union exacerbated such conflict because it introduced
arguments over the right of men to unionise.
Given this dichotomy the union fell back, more and more, on
its rule book which stated that all disputes must be approved by

the general secretary before they could receive union support. This was clearly out of the question, since time was of the essence in most bargaining and personal conflict was, by its nature, not amenable to cooling-off periods. Thus the union's executive supported some disputes and not others.[79]

The union's problems in relation to structural conflict were ultimately solved by the disappearance of such conflict and, crucially, the appearance of the Wages Board. Although this removed the possibility of the lightning strike, it gave the worker protection. It was not uncommon, for instance, for labourers not to be told what the rate for the job was, as we have seen above. But overriding all was the sense of fear. As Jack Leeder of Happisburgh said,[80]

> They were afraid you know, that was understandable. But the
> union did alter that kind of thing, that was a good job,
> negotiated harvest wages, and your weekly wages and that.

Beneath the apparently calm and ordered relationships of what is called a paternalist and deferential society there was endemic conflict. Like much conflict in the nineteenth century in rural as well as urban societies it found an institutional form – the lord and the team-man – which is not easily recognisable to the historian or sociologist seeking the usual models of class conflict. This conflict was local, limited and difficult to generalise. Its centre was the individual farm. Its widest support area the village or its surrounding district. Yet, in many ways it was remarkably effective. I want now to turn to that local world and see how two generations tried to generalise their struggle.

3   Radicalism, the first phase: The chapel

If there were to be any one text of the early years of Norfolk radicalism, it would not be a union speech or a political pamphlet, but a hymn:[1]

> Ho, my comrades! see the signal
> Waving in the sky,
> Reinforcements now appearing
> Victory is nigh!
>
> Hold the Fort, for I am coming!
> Jesus signals still;
> Wave the answer back to Heaven,
> 'By Thy grace we will'.

'Hold the Fort', P.P. Bliss's great hymn of the American civil war which, popularised by Sankey in the 'Second Awakening', became the battle hymn of English nonconformity. It shared that title with a yet more redolent sacred song,[2]

> Standing by a purpose true,
> Heeding God's command,
> Honour them the faithful few
> All hail to Daniel's band.
>
> Dare to be a Daniel,
> Dare to stand alone,
> Dare to have a purpose true,
> Dare to make it known.

'Daniel's Band', also by Bliss and popularised by Sankey, is perhaps the most defiant and most historical of all nonconformist hymns, with its echo of past persecutions and heroes as well as the fight to come.

Assailed, embattled, struggling but victorious, the rhetoric of popular nonconformity points directly to its strength and appeal to the poor of rural England. Yet it was a rhetoric which, since the end of the heroic age of English dissent in 1688, had lapsed, grown fat and comfortable, even cultured. In Norfolk the Octagon chapel in Norwich, 'the most elegant meeting house in England, or perhaps in Europe',[3] symbolised this period. The Martineaus, the Taylors, the Aldersons and Dalrymples, despite their initial enthusiasm for the French Revolution, were not men of the people, they were a cultured and elevated provincial elite.[4]

Even the Wesleyan revival made little impact in the rural areas of Norfolk except, perhaps, by leading to a slight revival of the old dissent.[5] Although he travelled through rural Norfolk on a number of occasions to deal with the fractious congregations of Norwich and Yarmouth, Wesley seldom stopped, and left few supporters behind him. As Cyril Jolly, the historian of Norfolk Methodism has written,[6]

Wesley preferred to work in the large towns where they would 'listen and repent', and he expressed a poor opinion of farmers, 'Of all the people in the kingdom they are the most discontented', and of farm workers.

Certainly some villages contained cottage meetings, usually short-lived. More importantly it seems on first impressions from the preaching certificates listed by Jolly that Methodism was appealing to farmers, tradesmen and occasionally artisans rather than to the labourers.[7]

The reasons for this are important and not far to seek. While not wishing to argue that late eighteenth-century Norfolk was a stable organic society, it is clear that it had not experienced severe social disruption. However, in the years from approximately 1800 to 1830 it underwent a major transformation. Central to this was the end of living in, a general collapse in regular employment on the land and an enormous increase in the size of the casual workforce. These changes, along with continued enclosure and engrossing of holdings, especially in the west of the country, were exacerbated by the relative loss of profits in Norfolk farming between 1815 and 1825.[8] As a result,[9]

By the early nineteenth century Norfolk opinion had become convinced that an intractable problem of surplus labour existed

in rural areas. While traditional ideas of social responsibility by
the propertied classes towards the poor dictated that everyone
should be kept from starvation the less affluent condition of
agriculture dictated that this must be done more cheaply than
before.

The solution adopted, before 1834, was the roundsman schemes
and labour rates.[10]
These factors created within Norfolk in the years from 1816 to
1832 a major crisis within the ideology of the poor.[11]

Good people give attention who now around do stand,
I'll unfold the treatment of the poor upon the land.
For nowadays the gentlemen have brought the labourers low,
And daily are contriving plans to prove their overthrow.

Come all ye sons of freedom, the world is upside down
They scorn the poor man as a thief in country or in town.

The poor replied in the only way they knew how, by riot. In
1816, 1822 and 1830–1 there were major outbreaks of rioting and
arson in Norfolk. But, and this is important, these outbreaks
should be seen essentially as responses within the traditional
framework of the 'moral economy of the crowd' rather than as
new responses occasioned by the manifestations of a change in the
social relations of production.[12] Only when riot, the traditional
ultimate appeal to authority, had failed did the full extent of the
anomie of the Norfolk labourer strike home.

In this situation, when the traditional 'norms' of social relations
had collapsed, the labourers looked outside their traditional roles
and institutions and found religion. They found it not as a
'chiliasm of dispair' but as a positive assertion of an alternative
society. As Brian Wilson has written,[13]

Change in the economic position of a particular group . . .
disturbance of normal social relations . . . are possible stimuli
in the emergence of sects. These are needs to which sects, to
some extent, respond. Particular groups are rendered marginal
by some process of social change; there is a sudden need for a
new interpretation of their social position or for a transvaluation
of their experience.

This 'new interpretation' has been described by Gilbert as 'a heightened demand for new associational and communal foci to replace those which have been lost'.[14] In the towns of the first industrial revolution this was provided by the Wesleyan revival. In the villages of Norfolk it was provided by the much more democratic and proletarian Primitive Methodists.

The Primitive Methodist Connexion had been founded in 1811 in Tunstall in Staffordshire by Hugh Bourne, William Clowes and James Steele. These three were ex-Wesleyans who were expelled from the old Conference for open-air preaching modelled on that of Lorenzo Dow and other American 'frontier' evangelists. They were also, consciously, returning to the model of Wesley.[15] They were from the start both more plebeian and more democratic than the parent chapel, burdened neither with a high Tory founder nor a history of respectability. Clowes, Bourne and Fletcher, for instance, were all self-taught working men preachers, and most of their early helpers came from the emerging proletariat of Staffordshire – miners, factory workers and labourers. Further, there was a strong feeling in the early years of the Connexion against a full-time ministry which, although it resolved into a half-way house solution of a ministry supported by collection from the membership, remained powerful and gave both the individual congregations and lay preachers great power within the Connexion. Thus the idea of 'Free-Gospelism' and that of individual inspiration regardless of rank were fixed. Although in later years these ideas receded, though not to the extent that a history of the Connexion written from a national perspective alone would suggest, they remained at the heart of Primitive Methodist belief.[16]

Between 1811 and the early 1830s Primitive Methodism grew and spread through the Midlands of England. Called the Ranters, a name which, intended as an insult, they took and gloried in, the Primitives stood against all. Wesleyanism, especially under Jabez Bunting, was a formidable enemy, characterising the Primitives as radicals and shifting blame on to them for any disruption within the Wesleyan body.[17] The Established Church brought constables, mobs and even the Army against them yet their progress was remarkable. Moving into areas largely uncovered by Wesley they established causes in many areas of rural England by the early 1830s including Norfolk.

In 1829 there were 1,917 Primitive Methodists in Norfolk, mostly in the east of the county and a few around Kings Lynn. In the spring of 1830 the Primitives of the tiny North Walsham circuit sent Robert Key, a reformed drunkard and former coal heaver from Yarmouth, into the dislocated society of central and west Norfolk. He preached, largely in the open air, an emotional doctrine of free and full salvation. George Borrow gives a fine description of a Primitive meeting in Norfolk in *Lavengro* which captures the spirit of the revival,[18]

> a tall man speaking as I arrived; ere, however, I could
> distinguish what he was saying he left off, and then there was a
> cry for a hymn 'to the glory of God' – that was the word. It
> was a strange sounding hymn . . . a thousand voices all joined,
> and all joined heartily. . . . The crowd consisted entirely of the
> lower classes, labourers and mechanics and their wives and
> children – dusty people, un-washed people, people of no
> account whatever.

It was not a cause, though, which flourished at ease. From the start Key and the other missionaries were subject to attack and persecution. As they would have seen it they were the successors to Pilgrim at Vanity Fair, abused and cast into the dungeons. Those who opposed Key in the villages of Norfolk were the same groups who were to stand against the Primitive Methodists in later years when they fought for the farm labourer, 'the middle and upper classes of society; persons who call themselves "respectable" '.[19]

However, from the first a substantial section of the poor turned to the 'Prims'. Even where they were not especially religious, Key found the poor of the villages came to his side when he was attacked. At Reepham, when he announced a return visit the local shopkeepers and minor gentry organised to have the fire engine turned on him, and assembled a mob to disrupt his meeting,[20]

> but [Key wrote] from most of the surrounding villages the
> roughs came up by scores, some of them armed with long
> sticks, and other weapons of war; for it was a common feeling

amongst those ungodly men, that I was a good man and meant to do them good.

Chapel society and structure

By 1835 there were 8,017 Primitive Methodists in Norfolk almost entirely in the villages of central and western parts of the county, the areas of Key's mission. The important factor is that it remained 'the faithful few'. In 1851 about 15 per cent of church attendances in Norfolk were Primitive and 35 per cent of the places of worship. Although their number remained static, population decrease in many villages probably meant that by 1900 upwards of 20 per cent of those who went to church belonged to the Connexion. Again in individual villages the figure may well have been much higher since the market towns, as we know, accounted for the highest proportion of Anglican attendance in 1851. Nevertheless they were still a minority, but think of 'Daniel's Band' again, a minority asssailed but triumphant, a minority in battle with the world. The church is a garden surrounded by a wall as in Watt's hymn but it is also a fort, armed and defended against Satan. This fort was the brick-built wayside Bethel, built against opposition from farmer and landlord, paid for with the pence of the poor, and maintaining a whole alternative culture. The rhetoric and the reality become almost indistinguishable. As Augustus Jessopp, Rector of Scarning in Norfolk, and no friend of the Primitives wrote,[21]

> Explain it how we will, and draw our inferences how we choose, there is no denying it that in hundreds of parishes in England the stuffy little chapel by the wayside has been the only place where for many a long day the very existence of religious emotion has been recognised; . . . the only place where the peasantry have enjoyed the free expression of their opinions, and where, under an organisation elaborated with extra-ordinary sagacity, they have kept up a school of music, literature and politics unaided by dole or subsidy – above all, a school of eloquence in which the lowliest has become familiarised with the rules of debate, and has been trained to express himself with directness, vigour and fluency.

The chapel, as is implied by Jessopp, had not one but two

structural existences. Firstly it was a citadel against Satan within the village, protected and protective. As Gilbert says, 'Chapel communities were able to meet associational, recreational and communal needs which in many cases would otherwise have gone unfulfilled.'[22] But it was also linked to a whole 'chain of forts' from which aid and support could come.[23]

> Fierce and long the battle rages,
> But our help is near:
> Onward comes our great Commander,
> Cheer, my comrades cheer.

Through the Connexion, missionary societies, magazines and conferences 'Daniel's Band' was linked into a wider world, a world far outside the narrowness of village life. Like the artisans of rural France in Eugene Weber's fine study they were 'more literate than their fellows, better informed . . . capillary vessels through which the national interest and the national culture rushed into the rural world'.[24]

It is important to have some social and personal sense of this key group. It is beyond the scope of this study to do this in any statistical sense. However, some indications can be given. Nigel Scotland's work, which is more thorough on this count than mine, suggests that chapel members were not, at least until the mid-1890's, noticeably either 'labour aristocrat' or petit-bourgeois, at least not in Norfolk.[25] This is born out by my own examination of those involved in the East Dereham area in the 1870s and 1880s. A number of key figures in the East Dereham circuit of the Primitive Methodist Connexion were labourers or ex-labourers. They filled all levels of local organisation from circuit steward (at the top) to chapel trustee and lay preachers. For example Benjamin Brett, circuit steward of the East Dereham circuit in the 1880s, had been a labourer but was dismissed for union activity. Robert Jude, a trustee of Beetly Chapel, and Josiah Bowes, a trustee of Elsing, were both labourers while the original trustees of Swanton Morley consisted of four labourers, two shoemakers, a butcher, a miller and a general dealer.[26] Perhaps most importantly, labourers often filled the crucial role of lay preachers. Josiah Bowes, R. Buxton, John Culley, George Edwards, Robert Girling, John Harris, and many many others were all labourers and lay preachers. The importance of this can be seen when we realise that in 1840 the East Dereham Circuit of the Primitives had 460 full-time members, 30 on trial and 6 doubtful who were serviced by only 3 travelling preachers but 48 lay preachers.[27] Even the travelling preachers on occasion could turn out to have unlikely connections with the labourers. For instance the Rev. H. Cooper, a Primitive Methodist Minister, speaking at a union meeting at Sparham in 1874,[28]

> soon demonstrated that his year of collegiate learning had not made him forget the struggles and hardships of his former fellow labourers . . . the old fire still burnt in his bosom, and the same noble spirit inspired him to raise his voice on their behalf.

Cooper was, though, an exception. The Cambridge Circuit actually opposed sending young men to college. 'We thoroughly disapprove of the proposed training scheme as dangerous to the piety of young men. What they will gain in light they will lose in heat.'[29] In Norfolk at least 'Daniel's Band' was most often labourers with a smattering of small tradesmen, those who sought a new ideology following the collapse of paternalism in the years after the French War and found it in the assailed Bethels of Primitive Methodism. These factors taken together, their class, the circumstances of their conversion, and the deliberately almost embattled stance of the chapel was a heady mixture and it led fairly quickly to radicalism.

Nationally, the Primitive Methodist Connexion was little more radical than the Wesleyan. Despite the fears of Jabez Bunting that the Ranters would lead a revolution of the saints, the Prims, as a connexion, kept well clear of direct involvement in politics. Indeed, in the crucial years of 1816–20 the Prims directly opposed radicalism in the areas of greatest strength, Staffordshire, Leicestershire, Derbyshire and Nottinghamshire.[30] Additionally, Hugh Bourne in particular among the founders was no radical. At the Tunstall Conference of 1821 he attempted, with some success, to have the radicals, who 'were speaking in public against the government',[31] expelled from the meeting. In the 1840s, and 1850s the Primitive Methodists seem to have stood aloof, at least in an organisational sense, from the anti-state church agitation, and their main 'political' move was to support first temperance and then teetotalism.[32] Only from the late 1870s did the Connexion move towards 'social work' as it was coyly put, and then firmly within the inner city and on lines of soup and God.[33]

How then did this nationally conservative body (for that must be our judgment until proper research is done) get such a reputation for radicalism that even Hobsbawm and Thompson have excepted it from their various condemnations of nineteenth-century nonconformity?[34] The key lies in the relationship between the centre and the periphery of the movement, between the conference, which was far from democratic at least until the 1860s, and the districts, and especially the chapels. Here we return to the chapel as a local unit. A Norfolk example can serve to demonstrate what I mean. In 1872–96 the Primitive Methodist chapels of Norfolk were used extensively for meetings of the farm labourers' unions. Not surprisingly this caused a good deal of comment and argument in the press and elsewhere.[35] On 17 March 1873 the Minutes of the Quarterly Meeting of East Dereham Circuit read[36]

That the complaint made against those Brethren who have used our chapels for the purpose of holding agricultural labourers meetings be floated until full board. . . .

That until the opinion of the General Committee be known as to the legality or otherwise of allowing Chapels for the use of Agricultural Labourers meetings, only those with a majority in a trustee meeting decide to allow it shall be used for that purpose.

This assertion of the trustees against the district and the general committee did not go unchallenged and it seems that a month later the general committee instructed the circuit to stop union meetings being held. However, the pro-union faction in the meeting, which was very large, moved, and got carried, a motion that since they had not asked whether to stop the meetings or not, but whether the union was political, the General Council had not answered their question. Therefore it was up to the trustees to decide as before.[37] Despite attempts to impose discipline this remained the position in East Dereham until the 1890s. Here we see the power of a democratic local and radical periphery exerted against national policy. The chapels in question could, of course, have been expelled, but given that East Dereham was certainly not alone in allowing its chapels to be used by the union this would have meant a major schism.

But this still does not answer the question. After all there was a similar relationship between centre and periphery in the Congregational Church, the Baptists and even among the Wesleyans, yet none of these chapels gave their support to the labourers in Norfolk to anything like the extent of the Prims. The answer lies in origins. Primitive Methodism came to Norfolk when it was still in the 'sect' phase, it was a new church. The sect, according to Brian Wilson,[38]

> is a voluntary association; membership is by proof to sect authorities of some claim to personal merit . . . exclusiveness is emphasised, and expulsion exercised against those who contravene doctrinal, moral or organisational precepts; its self-conception is of an elect, a gathered remnant, possessing special enlightenment; personal perfection is the expected standard of aspiration . . . it accepts, at least as an ideal the priesthood of all believers; there is a high level of lay participation; there is opportunity for the member spontaneously to express his commitment; the sect is hostile or indifferent to the secular society and the state.

'A gathered remnant', Daniel's Band, the heroic age of Primitive Methodism was all this and more to the first one or two generations of chapel members, more because the world was not only spiritually but physically hostile. The farmers and landowners who pulled down cottages to prevent settlement under the poor laws, and who maintained a poverty-stricken casual workforce, were the same men who refused land to build chapels, discriminated against nonconformist workmen; and the same men who supported the Church of England and the Tory Party. Thus we see two separate chronologies with Primitive Methodism, one a central one of a chapel moving along the line of respectability towards becoming another denomination; the other a local one, lagging behind still in its heroic phase, still one of the 'churches of the disinherited'.[39]

Thus early meetings had an ease of language and a freedom of emotion which was profoundly democratic.[40]

They talked familiarly about Jesus Christ, as if He were a farm
labourer keeping a family on nine shillings a week. He was
invited to come among them in a chariot of fire and water His
people with a holy waterpot. "Brush us with thy heavenly
besom and we shall be clean."

This use of the vernacular and the high level of lay participation in
the chapels' affairs opened the doors to that most radical of texts,
the Authorised Version. Moses, Leviticus and the Prophets were
evoked, as well as the more familiar New Testament texts, to
glorify not only the gathered remnant but also the poor:[41]

it had been rumoured that these prayer-meetings were more
political than religious. The landlords and some of the farmers
were prayed for by name. 'Cursed is he who removeth his
neighbour's landmark, and oppresseth the poor and needy and
joineth land to land' . . . these sentences always met with
hearty amens.

However, it was not far from a radical reading of Isiah to much
greater concerns. George Edwards came on to the preaching plan
in September 1872, at about the same time as he appears at a
union meeting at Alby Hill described as a 'brick-maker'.[42] In his
autobiography he wrote about this point in his life,[43]

Up to this point I could not read, I merely knew my letters, but
I set myself to work. My dear wife came to my rescue and
undertook to teach me to read. For the purpose of this first
service she helped me to commit three hymns to memory and
also the first chapters of the Gospel according to St. John . . .
when I returned home from work after tea she would get the
hymn book, read the lines out, and I would repeat them after
her.

But this was not enough. By the spring of 1873 Edwards had
mastered reading and sought more knowledge and gradually
acquired more books; Johnson's *Dictionary; The Lay Preacher* in
two volumes; *Harveys Meditations among the Tombs* and *Contempla-
tions of the Starry Heavens*; a Bible Dictionary and a *History of Rome*

(sic).[44] Later he added Adam Smith, Thorold Rogers and Henry George to his library.[45] However, it was the Bible, on which his radicalism was founded, which remained at the core:[46]

> With my study of theology, I soon began to realise that the social conditions of the people were not as God intended they should be. The gross injustices meted out to my parents and the terrible sufferings I had undergone in my boyhood burnt themselves into my soul like a hot iron. . . . Many a time did I vow I would do something to better the conditions of my class.

As the Rev. Tonks wrote, 'Where Primitive Methodism triumphs the brain fetters must be broken, and this not for narrow sectarian purposes.'[47] Reading and self-education lead men and women into a wider intellectual and political world. By the 1860s the nonconformist conscience, although the Methodists as a body nationally stood slightly apart from it, was a real fact in British politics.[48]

At local level it was battles over ritualism and charities, the latter often seen by nonconformists as a village right appropriated only to churchgoers, which brought chapel men and women into battle with both religious and secular authorities. In East Dereham the mildly tractarian Rev. Benjamin Armstrong faced, from the 1860s, an increasingly well organised nonconformist attack on both his High Church principles and his partial management of the town charities. The opposition took many different forms. It stretched from the harmless, as in May 1861 when two dissenters stood up and walked out of his sermon, to more organised attempts to wrest control of the vestry by dissenters in May 1858, April 1857 and April 1865. He also met opposition, probably from the same group, on his High Church principles, and 'feared' in January 1869 a clash between the church and dissenting parties on the design of a chapel for the new burial ground. At the vestry of 1873 these two prongs were brought together in a single attack when a nonconformist called Thomas Gidney, a coal and coke merchant, stood against the vicar on the issues of charities and 'rampant ritualism'. Gidney was defeated much to Armstrong's delight; he called the election 'the greatest triumph of Church principles I have ever known in Dereham'.[49]

His hoped-for peace did not follow though. In 1874, in

conjunction with a national campaign run by Joseph Arch's National Agricultural Labourers' Union, Armstrong faced the much more formidable figure of Benjamin Brett, 'furniture dealer and broker' of Quebec Street, East Dereham. Brett had been a labourer, was a member of the union committee, and was a Primitive Methodist. Brett found himself at the head of a much wider campaign because of the 'enclosure' of Rush Meadow. This had been allocated under the enclosure award of 1815 as common land for the poor. While it was not cultivated it was used for grazing particularly, according to Armstrong, by 'horse dealers, "dicky" [donkey] buyers, fish cart people, and Hucksters',[50] in fact precisely that group from which so many Primitive Methodists in Dereham came. In 1874 the vicar and church-wardens proposed to let Rush Meadow to 'a London man' to grow watercresses. Brett and the union and nonconformist interests in the town opposed this and found themselves at the head of the poor of the town. At an uproarious meeting the vicar was defeated and the vicar and his nominee, Mr Evrington, left the meeting amid cries of 'No enclosure!' and had to be protected by the police.[51]

In the following year the movement continued when Gidney fought the school-board elections and brought a lecturer from the antitractarian Church Association to Dereham and held a 'packed' meeting in opposition to Armstrong.[52] In 1877 Brett stood again as people's warden but was defeated because the vestry, 'according to practice', was ended at 7.00 p.m. before most labourers finished work.[53] Similar cases, though not so well documented, can be found all over north Norfolk in this period, in which an organisational base within nonconformity began with traditional dissenting grievances and, willingly or unwillingly, moved into local politics.

Temperance and friendly societies were movements which took the village chapelgoer along the same route. In mid-Norfolk there were particularly close links between the chapel and friendly societies which in turn led to trades unions and Liberalism. The main mid-Norfolk 'club', the North Tuddenham Friendly Benefit society, and known locally until the Great War as the 'Ranters' Club',[54] was founded in 1834 specifically for Primitive Methodist local preachers. By the mid-1850s it had opened its doors to anyone. Its special appeal was stated clearly by the secretary in

1882 when he wrote in the *Eastern Weekly Press*[55]

> It was the imperative duty of every young man to make himself
> a member of a good sick benefit society and he would strongly
> recommend them to join the North Tuddenham Friendly
> Society, with its no fines, no fees, no public house meetings, no
> great guns to pander to and be alarmed at.

In 1875 the secretary of the North Tuddenham Society was
George Rix, grocer and general dealer of Swanton Morley near
East Dereham. Rix, whose name was probably as well known
in Norfolk as Arch's, and who will figure large in the next
chapter, said in 1875 that he had been 'a member . . . for
upwards of thirty years, on the committee for many years; [and]
one of the auditors for several years.'[56]

Rix remained an officer of the North Tuddenham Society until
at least the mid-1890s, but his career, like many, spread wide. He
was a Primitive Methodist preacher, Sunday school teacher and
superintendent, and trustee, at different times, of two chapels. He
was born the son of a labourer and worked as one himself until
1851 when he set himself up as a higgler. He founded the
Primitive chapel at Elsing and moved to Swanton Morley in
1873.[57] He was also district secretary of the East Dereham district
of the National Agricultural Labourers' Union, was active in the
Liberal Party, as we shall see below, and sat as a Parish and
County Councillor.[58]

Nor was he unique. Robert Jude, of Gressenhall, was also on
the committee of the North Tuddenham Society, a Primitive local
preacher, branch secretary of the Beetly branch of the NALU.
John Culley of Guist was on the committee of the North
Tuddenham Society, a local preacher and on the committee of the
Norfolk Federal Union after 1878.

But it is perhaps in a less clearly definable area that the most
fundamental contribution of Primitive Methodism was made.
Chapel was a disciplined training ground in democracy. Not only
did it give the poor responsibility and training in office-holding,
and it is no coincidence that the union structures of the 1870s and
1880s closely followed those of the Primitive Methodists, but it
taught them self-discipline in a hard school. Sobriety, neatness,
plainness in dress and good behaviour were all essential to

membership of the Primitive chapel. These virtues were of course double-edged. 'Everywhere Methodists grow rich,' wrote Wesley,[59] and there is little doubt, as we shall see shortly, that respectability became a curse. But initially it gave men pride to stand and face their betters, money to 'stand alone', and organisational ability to lead their fellows.

It was also, as Rev. Augustus Jessopp tells us, 'a school of eloquence'.[60] Rix knew this, Arch knew it and George Edwards knew it. But it was not dead even in later generations. Bert Hazell, team-man, union leader and MP, got his introduction to politics and public speaking through Christian Endeavour:[61]

> [The Chapel] . . . was the centre of activity, especially in the more remote, rural areas, it was only place where lads could go to. . . . We had the Christian Endeavour, and no matter what your background, everybody was invited to participate . . . it was an opportunity because you were always encouraged, shall I say urged, to take part. I suppose my first speech was made at Christian Endeavour, you gain a degree of confidence. It may have been a lot of tripe that you said, but that's neither here nor there, the fact was you got on your feet and you discussed afterwards. . . . It was, in a certain sense, educational because formal education came to a dead halt at 14 and chapel provided an outlet.

Deeper still was the chapels' concern with human dignity. As the Rev. Tonks wrote in 1907[62]

> In these days, there is once more hope for the farm labourer. God Grant he may not again be disappointed. Meanwhile, let him do as thousands of Primitive Methodist farm labourers have done in the past – trust in God, preach a gospel of Brotherhood in Christ, and fight hard for his rights – his rights of manhood, and what is requisite to sustain it.

'His rights of manhood' – this theme occurs again and again. It is sounded in one of the songs written for the unions of the 1870s by Henry Taylor:[63]

'Get wisdom' – true nobility,

'Knowledge is power', obey the call.
Rise in your manhood, men be free!
Knavery and arrogance must fall.

The decline of radical nonconformity

But dignity and manhood were ambiguous concepts. Sobriety and
thrift bred not only pride but social mobility. Even in the
generation of the 1870s and 1880s we see the signs of a religion
which looks more like that of Cromwell than that of the Levellers
or Diggers. Many of the local leadership of the Primitives were
labourers, many, like George Rix, had their first foot on the
ladder. In a famous court case connected with the vestry dispute at
Swanton Morley in 1876 Rix told the court, with some pride, that
he had 'property in Elsing which cost me for land and building
£200, which is mortgaged at $4\frac{1}{2}$%. But I own other property
where I live, which is not mortgaged, and I have the deed at
home.'[64] By 1890 a new generation of trades unionists was
beginning to find 'Old George' a little too respectable,[65] and by
1892 even Edward James, a unionist of the same generation,
wrote to the local press with reference to Rix's anti-strike line and
membership of the County Council, 'I am afraid my old friend
Mr Rix has not improved since he has sat with squires and
farmers.'[66] Rix did not reply but occasionally pronouncements
show that his attitude had changed. He remained 'firm' in politics
but by 1895 he had vanished from union affairs.

But it was not an individual matter. As Rix can in some ways
stand for the leadership of Primitive Methodism in its heroic days,
so too can he be seen as a symbol of a more general change within
Primitive Methodism in Norfolk, and also nationally. At a
theoretical level we might offer a loose combination of Niebuhr
and Weber. As Niebuhr writes of the 'churches of the disinherited',[67]

one phase in the history of denominationalism reveals itself as
the story of the religiously neglected poor, who fashion a new
type of Christianity which corresponds to their distinctive
needs, who rise in the economic scale under the influence of
religious discipline and who, in the midst of a freshly acquired

cultural respectability, neglect the new poor succeeding them on the lower plane.

If we add to this the notion which linked the individual self-improvement to the doctrines of Protestantism put forward by Weber we come to some sort of explanation of the changes in the Prims in Norfolk in the last decade of the nineteenth century and the first decades of this.[68] 'Everywhere Methodists grow rich.' In the language of more recent religious sociology, Methodism had passed out of its sect phase.[69] This is not to say that the Norfolk Primitives ever reached the level of Manchester Congregationalism with its 'millionaire' patrons[70] or, for that matter, the urbane riches of Norwich dissent, but that slightly and slowly things changed.

The most obvious sign of this, in the first instance, was the decline in the number of chapel meetings held by the union. In the early days, most meetings were held in chapels and nearly all had a religious tone. Even by the early 1890s this was beginning to change. The reasons for this are difficult to trace but the impression is that more and more trustees were unwilling to side openly with the union. George Edwards said as much in 1895:[71]

I will admit at once that the Nonconformists have not moved along so fast these few years as some of the more ardent spirits amongst us could have wished, and that they have far too much ignored the fact that Christ came to redress social wrongs as much as to prepare the way for a higher life.

The local perspective here appears very different from the national. It is precisely at this point that it is argued both by the denominational historians and more recent writers like Inglis and Young[72] that the chapel began to take on a social face. Certainly by the 1890s the Primitives had opened inner city missions and had begun 'social work', especially in the East End of London,[73] and certainly conference began to discuss issues, like old age pensions, which were outside the usual run of those discussed, which more usually centred on disestablishment and temperance. The overwhelming impression remains that as the chapel nationally became a political force, locally it withdrew from confrontation on political issues, adopting a 'neutral' stance of moderation and justice to all sides. Certainly by 1907 Edwards was protesting that he had 'been boycotted from more than one pulpit in consequence of my advanced opinions'.[74] Later in the same year the Primitives at Sprowston refused the use of the chapel for an ILP meeting during the Norwich municipal elections, despite the ILP's insistence that 'They wanted a Brotherhood which would bring in the Kingdom of God'.[75]

That last phrase points to a continuing ambiguity. Although the chapel seems to have turned against radicalism in an institutional sense in Norfolk in the early years of the twentieth century, the notion of a democratic God and a close association between a chapel upbringing and radicalism remained. Even Edwards, after attacking the nonconformists, more vehemently denounced the condition of the labourer as 'not in accordance with the will of God'.[76] The language even of those unionists interviewed for this study, most of whom were only born in the 1900s, was firmly that of chapel, and most saw a link between radicalism and the chapel which would have been familiar to Rix and Edwards.

Thus the chapel remained an abiding influence on radicalism throughout the period up to the mid-1920s. In the early 1870s it was more than that. It provided the rural proletarians of Norfolk with a leadership, a language and an ideology. The wayside Bethel gave to the trade unions a model of organisation, and the training and ability to speak and argue in public. The alternative culture, for it was genuinely that, suffused their whole being and through it they dominated the local world of the labourer. This influence made sure that the first years of trades unionism were akin to the revivals of the 1830s – passionate, enthusiastic, occasionally millennial.[77]

> Do not tarry, do not tarry,
> Now's the great momentous time.
> Join the union's ranks in thousands
> Swell the numbers of its line,

ran a union hymn which, almost as accurately as 'Daniel's Band', spoke to the labourers of 1872 and gave voice to their aspirations.

4 Radicalism, the first phase: The local unions 1872–96

When Arch beneath the Wellesbourne tree,
His Mighty work began,
A thrill of hope and energy, all through the country ran.
The farmer, parson, lord and squire, looked on with evil eye.
Some looked with scorn and some with ire,
And some in dumb surprise.[1]

Rural radicalism from 1872 to 1896 is dominated, historiographically at least, by the figure of Joseph Arch. The Warwickshire hedger and ditcher, and Primitive Methodist preacher, founded and became leader of the first agricultural labourers' union (the National Agricultural Labourers' Union) in the spring of 1872. During the next twenty years he rose from local notoriety as a radical[2] to national prominence as an MP. It is with Arch then that we must begin any account of these years, not because of his importance to Norfolk, although he was important in our county, but because of the prominence given to him by historians of the labourer, a prominence which I would wish to suggest is perhaps greater than is deserved.

This prominence, even preeminence, comes from two major factors; first the character of Arch himself. He was an able self-publicist. He appears to have had local and informal links with Warwickshire Liberalism dating back to before the foundation of the union[3] and within two months of the union starting the influential *Daily News* sent Archibald Forbes, one of its best-known correspondents, to cover the Warwickshire strikes. But more than this, his vision of a national union, respectable and well organised with full-time officers, a bureaucracy and a national headquarters, accorded firmly with the 'new model' unions of the engineers and carpenters, which were increasingly allied with the Liberal Party. Finally Arch's own rise to Parliament in 1885 and a

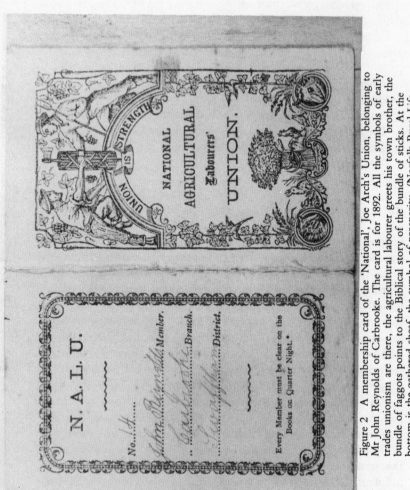

Figure 2   A membership card of the 'National', Joe Arch's Union, belonging to Mr John Reynolds of Carbrooke. The card is for 1892. All the symbols of early trades unionism are there, the agricultural labourer greets his town brother, the bundle of faggots points to the Biblical story of the bundle of sticks. At the bottom is the gathered sheaf, the symbol of prosperity. (Norfolk Rural Life Museum, Gressenhall, Norfolk)

position as a kind of informal Liberal spokesman on agriculture kept him in the public eye.

But it is not only Arch's character and life that led to his preeminence in the history of these times. He left, in 1898, a full and detailed autobiography which has shaped writing about the 1870s ever since. Additionally other printed accounts from the last years of the nineteenth century like those by Hasbach and Clifford also gave Arch, and the National Union, pride of place.[4] Furthermore the dominant tradition of labour history in this country was created by, and to some extent is still in the shadow of, the Webbs' monumental work on the history of trades unionism.[5] This profoundly Whiggish work sees a linear progress from the barbarian age of local unions, violence and disorganisation at the end of the eighteenth century through to the civilisation of the 'new model' unions. Henry Broadhurst, Liberal, Temperance, a paid official with a gold watch and chain, becomes the epitome of all that is good. The ultimate aim of the unions was, and indeed should have been, a place in the state. In this view the big unions are seen as a force for progress, each unification congress is analysed, and the disappearance of the 'impractical' and 'old-fashioned' local unions is greeted with an academic joy which once characterised the style of a Whig historian looking at nineteenth-century social reform.

The history of the labourers' movement has, by this process, largely become the history of Arch and the National. There are exceptions, especially recent work on Kent and Sussex, the north-west and the north-east of Scotland, but in essence the position remains unchanged.[6] For instance Pamela Horn, in a short article published in 1981, still places Arch and Warwickshire as the 'prime inspiration of the rural union movement'.[7]

In the course of this process the real strengths of local unionism have been largely ignored and those unions which remained firmly local in their orientation condemned as at best backward and at worst sectarian. Again this follows precisely Arch's own position when, after 1874, a number of areas of the National split away to form local unions.[8] Yet the labourer, both in his work and in his social relations, lived in a local world. As I argued above, work relationships were close and dictated by local conditions. The chapel, while it had an ambiguous existence, was at least in part a firmly local grouping. These factors tended, especially in the case of workplace relations, to generate animosity which was local and often personalised.

In the case of Norfolk this localism was further reinforced by the nature of the county and by local tradition. We saw above how rural population changes had, through the nineteenth century, created a virtual desert, in terms of settlement patterns in the west of the county with great distances between villages.[9] But the county as a whole was isolated. The vast majority of the land of Norfolk lay off the main thoroughfares of nineteenth-century commerce which linked north and south, and while both Norwich and Yarmouth had important economic roles these had little effect on most of the rural areas. Additionally the railways came late to many rural areas and never covered them totally. The Midland and Great Northern Joint Railway, for instance, was a more or less total failure except as a holiday route from the Midlands.[10] Even in the 1890s, after the coming of the railways, the Cromer holiday guide refers constantly to the isolation of the town as one of its charms.[11]

This localism was not only economic and social but also cultural. Norfolk people have a reputation for being close and secretive, a reputation which is completely undeserved, but which is reinforced by the strength of the dialect and the persistence of local culture, all of which were pointed to by Marion Springhall in 1936.[12] Further, folk tradition had a remarkable survival rate in Norfolk. Both traditional music and song seem to have played a vital and central part in the community until the 1950s.[13] But it was not only the rural poor who inhabited a local world. Even within the local ruling class the centres of social and cultural life for much of the nineteenth century, for the farmers, tradesmen and minor gentry at least, remained the market towns. East Dereham in 1896 had its own Corn Hall, Assembly Rooms, Institute, Liberal and Conservative Clubs. It was also the seat of the Mitford and Launditch Petty Sessions and a County Court District, the headquarters of the 3rd Norfolk Rifle Volunteers, had two churches and five chapels, and shops which could provide every need.[14] At the centre of it all it had a market. As *Kelly's Directory* for 1896 said,[15]

The position of the town, in the centre of a fertile and highly cultivated district, and its distance from any other market of any consequence cause Dereham to rank among the best markets in the county.

Dereham was at the centre of a local world and provided for that world most of its needs, social, economic, political and cultural. It defined that world geographically by the parish, the Methodist Circuit, the Poor Law Union and the Petty Sessional District. It defined it economically because of its market. It defined it socially and culturally by its clubs, meetings and balls. Crucially, for us, it defined its radicalism as the centre of a trade union district. It was a world which was 12 to 15 miles from east to west and the same from north to south.

Local and national unionism: East Dereham district

In the spring of 1872 the local paper, the trusted Liberal *Eastern Weekly Press*, brought news into this local world of stirrings 'in the Shires', as the rest of England was inevitably called. On 31 March that year the paper carried a leader on the strike by Warwickshire farm workers, and then, in the following week a 'sketch' of Arch and a further account of the Warwickshire movement.[16] At this point the role of the *Eastern Weekly Press* was crucial. Unlike its current near namesake, the *Eastern Daily Press*, the 'Press' was a radical paper. It had been founded in 1867 by a group of Norwich Liberal businessmen including J.J. Colman, Thomas Jarrold and Henry Tillett. From the first, its aim was, ' "to guide the working classes politically and morally". It devoted its columns to the affairs of the agricultural labourer and to under privileged members of the community.'[17] Its editor from its foundation until 1897 was James Spilling. Spilling was born in Ipswich in 1825 and was, in the 1840s, according to his obituary, 'an agnostic and a revolutionist of the most uncompromising order'.[18] He later became a Swedenborgian but retained a deep personal sympathy for the rural poor which was echoed in the *Press*: 'Leaders, special articles of rural interest, stories dealing with rural life, and illustrating the hardships of the labourers' lot flowed from Mr. Spilling's pen.'[19] Spilling wrote every week under the name 'Cherub' a column called 'Local Topics' which frequently contained *exposés* of conditions in the rural areas.[20]

Under Spilling's editorship the *Press* was placed, in the spring of 1872, at the 'disposal' of the labourers' movement 'as an organ for expressing their grievances and reporting their proceedings'.[21] But no newspaper alone, nor the example of Joseph Arch in distant Warwickshire, could have caused the revolt of the field in Norfolk, it was much more 'a great momentous time'. We saw in Chapter 1 how relationships between master and man had changed during the years before 1870 with the workforce growing more and more casual. We also saw how, in the course of this change, the chapel moved into the vacuum created by the collapse of the old ideology of paternalism and gave the labourers' organisation language but above all belief in themselves. We also saw how this religious belief could, and did, lead to social and political action. In these senses the labourers had a cause and the beginnings of a leadership.

There were also short-term factors. In 1867–70 there were a number of local disturbances connected with enclosure, as at Fakenham, and with charities as we saw at East Dereham.[22] In both these cases, Fakenham and Dereham, local organisations were created and a local leadership emerged which was to revive in 1872.[23] Following the industrial downswing in 1862–4 a number of migrants returned to Norfolk not only swelling the labour force but bringing with them organising ability and more militant attitudes. At the founding meeting of the union in the East Dereham area, for instance, one of the speakers was a Mr Wilkin, 'a labourer from the North'.[24] From 1865 there was a long series of bad harvests which reduced the actual level of harvest earnings, while in 1868 real wages fell drastically, a fall felt more severely because of the relative prosperity of the previous ten years.[25] Although they rose again in 1870, figures produced by John Cook, and as yet unpublished, suggest they fell again from 1870 to 1872 at least in some areas.[26] Thus when J.P.D. Dunbabin talks of 'a revolt of rising expectations'[27] these expectations must be seen in the long term and must extend to the cultural sphere, in the sense of the changes in ideology in Chapter 3, as well as simple economic changes. Further it seems that in Norfolk at least there was an actual drop in wages in the years before 1872.

It was also spring. As we saw above this was one of the points when the yearly cycle moved in the men's favour and when, traditionally, wages were increased as summer hours started. It was precisely in the last couple of weeks of March, when this change took place by custom, that the union started in Norfolk. But it was not only custom. In the months following the foundation of the union in Norfolk the season moved strongly with the labourer. Spring ploughing, sowing, weeding, haysel, harvest, formed a period of six to seven months when labour was at a premium, the best time to strike and to build an organisation.

And so, 'the great momentous time' began. The first meetings were in the south of the county but very quickly the west and central areas of Norfolk, those where high farming and rural depopulation had gone furthest, came to dominate. By the beginning of 1874 there were branches all over the county totalling some 18,000 members.[28] The story of most of these branches was essentially similar and I want to take one area, the 'land' of East Dereham described above, to look at the progress of the union through the twenty-five years after 1872.

The union in the East Dereham area was founded at a meeting in the Elsing Sand Pit, a kind of rough, small common in the centre of the village on Saturday 22 April 1872. Its origins lay with George Rix, the Primitive Methodist shopkeeper whom we met in Chapter 3. According to the newspaper report, 'the proceedings . . . [were] commenced by singing and prayer.'[29] This was characteristic not only of the East Dereham area meetings but of all the meetings of the unions of the 1870s and 1880s. We do not know what the hymns were but it is likely they included 'Hold the Fort', a perennial favourite much used at later meetings, 'Stand like the brave' and 'Daniel's Band', both of which occur time and time again. The prayer was most likely extempore as at Dereham itself in early 1873 when H.J. Gibson of Swaffam, '[read] the 1st Psalm (Blessed is the man that hath not walked in the council of the ungodly . . .), and afterwards pray[ed] to God that if the Union were of man it might fail but that if it were of Him it might prosper'. Later in the same meeting James Culley said, with characteristic millennarian feeling, 'The Union would bring the fullness of Gentiles into the Church, and then Israel would be restored.'[30]

The newspaper report names only three people as speaking at the founding meeting, George Rix, Mr Wilkin and William Lane of Elsing, a brickmaker. John Culley of Elsing was in the chair.[31]

Lane was a Primitive Methodist lay preacher who became a full-time union official and organiser for the East Dereham District of the National Agricultural Labourers' Union (NALU) in January 1873. John Culley was also a Primitive preacher and had been active in the Dereham Circuit since the mid-1860s. In 1875 he is described as 'a farmer' but he was working as a labourer in Guist, a closed village about 4 miles north of Elsing in 1872.[32]

Who the others elected to the committee of the first union in the Dereham district were it is not possible to say with certainty. Basing ourselves on the first full committee list from May 1874, and speakers at meetings up to that point, we get some idea. The president of the district in 1874 was David Reeder of Elsing. He spoke at Swanton Morley at the union's second meeting in the first week of June 1872 and was described as a farm labourer. In July he was elected president of the district. In December 1872 Reeder was one of a group of labourers on strike in Elsing. The strike, which seems to have been against wage reductions, ended in February 1873, and was claimed as a victory by the union. Reeder was blacklisted and although he was described as a labourer a few weeks later, he subsequently always referred to himself as an ex-labourer. Reeder was also a Primitive preacher, a committee member of the Lenwade Union and Primitive Methodist Preachers Benefit Societies, and continued as chairman of the Dereham union until the end of the 1880s.

Treasurer in 1874 was William Hubbard of Swanton Morley. He was described in September of that year as being on strike because of victimisation, which suggests he was a labourer. However, he also owned property in Swanton Morley and was George Rix's landlord for a time after Rix had been evicted from his cottage and shop in Elsing because of union activity. Hubbard's land was big enough to put a marquee on for the District Meeting of 1874. Rix, in his autobiography, refers to Hubbard as a 'cockle seller', and he was described as a 'dealer' in 1877. He was still selling 'seafood' in 1900 when he was killed falling from his cart. He also seems to have been one of the 'higglers' who opposed the Rev. Armstrong in the late 1860s.

John Harris of Lyng was also on the 1874 committee. Like Hubbard and Rix he was a Primitive preacher. He was also, like David Reeder, a committee member of the Union Benefit Society at Lenwade and the North Tuddenham Friendly Benefit Society.

Finally, he was a trustee and treasurer of the Primitive Methodist chapel at Lyng. In 1872 he was described as a yardman, but by 1874 it was said he had formerly been a labourer but was now a tradesman. By 1881 he was 'a carpenter working on his own account'.

It seems likely that the four remaining members of the 1874 committee also served in 1872. Benjamin Brett we have already met in Chapter 3. Robert Jude, also an ex-labourer who, 'after arriving at manhood learned the boot and shoe making trade', was a considerable figure among the Primitive Methodists in Norfolk and when he died in 1902 the circuit plan was put in mourning in his memory. He was branch secretary at Beetly and sat on the union committee until 1888. He was also on the committee of the North Tuddenham Friendly Society.

Of the two remaining members of the 1874 committee we know even less. Archibald Pearce of Hingham remained on the committee until 1877 and is recorded speaking at a meeting in his own village a year later. After that his name vanishes. William Horne, who was secretary of the Mattishall branch appears to have ceased his activity in 1875, but remained on the financial committee of the Norwich district of the Primitives until at least 1879.

This group, which remained at the core of the union in East Dereham until the early 1890s, was extremely important in shaping the union's activity and attitudes. Like the Primitive Methodists in general they were highly respectable and self-improving. George Rix, along with others, constantly advocated temperance and non-smoking. He disliked violence and was in favour of arbitration in union affairs, even though this was usually impossible since the farmers refused to recognise the union. Order and sobriety were his watchwords. As a group these small tradesmen who led the labourers tended to be socially mobile but we must beware of taking this too far. They remained at the upper end of the labouring class although they had usually acquired, through their own efforts or chance, a small business. These were seldom stable – higgling and dealing especially were chronically prone to failure. However, they did have a crucial freedom from victimisation either in the form of losing jobs or homes. (This could be tenuous enough though. Rix claimed his fish-hawking business had been ruined 'as the rich would no longer buy my fish'.) They were also men of many occupations, moving from one to the other at different times, sometimes labourers, sometimes higglers or builders, sometimes even shopkeepers, and were certainly not even petit-bourgeois in the sense we understand that term today. They occupied a twilight zone between the regularly employed among the labourers and the small tradesmen of the market town and, like the Primitives, which they so often were, this put them in a unique position in village society. They were in it, and of it, but also linked to a world outside it by their slightly better social position and self-education.

They were also, by and large, older men. Most of them seem to have been in their late forties or even fifties when the union began. This is not surprising since some status must have been required to be even a branch secretary. Yet it is in marked contrast to the earlier generation, particularly those involved in rick-burning and machine-breaking. It has been noted several times that those involved in these incidents tended to be young.[33] This also had important consequences for the 'second' union as by 1906 many of the local leaders were dead or infirm, and so there was little continuity in the middle rank of the leadership.

However there clearly were labourers active as officers in the union. A number of the committee members had been labourers originally and had been forced into other professions because of victimisation and were often helped by collections around the union branches. Others remained labourers like Stephen Hudson of Lyng, who served briefly on the district committee. Labourers are frequently present on union platforms, often taking the chair in their own village, suggesting that they probably held some kind of branch office, for example, a man called Buxton from Bawdeswell, who was a Primitive preacher and whom Rix described as 'Our old and long tried friend', and John Durrant of East Tuddenham, Carson of Lenwade, or Gooch of Swanning-ton.[34]

Although the initial growth of what soon became the Elsing Agricultural Labourers' Union was slow, its experience was repeated all over the county of Norfolk. Trades unionism swept the county like some massive religious revival. It was a spontaneous movement which transcended this spontaneity via the new leadership provided by chapel. The experience of the

Elsing unions was probably duplicated all over the country in what followed. In January 1873 it seems not to have spread much beyond Elsing, Lyng and Swanton Morley. However, at this stage it had made a firm stand for independence. Arch had first visited Norfolk in August and from that date the local unions begin to group together either around the Lincolnshire League or around the larger National. Elsing, however, refused. A report of a meeting in the first week of September 1872 said 'a decided opinion was expressed that Norfolk could and ought to stand by itself'.[35] Outside events intervened and rendered this resolve an empty gesture for six years. In October it was announced that the Elsing union was to become part of the Eastern Counties Union, an organisation which immediately vanished. Crucially in the first week in December four or five farms in the Elsing area struck work, probably against winter wage reductions. The union at this stage had only 250 members.[36] The Elsing union could not support the strike and financial assistance was given by the Aylsham and Swaffam districts of the National. In the later acrimonious debate between Zachariah Walker and George Rix, Walker claimed that the National had rescued the Elsing union while Rix claimed he was forced to join the National against his will by his committee. He wrote in 1879 '[he was] . . . the last man in the East Dereham District to consent to join the NALU. . . . He did join very reluctantly in April 1873.'[37]

What seems to have happened is that the National started a campaign based on the existing Swaffam district to form an East Dereham district with William Lane as organiser. The National held a meeting in Dereham in the first week of January 1873 for this purpose which was addressed by Henry Gibson of the Swaffam district and through January and February more and more branches in the Dereham area announced that they were affiliating to the National. In the second week of February Elsing finally joined and became the East Dereham district. It is significant that in the report that contained this announcement reference was also made to the help of Swaffam and Aylsham in 'the recent strike' and further that the strike was over and apparently victorious although David Reeder was unable to find work.[38]

Following its affiliation to the National the East Dereham district (as it now was) grew steadily, chiefly through the work of

Lane as full-time organiser. By April 1873 the district committee claimed 1,000 members and they seem regularly to have held meetings of 500 and could muster 1,200–1,500 for special occasions. In February 1874 membership had risen to 1,500. The area covered by the union can only be given approximately but at its greatest in 1877 it stretched from Hindolveston in the north of Hingham in the south, from Mileham in the west to Reepham and Ringland in the east. The size of the union can be charted in a little more detail and this is set out in Figure 3. All figures are from the press and are therefore 'claims', and are obviously rounded off. All are from the *Eastern Weekly Press*.

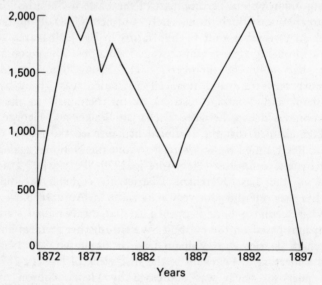

Figure 3   Membership of unions in the East Dereham area 1872–96

If we compare these local figures with the national figure for the NALU in Dunbabin[39] we see that they show a rather different pattern. First the fluctuations are not nearly so violent (although this could be accounted for by optimistic membership figures of the NALU in 1872–3). Second the national figure shows a sharp decline in membership after 1874, rising briefly in 1876, then declining steadily until 1890. Dunbabin places the cause of this decline firmly with the defeat of the union in Suffolk and

Cambridgeshire. 'Only a minority of the union's members . . . had been directly involved. . . . But the psychological effects were more widely felt',[40] while the increasing tempo of the depression made strikes less likely to succeed and moved the union into emigration and benefits which could be, and were, fulfilled by other organisations. Dunbabin also thinks the splits within the National may have added to the disillusionment of the members, as does Horn who also states that the union's increasing preoccupation with 'politics' may have alienated the membership.[41]

This is not so obviously true of Norfolk as it is nationally (if indeed it is true then). First the Dereham membership reached its peak in 1877 and probably remained fairly constant around 1,800 members from mid-1879 with the lockout having no noticeable effect. The depression probably did affect membership but there does not seem to have been a real decline in number of disputes until 1883, which was the first year since the Union's formation with no recorded disputes. Table 2 gives some idea of the level of union activity in different fields over the period up to 1889.

The general trend in the Dereham district while towards less strike action shows no sudden cut off after 1874, indeed the high point comes in 1876. Further, disputes about harvest wages (see Chapter 2) are a constant factor, as they are in periods of non-unionisation and during the period of the second union.

The Dereham area also seems to differ from what historians have regarded as the national pattern in another significant respect – that of non-industrial or 'political' activities. It has been suggested the one factor in the decline of Arch's union was Arch's own, and the union's, increasing concern with politics. But I would suggest that the movement should be seen as a 'freedom' or a civil rights movement and as such it should have been concerned with a wide range of issues from the first. This is in fact true of the Dereham district. The issues in Table 3 represent the concern of working men and women in East Dereham area with local and national politics. Local politics are covered mainly under the headings Charities, Common Rights, Benefit, Schools; national politics, by Game Laws, Franchise and Politics. A bridge between the two is provided by Vestry/Guardians and County Council. Allotments and Immigration do not clearly fall into any of these groups but were an integral part of the union's role as a civil rights movement. However, local communities clearly do respond to national events and are shaped by them. A glance at the table shows a marked upsurge in political activity between 1885 and 1887 which can be explained first by the election of 1885, then by the Irish policy of Gladstone, and finally by the defection of two of the Norfolk Liberal members (elected on the farm workers' vote) to the camp of the Unionists. Similarly the upsurge in vestry fights in 1877 was in response to the national policy of the NALU, as was the rise in the number of charity

TABLE 2   Labour disputes 1872–89 involving withdrawal of labour (*Eastern Weekly Press*)★

Year	Reason for dispute	
	Weekly wage	Harvest wage
1872	1	
1873	1	3
1874	8	
1875	7	2
1876	8	4
1877	3	1
1878	4	2
1879	7	
1880	3	30 men paid
1881	1	2
1882	1	
1883		
1884		1
1885		2
1886	2	3 'and others'
1887		1
1888		
1889		1

★   These numbers refer to disputes. The number of men involved is impossible to estimate as it is seldom given. On occasions as many as 30 or 40 men could be out (Longham and Mileham 1878), on others only one or two. If there is an average it could be estimated at around 10–15 men. Second it is probable that there were other disputes in the area which went unreported. For instance the phrase 'and others' in 1885 could mean almost anything. However it is unlikely, in view of the support given to the union by the *Press* and the fact that Rix himself wrote the union reports, that many were missed.

meetings in the same year. Also it was obviously impossible to fight county council elections before 1889.

Probably the most important aspect of the union's involvement in politics was its central part in organising the farm labourers of Norfolk in relation to the franchise. This is a complicated problem and I have dealt with it in greater detail elsewhere.[42] However the broad outlines of that involvement should at least be indicated.

From their foundation the unions of the 1870s all were closely concerned with the extension of the franchise to the labourer and from 1874 onwards a series of campaigns and petitions were organised at both national and local level. In Norfolk Rix, himself a Gladstonian Liberal, took an important role in these campaigns and when the vote was finally granted in 1884 he led the labourers into the Liberal Party. The results were striking. From 1885 to 1914 Liberalism dominated Norfolk county politics. By an inspired linking of chapel – union – Liberalism Rix created a firm base on which the Liberal grandees were returned to Parliament. Even in 1900 Norfolk went against the national trend showing a much lower swing to the Conservative Party and even in one seat, South West Norfolk, the Liberals increased their vote. In 1906 every Norfolk seat returned a Liberal member to the House of Commons with the exception of Norwich where one of the seats was won by Labour.

At the beginning of 1888 the union's position was weak in East Dereham. However, long before that date important changes had taken place within the union which ensured that it at least still existed when, throughout East Anglia as a whole, the labourers' unions had collapsed. From the middle of 1875 onwards problems were beginning to appear in the relationship between the East Dereham district and Leamington, the union's national head-quarters. After the conference of that year, although Dereham supported the expulsion of the anti–Arch faction, they rejected the notion that only *bona fide* labourers should serve as delegates. Rix wrote that this was simply an exercise by the executive to hold on to its power, 'a thing every district in the Union would do well to keep its eye upon, and insist upon retaining the power in their own hands of sending their own choice, irrespective of calling'.[43] The following year the dispute with Leamington took on a more serious tone when the East Dereham district insisted on paying a number of men who had struck work at harvest £7 10s (the

TABLE 3 Issues raised in the Dereham district of the union other than wages, conditions or housing, 1872–89[1]

Year	Charities	Immigration[2]	Franchise	Politics	Common Rights	Benefit
			Number of meetings			
1873	1					
1874	1	3		1	1	
1875	4			2	1	1
1876		4	3			
1877	13		3			
1878	1	1		3		
1879		2		1		
1880	1					
1881	3		1	2		
1882		2		1		
1883	2	'series'		1		
1884						
1885	1			10[3]		
1886				20		
1887				19		
1888				3		
1889						

[1] Again this is a far from complete list. Most of these topics would have been dealt with by visits to the branches and since branch meetings are seldom reported in any detail these are lost for ever.

[2] This is clearly an underestimate since it was usual simply to announce that the agent was in the area and holding meetings. It is unlikely though that there were union sponsored meetings in the district in any other years.

[3] This figures does *not* include election meetings.

Norfolk rate that year) against head office instructions to pay only £6. In this argument a new and bitter tone entered Rix's writing,[44]

> We would patiently bear the reproach and condemnation of a thousand such men as formed that committee [the NEC]. We have had during this agitation plenty of enemies to contend with and conquer without have to fight with our professed friends.

From 1876 onwards Leamington began to retaliate. The doings of the East Dereham district figure less and less in the union paper,

| Year | Game Laws | Schools | Number of meetings | | | |
			Vestry/ Guardians	Allotments	County Council
1873	1				
1874	4	1			
1875		1	1		
1876		3	1		
1877			12		
1878	1		2		
1879		1			
1880					
1881					
1882					
1883					
1884			1		
1885					
1886					
1887			2	4	
1888					
1889					6 candidates and a series of meetings

only appearing when it suited Arch's purpose to distort the position of Rix and the Dereham district on the question of local power which was rapidly becoming a major issue. After the conference of 1877 Rix wrote,[45]

> he found that all the evils of centralisation would soon become apparent. To place such unlimited power in eleven men's hands, and those eleven all paid officers of the Union was, in his judgment, a most unwise thing.

The reason for the final break though was the appointment of William Lane, a paid official, to improve the ailing fortunes of the union's paper the *English Labourers' Chronicle* by selling it in the Dereham area. This was done without consulting the area committee and all saw it as an attempt to overthrow a democratically elected local body by the paid agents of national office (which it almost certainly was). There followed a bitter public dispute between Lane and Rix in the pages of the *Eastern*

Weekly Press which showed just how far the East Dereham district had moved away from Arch.[46]

The split between Rix and Leamington was quickly duplicated in the branches. Lane began holding meetings in the district on a pro-Arch, anti-Rix basis. Mattishall branch split and a new branch was set up with a pro-Rix leadership. Robert Jude, a pro-Rix secretary, wrote in to say that he attended a number of Lane's meetings which were failures and attracted hardly any union men.[47] Outside the Dereham district though, Rix found little support, initially at least. Swaffam district passed a motion condemning his action and supporting the national leadership, as did other Norfolk districts.[48] The scene was set for a final separation, which Rix presented with the phrase 'The days of man worship and despotic rule are numbered among the dead . . . '. On 1 October 1878 Rix, and other local leaders who were dissatisfied with Arch, set up the Norfolk Federal Union.[49] The reasons given were clear, they were dissatisfied with 'the conduct of business at central office, and the salaries and wages paid to a number of national and district officers'.[50]

The position was put more firmly still in 1879 when Arch appealed for a vote of confidence. In a letter to the *Eastern Weekly Press* 'An Old Member of the Labourers' Union' wrote in an open letter to Arch,[51]

> We shall not forsake our old and tried leaders to please your whims and fancies. . . . We have summered and wintered them long before we had heard of your existence . . . We would rather a thousand times forsake you than our present faithful leaders.

Rix's response to Arch's appeal was more forceful still. He wrote 'Centralism is Toryism rank and rife. Federation is Radicalism pure and simple. As a district we must profess to be of the radical type, and we must be loyal to our convictions'.[52]

The split with Arch was seen by Rix and his supporters as a move towards a more democratic and radical form of union organisation. Behind it lay the belief that ultimate control should lie not in head office, but in the branches. This approach seems to have found a response in Norfolk and the East Dereham district remained consistently strong in membership throughout the 1880s when the National all but disappeared both at a national and a local level.

Through the 1880s the union's fortunes fluctuated. The various campaigns organised around the franchise, the 1885 election and particularly Home Rule after 1886 caused temporary revivals as did local strikes but, by the beginning of the second revival in 1889, things looked very bad. In the spring of that year East Dereham district seems to have been reduced to less than a dozen branches and, although activity centred on the first County Council elections and continuing propaganda on Home Rule, things were basically very quiet.

In March 1889 the revival started. First to notice it were the shattered remains of the National which were confined entirely to the area around Zachariah Walker's home village of Docking. This may have been stimulated by the County Council elections in which Walker stood although he was defeated. Certainly meetings were organised around his candidature which could have served as a stimulus. In the first week of March 1889 Walker wrote to the *Press* that 'a large number had rejoined the Union'.[53] Since in March 1889 the dock strike had not begun, it seems that the beginnings of the revival in Norfolk are to be sought, not in stimulus from new unionism, but in the County Council elections bringing back into operation a semi-defunct organisation.[54] The revival of the National really got under way after harvest and at that point East Dereham entered the fray. In November, George Edwards, formerly a branch secretary in Arch's union, wrote to the press that he had been 'approached' to set up a union in the Cromer District on the 'same principles' as Rix. Accordingly he organised two meetings at Cromer and Aylmerton, his own village.[55] At that point the National was organising widely in north-west Norfolk and although Rix mentioned the example of the dockers in a letter to the *Press* it seems the stimulus came from local forces rather than national.[56]

The two meetings addressed by Edwards and Rix founded the Norfolk Federal Union (Cromer district) which was formally associated with Dereham and Harleston, another strong 'Federal' area. It was to be a short-lived association. Rix was getting old and his work as a County Councillor took a lot of his time. He wanted to pass control to 'younger and abler advocates and leaders of the working class'.[57] It was also suggested that his term on the council was making him less inclined to be a militant labour advocate.[58] Further, although Edwards was strongly opposed to centralisation ('Is not centralisation Toryism? . . . Don't let funds run away from Norfolk to the fashionable town of Leamington'), in 1890[59] he felt that the districts of the Norfolk Federal should come closer together ('I . . . was convinced that we should never be a force strong enough to meet the farmers . . . so long as we remained in little Unions'.)[60] In this he was opposed by Rix and Edward James of Harleston.

It was the death knell of the Federal which had stood so long and so firmly for the labourers' rights. In October 1890 Edwards called a general meeting of the Cromer district at which it was decided to join with the Norwich Labourers' Union, a predominantly urban general Union led by Edward Burgess who published a satirical magazine in Norwich called *Daylight* and had been a socialist.[61] James remained outside and kept his section of the Federal going until 1896. Rix left the scene and East Dereham gradually moved over to the new union now called the Norfolk and Norwich Amalgamated Labourers' Union with Edwards as secretary.

Initially the Norfolk and Norwich seems to have grown rapidly. Edwards claimed that by the end of 1891 they had 3,000 members. Estimates are difficult but it seems that by the end of 1890 the Norfolk and Norwich, the National and the rumps of the older unions had between 9,000 and 15,000 members in Norfolk. As the temporary improvement in agriculture of the late 1880s vanished the farmers themselves formed the first effective farmers' organisation in Norfolk, the Farmers' Federation, in 1890. This organisation, as the Royal Commission on Agriculture noted, was 'avowedly maintained for the purpose of promoting common action among farmers in regard to wages and conditions of employment, and for mutual assistance in the case of strikes'.[62]

Inevitably strikes started again. The Farmers' Federation claimed that in 1892–3 they had fought twenty-two disputes on behalf of their members, although this is a figure for the whole of Norfolk.[63] Table 4 gives a broad idea of industrial activity in the 1890s. The strikes in 1891–2 caused a good deal of bitterness, especially those in the winter of 1890–1 (which was particularly hard) when the farmers reduced wages from 12*s* to 11*s*.[64] The *Press* reported in January 'We are just now passing through the rigours of a winter of exceptional severity.'[65] At Salthouse there were evictions in February when the men struck against reductions, while at Thorpe Market and Bradfield fighting broke out between strikers and blacklegs.[66] The strikes were attended by considerable controversy amongst the union's supporters over winter strikes. Then at the beginning of April 1892 a strike began in north-west Norfolk for a wage increase to 13s which was supported by the National Union.

TABLE 4   Industrial disputes 1890–5 involving the withdrawal of labour
(*Figures refer to the Norfolk and Norwich Labourers' Union (Cromer District)*)*

Year	Reason for dispute	
	Weekly wage	Harvest wage
1890	2	2
1891	3	
1892	1	
1893	3	1
1894	1	1
1895	2	

*   Figures based on reports in the *Eastern Weekly Press* and
    Eastern Weekly Leader

It quickly spread to the east and into the territory of the Norfolk and Norwich union. The strike was unevenly supported and the Farmers' Federation soon brought blacklegs in, including Yarmouth fishermen, who were soon to become one of the traditional groups of Norfolk strike breakers. At Longham they were met by the women and children of the village who 'rough musiced' them with 'derisive cheers, tin kettle music, hooting jeers and jibes'.[67] At Burnham Thorpe the men went out into the fields, as they were to do in 1923, and stopped men working: 'a harrow was discovered hanging in a tree, whilst another was found thrown down in a meadow nearby.'[68] The strike though was a serious defeat for the labourers. By July all the men who were going to be taken back were back at the old rate. Yarmouth fishermen were again used in 1894 to break a harvest strike at St Faiths and were again met with rough music. On this occasion six St Faiths men were tried for riotous assembly and one of them, William Furness, received two months in prison.[69]

Less conspicuous in the 1890s was political activity on the union's part. Although the union continued its close relationship with the Liberal Party the issues adopted were more 'trade union' oriented than in the past. Unemployment, for instance, figures large in its concerns, and the Norfolk and Norwich affiliated itself to the TUC. Nevertheless the tie-up was still definitely there. There was, for instance, a slight union revival around the time of the 1895 election which seems to be directly connected with the election.

However, from the defeat in the summer of 1892 the union's days in Norfolk were numbered. Agricultural depression once more set in and with the farmers well organised around the Farmers' Federation the union's position became weaker and weaker. In the first week of 1894 Edwards attacked the farm labourers in a bitter tone, which was to become increasingly common from both him and Zachariah Walker, and accused them of apathy which led to their own defeats.[70] At the end of 1894 he met with Arch and Walker and decided to give it one more year and to attempt with the aid of the English Land Restoration League's Red Vans to revive the union.[71] Despite a revival around the election, the attempt failed and the Red Vans met with a good deal of hostility in the villages.[72] By May 1895 the National was in serious trouble. Walker wrote, 'I have not forsaken them but they have forsaken me.'[73] On 2 February 1896 Edwards formally gave up the union. Walker followed within a matter of weeks.[74] The first phase of Norfolk rural trade unionism was at an end.

The year 1872 has been compared to a religious revival, spontaneous and wild, moving relentlessly across the country, sweeping all before it. Certainly it had those elements. Indeed based as it was, in Norfolk at least, so firmly within Primitive Methodism, itself barely out of the revivalist phase, it would be surprising if it were not. In common with revivals it is usual to see this movement as short-lived. Mortally wounded in the bitter months of the great lock-out in 1874, it lingered on painfully until 1896. This may be the picture of the National Union of Agricultural Labourers, it is not the picture at local level. In Norfolk, as in Kent and Sussex, and parts of Lincolnshire and Oxfordshire, the move to a local federal structure in the late 1870s ensured that the unions survived, if not always healthily.

The reasons for this are, I hope, clear. The labourer, both in his workplace and in his social and cultural life, inhabited a local world. Strikes like everything else including hours, wages and conditions, were local, seldom the same even within one county. Given this, it was not only that the Norfolk labourer was isolated from national consciousness to some extent, but it was sensible for him to behave in a localist way. The local unions of the 1870s have been missed by history; they deserve a better fate. If their ideas seem to be wrong it is because we look through twentieth-century labour history spectacles at them. In East Dereham in 1878 they made good sense.

Nor were the local unions so concerned about simply being unions as was the National. Their range of concerns, although local in focus, extended well beyond wages, hours and conditions. Above all they were political, seeking in a sense like the Primitive Methodist Church, to raise men, to civilise them. In this the fight for the vote, for full civil rights for the labourer, was central. With the vote, Protestant religion, a good union and the help of a friendly society, the radical working man of Norfolk could 'Stand like the brave with his face to foe' and fear no one.

5 Radicalism, the second phase: The second union

On 5 May 1900 Zachariah Walker died. His local world lay to the north-west of George Rix's and they were as often antagonists as comrades, yet his death marked the end of an era for Rix and the men and women of 1872 as firmly as if Rix himself had died. Walker 'passed over', as his contemporaries in the Primitive Chapel would have had it, at a meeting of the Christian Endeavour Society in Kings Lynn.[1] His funeral brought together, perhaps for the last time, all the elements of the unionism of the period 1872–96. There, apparently at ease with one another, marched the Oddfellows, the Primitive Methodist chapels and Sunday schools of north-west Norfolk, Norfolk liberalism and what remained of rural trade unionsim, in total 600 or 700 people at the graveside.[2]

In the months before his death, Walker and others had sensed a change in the air. As we saw in Chapter 1 the labour market was moving slowly back in the labourer's favour as the depression temporarily lifted in 1898–9. Rural depopulation had done its work and farmers all over Norfolk were crying out for good men.[3] There were other signs too. In March 1899 County Council bye-elections in north Norfolk returned liberals against the national trend, and were hailed by old George Rix as 'a working man's victory'.[4] Nor was the Boer War popular, in Norfolk, it was, in the words of one Primitive Methodist, 'unrighteous, without justification in morals or diplomacy'.[5] Socialists and Liberals stamped the rural areas holding anti-war meetings and often met with considerable support.[6]

As always, however, it was the weather and the state of agriculture in each tiny local world that really determined action. In the summer of 1899 there were harvest strikes in Cambridgeshire and the following summer they spread to Norfolk. As a result there was an attempt to restart a union. The initiative came from the labourers themselves and by the middle of June 1900 they had sufficient support to hold a public meeting in the Swaffham Temperance Hall.[7] The union was a failure as a trade union at least. Despite a series of strikes that summer the leaders of the abortive attempt to revive trades unionism seem not to have been able to link up with the men on strike, most of whom came out on the basis of intensely local disputes at farm level, and quickly won their demands.[8]

However, in the medium term the meeting was of considerable significance for it brought Richard Winfrey into the labour movement. Winfrey was born in 1858 in Long Sutton in Lincolnshire, the son of a farmer. He trained as a chemist in London where he was converted to Liberalism. In 1885 he returned to Lincolnshire and set up as a newspaper owner, starting the *Spalding Guardian*.[9] In the winter of 1887–8 Winfrey became involved in the agitation for allotments following the passing of the Allotment Act. It was the beginning of a lifelong concern with the land question.

From 1887 onwards Winfrey's political ideas were dominated by his belief that only by settling the labourer on his own land as a smallholder or by the granting of allotments could the fundamental problems of rural poverty be solved. In 1894, with the aid of the Liberal peer Lord Carrington, and a number of eastern counties Liberal grandees, he leased a 230-acres farm at Deeping Fen near Spalding, Lincolnshire and let it to 60 labourers as allotments and smallholdings.[10] Encouraged by the apparent success of Deeping Fen, Winfrey urged the Swaffham labourers to follow suit and in July 1900 he purchased 'on behalf of the Norfolk Small Holdings Syndicate' a farm of 132 acres near Swaffham.[11] As at Deeping Fen Winfrey drew heavily on the support of local Liberals, including three present or future Liberal members for Norfolk constituencies.[12]

In the meantime, in August 1893, Winfrey had been selected as Liberal candidate for the south-west Norfolk constituency and he began what he described as a series of 'Liberal Crusades' in the area. Travelling on horseback or using a caravan ('The Sunrise Van') Winfrey held village meetings every autumn and spring for the next ten years. In 1895 he was beaten by 206 votes, but in 1900 he reduced the Tory majority to only 66 against the national trend.[13]

There can be little doubt that Winfrey spoke clearly to the

Norfolk labourer. He was a chapel man and an East Anglian. He lived in the constituency and worked hard and long to win the labourer's vote. In his advocacy of 'the land for the people' he found a ready following among a section of the labourers and the artisans of the country towns. Winfrey's radical vision was, however, restricted. He appears on the land question as a radical, as he did on the Boer War. But it is interesting that we find no mention of him in connection with the trades union movement before 1900, although he was active in South West Norfolk constituency from 1893. His central belief was in smallholdings and allotments and he was opposed to strike action for higher wages which he regarded as counterproductive. Thus he argued in 1900 that wages were 'not the only important question', but that voting and smallholdings were equally important since 'just taxation' and the 'exodus of farm labourers' could only be dealt with by these means.[14] To Winfrey, as to many of the Norfolk Liberals, the question of the labourer was a political question, and resolved itself only via the Liberal Party.

A figure missing from the platform of that meeting in 1900 which sought to revive trades unionism among the farm labourers was George Edwards. After the collapse of the union movement in 1896 Edwards retired, bitter and disillusioned, from the fray. For a time he was employed as a speaker by the Liberal Party but by 1900 he was back at his trade as a brickmaker.[15] He attended Zachariah Walker's funeral but seems to have taken no other part in the movements of the summer of 1900.[16] He did remain active in local politics, serving on the Erpingham Rural District Council and on the Board of Guardians.[17] He also remained a member of the Liberal 'Hundred' and a Primitive Methodist preacher. In 1902 his health failed and he was forced to work as a general labourer.[18] There seemed little hope for him or for the labourers' cause. 'I was' he wrote, 'a disappointed man, having lost all faith that my class would ever be manly enough to emancipate themselves.'[19]

But then, in 1902–3, in what appeared to many contemporaries a time of total darkness for the labourer, things again began to stir. Two separate sets of factors can be seen at work; local ones concerned directly with the labourers' conditions and national ones concerned with Liberal politics in relation to the rural areas. These two sets of factors were to come together in the early summer of 1906, but in 1902–3 they appear as quite separate.

First, the local conditions. From 1898–9 to 1902–3 the Norfolk labourer enjoyed a period of relative prosperity. Wages were not bad, and, more importantly, harvest earnings were high and work was regular. As part of the switch away from a casual workforce fewer and fewer men were laid off in winter or wet weather. It seems possible that customary winter wage reductions were stopped in some areas. Against this background the Norfolk labourer seems to have gained in confidence and independence. For instance, Clare Sewell Read, probably the most prominent spokesman of the Norfolk tenant farmers,[20] told a Norwich Diocesan Conference in 1902 that 'the clergy had lost the influence they once held over the agricultural labourer' and blamed this on Arch's union.[21] Arch's union was blamed by a Dorset clergyman for a much more general change in the labourers' attitudes: 'the Revolt of the Labourer began under Arch. And by revolt I mean the expression by every means in his power of his independence of the classes to whom he had hitherto been in submission.'[22]

'Dare to be a Daniel' had become more than an exhortation. Other evidence bears this out. The willingness, for instance, of the Norfolk labourer to vote Liberal both in 1900 and in 1906, testifies to the growth of political independence, as does the growth, however limited, of rural Co-ops and even socialism. More tangible is the apparent increase in prosecutions under the 'master and servant' legislation. This was mentioned above, but it should be stressed just how important a step it was to leave a 'master' and even, on occasions, a tied house. It not only put the individual at risk economically, but broke decisively with quasi-paternalist notions of a personal bond between master and man, and replaced them with a cash nexus.[23]

However, as in the case of 1872, these improved conditions and increased aspirations were not to hold. From the winter of 1902–3 unemployment began to increase again and wages were reduced. Even in February and March 1903, when demand for labourers should have been on the increase, the *Labour Gazette* noted that there was 'not much demand' for casual workers.[24] In Cley in December 1902 the *Eastern Weekly Press* wrote,[25]

the near approach of winter will make itself felt by a reduction of the men's wages, and already some of the labourers have received an intimation that from next week their wages will

bear a reduction of one shilling. The pay of an agricultural
labourer in this neighbourhood is 13s weekly.

The summer of 1903 saw this customary 1s drop restored in most
areas but winter again brought problems. By 1904 there was,
according to the *Labour Gazette*, unemployment for day labourers
even at harvest.[26] This situation gradually got worse in the next
two years. By the early summer of 1906 the Norfolk labourer had
been faced with two years in which unemployment had been a
constant factor. Further, wages, from 1905–6 onwards showed 'a
very slight downward tendency'.[27]

It was not only local factors of supply and demand or wage
rates which were changing from 1903–4 onwards. In 1902 the
Tory government passed a new Education Act. This was seen, by
nonconformists, as providing 'sectarian education' on the rates,
since all denominational schools were now brought under local
government finance. However, a much more serious problem in
fact lay in those areas, most of them rural, where the only school
in the parish was an Anglican one. Here nonconformists saw
themselves as directly contributing to the 'Anglican supremacy'
through their rates.

From the early months of 1902 onwards the nonconformists
and Liberals of Norfolk began to organise against the Education
Bill. Initially this took the form of public meetings, but quickly
the notion of 'passive resistance', the non-payment of a part of the
rate, followed by seizure and sale of goods, gained adherents in
Norfolk as elsewhere. During the next three years most of the
Liberal grandees of Norfolk were involved in some way in passive
resistance, including Richard Winfrey. But it was not only the
grandees. Though very few labourers were involved, for the
simple reason that few paid rates, small tradesmen and farmers
often were, including a few who were to emerge, after 1906, as
local figures in the union movement.

The direct effect of the campaign of passive resistance, the last
fling of the nonconformist conscience, was probably much less
than the indirect. Growing from the campaign against the
Education Bill there was a period of intense political activity by
Liberals and nonconformists in the Norfolk countryside. For
instance, after harvest in 1902 Winfrey held 'a great village
crusade' throughout south-west Norfolk. This was sponsored by

the Eastern Counties Education League, the Eastern Counties Liberal Federation and the South West Norfolk Liberal Association, and centred on the Education Act.[28] But the subjects covered in the meetings ranged far outside that area into pensions, the South African War, Free Trade, and so on. The effect was one of a massive political awakening.[29]

Passive resistance brought the money and support of the nonconformist conscience to Winfrey and the other rural MPs and Liberal candidates, but at the same time, at national level, the Liberal Party was looking more and more to the rural areas. The growth of labour and the loss of some sections of the middle-class vote, on the one hand, and the ability of the Tory Party to hold on to sections of working-class voters in urban areas like Lancashire, London and the Midlands, at least before 1906, meant that the Liberal Party came to rely more and more on the vote of the rural poor. This reliance was reflected in Norfolk in campaigns like Winfrey's 'great crusades'.

In the early weeks of 1906 the local factors, a short-term drop in wages against a background of increased independence and expectations, came together with the national factor – a decisive general election. In Norfolk, as in the nation as a whole, the general election of 1906 was a resounding success for the Liberal Party. Every Norfolk seat returned a Liberal and in the two-member Norwich constituency the 'balance' of one Liberal, one Conservative, was destroyed for ever with the election of a typographer, G.H. Roberts of the ILP, as Labour.[30] In the county it was the labourers' victory, while the small towns voted against the Liberals. Downham Market, for instance, was 'a hotbed of Toryism'[31] and all Winfrey's meetings there were disrupted in 1906.[32] Lord Wodehouse, the Liberal candidate, was shouted down in East Dereham and there was 'continuous disorder' and fighting in his urban meetings.[33] Nevertheless, he increased his majority in Mid-Norfolk as a whole and his Tory opponent, while thanking the voters of Dereham, referred to 'the people in the villages who voted against me'.[34] R.H. Mottram has left a fine vignette of that election in North Walsham which is worth quoting at length:[35]

the townsmen stood solid for the Conservative interest because it was respectable . . . the farmers were fixed . . . and the voting went on all day, to the accompaniment of cheering from small boys, but, once six o'clock had come, a steady procession came rolling up to the polling booths. It was composed of farm waggons loaded with labourers. They poured into the booth, recorded their 'wut', and streamed off to the lesser public houses. There was no stopping them. Something influenced them for a few hours, something left over from Litester's Rebellion and Kett's Rebellion . . . [they] recorded their 'wut' and felt they had got back at all the rest of the world, for all the pheasants they had not poached, all the beer they had not drunk, all the money they had not spent.

When the shouting had died down it was not so easy. Firstly, victimisation was widespread. As the *Eastern Weekly Press* reported from the declaration at Dereham,[36]

'Cut their wages down a shilling a week', one man shouted, referring apparently to the agricultural labourers, and one gentleman, who did not appear to be a huge employer of labour, announced his intention of cutting his beggars at least 2s a week.

Although the tone of the press here is part facetious, there is no doubt that victimisation did take place. Edwards wrote in his autobiography of cases immediately following the election,[37] and he said at the founding meeting of the union in July 1906,[38]

a gentleman writing to him from South Norfolk some weeks since said the system of boycotting was carried to such a length that men dare not attend a parish meeting nor sign a nomination paper for a district councillor. Scores of cases had been reported to him of men being discharged and of others threatened that when winter came they would suffer an extra reduction in wages.

In this situation, Edwards later wrote, former members of Arch's union and the other Norfolk unions wrote to him urging him to restart the unions as defensive organisations.

However, it seems unlikely that the new union was a simple defensive response. Indeed Tom Barker of Erpingham says that his father and grandfather (John Pightle) were meeting in Gresham along with Edwards, Israel Lake, Walter Louder, Herbert Harvey and Jimmy Coe from 1905 onwards with the thought of restarting the union. Although no other account mentions these meetings (which were secret for fear of victimisation), Barker's account makes good sense. All those mentioned were active in the early years and the idea of the union simply emerging with no planning has always seemed a little too straightforward.[39]

The year 1906, more than any other time since 1872, had a millennial feel to it, it was almost as if the shores of the promised land had been reached. At such a moment no organisation was going to be simply defensive, and to see the new union of 1906 as born out of victimisation alone is clearly wrong. It has that aspect, but it should be seen as a continuation, in the first instance, of the hopes created by the electoral victory of 1906.

It was not only the labourers themselves who were interested in organisation. Although the labourers had voted firmly for the Liberals in 1906, there was no permanent organisation which could build on that alliance. Worse than that, the Tory Party had the Primrose League, aimed specifically at the poor, and the new Labour movement had the trade unions, on paper at least. For these reasons the Liberal grandees of Norfolk, and elsewhere, supported the new union.

The founding meeting of the union was held at the Angel Hotel, North Walsham, on Friday 6 June 1906. The Angel still stands, a large, grim public house just down from the Market Square on the old Mudesley Road. Upstairs in the 'assembly rooms' on that June Friday gathered a mixed bag of Liberal grandees and farm workers. Some of them, like Josiah Sage from Kenninghall, William Codling of Briston, and George Edwards himself, were survivors of the earlier unions. Although the bulk of those at the meeting were from Norfolk, there were men, and one woman, from Lincolnshire, Suffolk, Cambridgeshire and Essex. There were also the 'friends' of the labourers. Richard Winfrey MP, George Nicholls MP, and Herbert Day. Winfrey we have already met, Nicholls and Day are new.

Nicholls was, in 1906, MP for North Northamptonshire. He had been a labourer and was one of the original settlers on Winfrey's Lincolnshire allotments. From the mid-1890s he acted

as a Liberal speaker and was employed by the Eastern Counties
Liberal Association and Winfrey as a speaker with the Sunrise
Van.[40] Herbert Day was a very different character. He was the
son of a Norwich boot and shoe manufacturer and was educated
at Rugby and Cambridge. From 1889–93 he was an associate of
Toynbee Hall. He returned from Whitechapel to his native
Norwich in the mid-1890s and became active on the 'left' of
Liberal politics. From 1900 to 1909 he was a member of Norwich
Town Council.[41] Day was different from Nicholls, and indeed
Winfrey, in other ways too, crucially in relation to politics.
Nicholls and Winfrey, though both 'advanced' radicals, were, in
the last analysis, Gladstonians. Their radicalism was limited by a
belief in individualism and, in the end, *laissez faire*, which meant
that their response to the problems of the labourer was within an
area prescribed by these beliefs.

Day, on the other hand, was of the 'new' generation of
Liberals. His experience in London had, no doubt, made him
familiar with the work of Booth and Rowntree, and with that
current of thought soon to be known as 'New Liberalism'. More
than this, though, he moved further to the left and from the late
1890s onwards he came closer and closer to socialism. In
December 1902 Day split with the Norwich Liberal Association
on the question of the 'living wage', with Day arguing that there
should be a guaranteed minimum apart from market forces.[42]

The motion before the founding meeting clearly pointed the
direction in which those who supported the foundation of a new
union wanted to go:[43]

> That this conference composed of delegates representing the
> agricultural labourers of the Eastern Counties take definite steps
> to form a union, the object of which shall be to enable the
> labourers to secure proper representation on all local bodies and
> the Imperial Parliament, protection from political persecution,
> and better conditions of living; and that a central fund be raised
> for organising purposes.

The ordering of the 'objects' is no coincidence. Winfrey, Nicholls
and those other Liberal MPs and grandees who supported the
foundation of the union saw it as a Liberal working man's
association. This essentially political role was emphasised by all

the speakers at the founding meetings. Richard Winfrey, for instance, evoked the unions of the 1870s and their role in getting the vote for the labourer. He then went on,[44]

> He wanted to see the labourers banded together so that they might assert their political rights without fear or favour. Even the humblest agricultural labourer had a right to his political opinions, and to express them without being submitted to interference by employers or anybody else.

Political protection and organisation under, one assumes, the benevolent eye of Liberalism, was one way forward but the main road lay through allotments and smallholdings, these were 'the greatest hope for the future of our rural districts'.[45] Finally, he dealt with the question of rural housing. Here 'there were plenty of Acts of Parliament on the Statute Book', all that was needed was organisation. If they organised around these proposals they 'would have the support of all reasonable people in the Eastern Counties'.[46]

George Edwards spoke next to move the founding motion. His speech, like Winfrey's, stressed smallholdings, allotments and political protection. There was no mention of wages, hours or conditions, the basis of all normal trades union organisation. Only in his concluding remarks did Edwards turn to this question when he said,[47]

> Another object of the new union must be to obtain a fair and living wage and better conditions of living – by peaceful means wherever possible, and arbitration, and not by the cruel methods of strikes and lock-outs.

George Nicholls went even further,[48]

> He said that at the outset at least it would be as well to say as little as possible about the wages question, because the demand and the supply of labour in the different districts must always decide the amount of wages paid. . . . He would advise them to keep out of their programme any reference to wages.

All the points raised at the founding meeting came essentially from the Liberal 'programme' for the rural areas, and this is hardly surprising. What is more striking is the negative attitudes to wages. In part this came from experience. There is little doubt that the disastrous strikes of the early 1890s had severely damaged both Arch's union and the Norfolk and Norwich Amalgamated Labourers' Union, and Edwards at least, clearly had bitter memories of that period.

For the others, especially Winfrey and Nicholls, the question was quite different. Initially, at least, both saw that putting wages to the fore in any programme would lead to conflict. Not only was the resolution of the conflict out of the labourers' hands and in iron laws of supply and demand, as Nicholls believed; but strikes would lead to a wider conflict with those 'reasonable people' of the Eastern Counties who were not labourers and whose economic interests as farmers, bankers, seed dealers, land agents, or whatever, could be actively harmed by the labourers striking and winning a wage increase. Strikes, wrote Edwards, 'ought to be avoided to prevent ill feeling and to increase the feeling of brotherhood'.[49]

This view of the union and its role was reinforced by the dominance on the union's first committee of Winfrey and Nicholls (treasurer and president respectively) and by the reliance which the union was forced to place on its Liberal supporters for funds. Edwards was paid a salary of 13s a week as organising secretary and Herbert Day agreed to provide funds for this.[50] However, beyond that, initial finance came from wealthy supporters. For instance of the balance in hand in October 1907 at the end of the first year's active work, i.e. £267 10s 0d, nearly a quarter had come from 'donations' made in the previous six months.[51]

The week following the report of the founding meeting the *Eastern Weekly Press* carried an announcement, signed by Edwards, announcing that 'active propaganda' work for the Eastern Counties Agricultural Labourers' and Small Holders' Union, for such was the new union's cumbersome title, would begin after harvest. And begin it did. Despite initial enthusiasm, building the 'second' union was hard work, and much of the credit for those early days rests solely with George Edwards. In fact, one can almost exactly trace the growth of the union in Norfolk in the winter of 1906 and the spring of 1907 in terms of

how far Edwards could ride on his bicycle in one day. Although
in his late fifties, Edwards gave time, energy and all else
unstintingly to the union. His figure, 'a little humpety-backed
man', as one labourer remembered him, bent by work and poor
diet, became more familiar to the Norfolk labourer than any other
farm workers' leader had ever been, or has been since. His vision
may have been limited and confused, in later years he may have
been an ambiguous figure in relation to younger leaders, but from
1906 to 1910 he had no equal.

The first branch of the new union was founded at Kenninghall
by 'Comrade Joe' Sage, a veteran of Arch's Union and a member
of the first executive committee. For his pains he was dismissed
from his work and even in 1912 was still finding it impossible to
get regular employment.[52] William Codling, also on the first
committee, was also dismissed within weeks of founding a branch
in Briston.[53] After harvest Edwards began his work in earnest.
Some branches appeared where the union had been strong in the
period 1872–96 and there were no doubt continuities here. St
Faiths branch, for instance, was founded on 5 September 1906 and
had William Norgate, George Hewitt and William Robert Furnace
as officials, all of whom had been involved in the 1890s.[54] At
Trunch, Herbert Harvey, 'Billa' Gee and a Mr Pardon had all been
in Arch's union in the 1870s,[55] and in old George Rix's village a
number of families carried through the tradition from one
generation to the next.[56]

But there were also breaks with the past. Crucially, the 'second'
union lacked the religious 'feel' of the first, despite the 1906
election. This was partly due to changes in the condition of the
labourers outlined at the beginning of this chapter, but it was also
very much to do with changes in the chapel. 'Everywhere
Methodists grow rich . . .', wrote Wesley, and by the 1900s that
had become all too real. No longer did the 'chapel' automatically
represent the poor of the village; many farmers were members
even of the Primitive Methodists, and the wayside Bethel found
its radical past increasingly uncomfortable. Edwards saw this
personally when he found himself 'excluded' from the preaching
plan for preaching radical social sermons.[57] It is also seen in the
ambiguity of memories about the chapel and politics. While all the
people interviewed for this book made a link between the chapel
and the union, the link was not the direct one of the 1870s. One

man, born in the 1920s, for instance, remembered his father-in-law being told not to deliver the union paper to chapel members after service on a Sunday.[58] Perhaps most striking was the switch away from the chapel as the union's natural physical home. The majority of meetings in the period 1872–80 were held in chapels, but by the 1900s this position had changed completely; in the first years of the union's growth in Norfolk less than half a dozen meetings were held on nonconformist premises. When I asked Mrs Rayner of Swanton Morley, whose father was a Primitive Methodist and a member both of Arch's union and Edwards's, if the union met in the chapel, she replied, 'Oh no never. I don't think my parents would have agreed with that, those meetings were held on a Sunday, but I don't think they would have agreed with that.'[59] In less than thirty years the 'union chapel' of Swanton Morley, built by George Rix, had closed its doors against the labourers' union. Instead, each Sunday evening they made their way to the clubroom of the Papermakers' Arms.[60]

It is difficult now to capture the feel of those early meetings. The only photographs I know of show a meeting at Swanton Morley. It is an open-air meeting in the 'Sand Pit', near the Chequers in the centre of the village, and probably took place in 1907–8. Photograph 2.7 shows the speakers standing on the rising ground at the back of the sand pit. Dominating them are the figures of George Edwards and James Arnett, Edwards's helper in those early years. Edwards holds a book, probably the Bible, the source of so much of his political thought and imagery. Photo 2.8, taken from behind the speakers, shows the audience who, given that the photographer was a village man, dominate the picture. Here we see them, the union's membership, or potential membership. Some of them seem to be wearing the 'union's favours', a bunch of ribbons in the union colours; all are in their Sunday best and have brought their wives and children. In the middle of it all is the village band who have clearly been providing the music for the meeting. What it was we don't know, probably 'Hold the Fort' or 'Hark the Gospel News is Sounding' but also now perhaps some of the 'labour hymns' written by Robert Green, co-operator and radical of Sheringham:[61]

Sons of labour, who've been battling
With the hungry moil of years.

> See upon the world's horizon,
> Demos in the light appears.
> Haste ye greet him in the sunlight,
> Born of hoped for better times,
> Crown him with the right to lead you.
> Swear allegiance to his line.

The words are stilted and strange (even the printer of the *Union Song Book* managed to turn Demos into Demons and nobody noticed!) but the tune would have been familiar enough, 'Hark the Gospel News is Sounding'. Or perhaps it was the other version of 'Hold the Fort'![62]

> We meet today in Freedom's cause,
> And raise our voices high,
> We'll join our hand in union song,
> To battle or to die.

Whatever, the music was there, and the village band have stopped to listen to the union message.

Scattered among the crowd are a few pony and traps: farmers come to listen to that 'D——d little trouble maker' perhaps, or maybe curious tradesmen. One 'dickey' (donkey) cart points perhaps to one of Swanton's many smallholders. Mrs Rayner, who owns the photographs, remembers being taken to the meeting as a 'little tot' and her mother making tea for some of the speakers afterwards: 'They had come from away to help start (the union), from other villages and I know we had three or four into tea that day.'[63]

Elsewhere the meetings were held in the back room of the village pub:[64]

'Well my two brothers, they was older than me, and they went I think to two meetings, one was in Bradenham, and I believe they went to one at Necton. . . . They went to a meeting there and I think they got a book, and there was six joined in my father's house . . . there was us four [brothers], my father and an uncle of mine. We had our first meetings at the "Hart" at Wendling, that's where we had our first meetings. Then we moved from there to the club room . . . at the "Railway Tavern", that was a good big room, and they got a good branch there.'

Through the next three years the union grew slowly but surely in Norfolk. Branches appeared throughout the country, mostly in the north, but by 1909 spreading down to the Suffolk border and even crossing it. To the west some headway was made in recruiting in North Cambridgeshire and especially into Lincolnshire. It was a slow process and hard, but real gains were made albeit at a cost. For instance from that start there were sporadic lock-outs of union members as individuals, usually branch secretaries.[65] Occasionally it was worse as at a group of West Norfolk villages, Mileham, Bindringham and Rockland St May in April 1908 when a larger group of men – between 15 and 20 were affected.[66]

These disputes along with another slightly larger one at Sedgeford in the same month were the signs of a changing mood among the membership of the union. Gradually branches seem to have been coming to feel that now they had the strength and funds they should 'go for a forward movement'. In 1908, for instance, the St Faiths Branch, who were soon to earn a permanent place in the union's history, passed this resolution[67]

> That this society do all that lay [sic] in its power to get the Labourers in the St. Faiths district in advance of 2/0 per week as they are just reduced 1/0 below the average wage they have been getting for two years, for it to commence on 21st March 1909.

The executive committee viewed this increasing militancy with alarm, especially since the farmers seemed to be responding to increased union membership by more frequent locking out. In 1908 and 1909 the numbers locked out on the union's books increased considerably. In October 1908 the executive issued an instruction which was to have far reaching consequences:[68]

> A letter was read from the South Creake branch secretary asking for support in consequence of loss of employment through refusing to move into his employers cottage. . . . Mr Arnett moved that the man be allowed 10/- per week for loss of time as the committee believe that he was standing up for one of the fundamental principles advocated by this union. . . . But

> that the general secretary be instructed to send a circular to
> every branch that in future no independent action by any
> member of the union can be recognised by the executive
> committee for financial support unless his case has been
> previously laid before the Executive Committee and the
> General Secretary and agreed by them.

Such a statement, which made some sort of sense in the context of
urban unionism, was absurd in the rural areas where only by
striking at precisely the right time could the men hope to win.

In the place of such action, the executive continued to advocate
smallholdings and political action. For example, in the middle of
the small strike at Sedgeford in 1908, Winfrey told a labourers'
meeting 'when they had the land there would be no occasion for
quarrels over the question whether a man should have 13s or 14s a
week'.[69] Time and time again in the executive minutes the rules
were insisted upon, but it seems that splits were appearing.
Edwards for instance, seems to have supported striking or locked
out individuals against the express wishes of Winfrey and Nicholls
on occasion. More serious was political dissatisfaction. In October
1908 Herbert Day and William Harris proposed that the union
seek affiliation to the Labour Representation Committee. There
was, not surprisingly, a heated discussion but they lost. However,
much to Winfrey's chagrin they insisted on their right to raise
affiliation as a motion to the Annual General Council. Here it was
resolved that this motion should be put to the branches, a decision
that Winfrey and Nicholls as Liberal MPs could not have
welcomed.

In the spring of 1910 all these emerging divisions became real.
At the general council meeting of the Lincolnshire branches in
March Harris stood for the post of vice-president of the union.
Harris was a member of the ILP and one of those who wanted the
union to affiliate to the LRC. Winfrey was furious. He 'strongly
deprecated' Harris's action and said at the meeting, 'They
received little financial support from Lincolnshire and now they
had been put to the expense of printing special ballot papers.'[70]
Harris's reaction was, not surprisingly, equally strong: 'To hear
Mr. Winfrey talk', he said, 'was to make them believe the union
was a one man union – an aristocratic instead of a democratic

body.'[71] This accusation was to get stronger and stronger during the following year.

Harris was not elected, but outside the executive things were coming to a different kind of head. From a high point around 1903–4 wages had been gradually falling while the cost of living seems to have been increasing. As a result there was growing dissatisfaction in the membership. Additionally, as I mentioned above, the farmers often responded to union membership by simply dismissing the man, or men, involved. During 1909 both these tendencies seem to have accelerated. In mid-1908 for instance, the union was supporting only three men 'locked out' and none on strike. A year later, in July 1909, there were upwards of twenty members either locked out or on strike.[72]

The crunch came in March 1910, first at Trunch and Knapton, north of North Walsham, and then at St Faiths, just outside Norwich. The problem was a familiar one. In all three cases the farmers had reduced wages for the winter, spring came and battle was joined to get the shilling back. However, at St Faiths the battle was joined on different lines. St Faiths was one of the union's oldest branches, it had had a militant even violent history from the 1870s and 1890s, and it had experienced leaders, two of whom, George Hewitt and William Norgate, were socialists who had received their baptism of fire in the 1890s strikes. Hewitt seems to have been a member of the Socialist League in the 1890s, and to have gone into the ILP in the early 1900s.[73]

From a decision of its general meeting of 1910 the union was committed to obtaining a general rise of 1s a week, on top of the 1s given on return to summer hours, and half day Saturday. It was on these demands that St Faiths fought. On 29 April the St Faiths Minute Book records the first moves in the dispute that was to bring the 'new' union into open conflict with the farmers and ultimately to split its leadership.[74]

Bro J. Chapman said he thought it was getting time there [sic] should be something done to benefit members in trying to securing [sic] more wages and shorter hours after some discussion it was moved by J. Britcher that next Friday week should be a Summons meeting [sic] to thoroughly discuss the matter.

The meeting was held on 13 May and was attended by Green, Edwards, Day and Thomas Thacker, in accordance with the union rules. The branch put forward a resolution to ask for 1s a week rise and half day Saturday. It was carried unanimously, and Edwards was asked to write to the farmers.

The response from the farmers was predictable – none even replied. Not surprisingly the men of St Faiths were, in the words of Edwards's minutes, 'very indignant'.[75] Hewitt put it more strongly, it was 'an insult' to the labourers and 'it was about time they told the employers they intended to have trades unions recognised'.[76] Notice was given and on 28 May 1910, 100 men walked off twelve farms in the St Faiths district. In desperation Edwards wrote to Willis, the secretary of the Farmers' Federation, the 'free labour' organisation set up in the 1890s, asking them to agree to arbitration.[77] Willis replied that the Farmers' Federation 'have no dispute with the Labourers' Union' and issued a public statement that the Federation was 'taking steps' to 'have the men's places filled up'.[78] On the Tuesday of the first week of the strike the blacklegs arrived, 'in a huge covered cart . . . while behind them in a dog cart, was riding Mr Willis, Secretary of the Federation'.[79] This was, said Hewitt, 'an open declaration of war.'[80]

And so the strike, which all the Liberal leaders of the new union had dreaded, came to be. For them it could not have come at a worse time or place. The first election of 1910 had seen the Liberal vote drop in Norfolk. On Liberal instructions, Edwards, and Tom Thacker, the other full-time union employee, had been withdrawn from organising to help fight the election, and this had caused bad feeling. There was also a growing militancy among the men, demonstrated by the fact that in the next six weeks two more major strikes began, at Swanton Morley and Litcham. Nor was St Faiths the place for a 'Liberal' strike. Hewitt was a socialist and, supported by Day, was willing to go much further along the road to confrontation than the executive would have liked. More important, the men, women and children of St Faiths were committed to winning and supported by the bitter memories of the failure of 1894.

This quickly showed. Even in the first week the Federation was claiming that there had been widespread damage to farm

equipment before the men had left the farms making it very
difficult to use,[81] and by the end of the first week of the strike six
foot and four mounted police had been stationed in the village as
'a precaution' after what had happened '16 years ago'.[82] As F.E.
Green wrote:[83]

> The Farmer's Federation had evidently impressed the chief
> constable at Norwich with the idea that the agricultural
> labourers were a dangerous class, or possibly this extraordinary
> exhibition of force was merely a demonstration such as we
> carry out among the hill tribes of India.

But perhaps the chief constable was not that wrong. The
relationship between master and man was close, and when it
broke it often took on the elements of a family quarrel. The
'usurping' of a man's birthright and place by a blackleg made this
still worse, and it was against them that the anger was directed.
Refusal to speak to blacklegs or their families, abuse and casual
intimidation, was replaced at the beginning of July by traditional
forms of social pressure. On 23 July, Rose Chaplin and Sarah
Carter were charged with assault at Norwich Shire Hall. They
had, like the women of 1894, led a group of women and children
in 'rough musicing' a blackleg from Yorkshire called George
Watling and his son. They threw a rope around him when he was
coming from work and surrounded him beating pans and kettles
and singing a union song. They were bound over to keep the
peace for six months.[84]

Rough music, or 'tinging', as it was called in Norfolk, was used
again in August, this time with much more violence. At the end
of that month twelve labourers from St Faiths were charged with
'following Charles Rayner in a disorderly manner with a view to
compelling him to abstain from working as a labourer'.[85] Rayner
was a St Faiths man, 'an elderly team-man', and during the case it
became clear that a number of other St Faiths men had been
tinged, to 'make them ashamed' as one of the defendants put it.
But it was more than that. Another St Faiths man had been
'knocked about' during the tinging, at the beginning of the
week.[86]

The 200 men, women and children who took part in the series
of tingings of the second week of August, with their pans, kettles

and musical instruments (a cornet and an accordion), were acting out a traditional ritual of social disapproval. Like many such rituals it moved quickly into personal violence. Like the strikers of 1894, they got short shrift and were fined £5 each or in default two months with hard labour. Herbert Day paid their fines and they were released to scenes of triumph.

There were also new elements present in 1910. From the start of the strike the Norwich labour movement, through the strongly socialist Trades Council, was involved in supporting the strike through meetings and collections. Time and again these literally kept the men going as union funds were low and strike pay meagre. More than that, they bolstered the traditional communal solidarity of the village in the face of massive opposition and an increasing unease on the part of sections of the leadership as to what to do with the strike.

In the summer of 1910 it seems the first serious rifts within the leadership began to appear. On a number of occasions in August Edwards, supported by the Norwich Trades Council in the person of 'Bill' Holmes, a socialist gas worker and ex-labourer, urged the extension of the strike to a 'general strike' of all labourers on farms where the farmer was a member of the Federation. However, come the autumn, and as the labour market closed with the approach of winter, Edwards, under pressure from Winfrey, changed his tone. From September he began to talk of full ballots of all members before strike action, and actually went so far as to refer to the St Faiths dispute as a result of 'more ardent young spirits'.[87]

At the November executive meeting it became clear that the union was in serious financial difficulties. For the first time there was a 'considerable decrease' in the union's accumulated capital, and Edwards suggested that a ballot should be taken of the whole membership as to what course the union should take. However, he also stressed that the strike had won them over 1,000 members, and that the union's stand at St Faiths had contributed to a number of settlements elsewhere in Norfolk where farmers were unwilling to enter a major dispute. 'Great care . . . must be taken in the matter,' he concluded, 'or we shall lose a great deal of the ground that we have gained'.[88]

A ballot was agreed upon. The wording of the ballot was unclear: it talked of negotiation by Mr Leadbetter, the village schoolmaster, and an honourable conclusion. It was tacitly accepted that this meant going back on the terms the men were on at the beginning of the strike, i.e. 13s per week and no half day – but it did explicitly state that all men should be taken back. The membership accepted 'honourable conclusion' by 1,558 votes to 756, but the St Faiths branch were unhappy. It is clear that despite the 'no victimisation' clause the executive, or part of it at least, were willing to see some members remain out of work. As Leadbetter, the self-appointed arbitrator, said in one of his letters[89]

> I think it is far better to keep the two or three left [out of work] on the Union funds than to keep on a hopeless fight, believe me it is hopeless, and I hope for the sake of the Union and the men that the end has come and your men can see it.

The executive then split and it was decided to send out a further and clearer resolution spelling out what was meant by an 'honourable conclusion'. This ballot reversed the previous decision, 1,102 were in favour of continuing the strike and 1,053 in favour of going back on the old terms. It was now up to the executive.

The executive split. Despite a clear instruction from the membership on a majority of 7 to 4 (Day, William Codling, Berry and Edwards) it was decided to 'use their endeavours to bring the dispute to a close on the honourable terms mentioned in the first ballot and that they have full power to act.'[90] In the first weeks of January just how honourable these terms were became clear. The farmers of St Faiths agreed to take back 33 men 'on the old terms' leaving 42 unemployed, with no prospects of work until March or April, and little enough then with 25 blacklegs still in the village.[91]

So the Liberals triumphed. Both Winfrey and Nicholls claimed later that they had been opposed to the strike from the start and that it had been started 'unconstitutionally'. The latter point is nonsense, the decision was taken, as per union rules, by the general secretary (Edwards) and the three executive members nearest to the dispute. The former point is certainly true. We saw above that both Nicholls and Winfrey were opposed to strike action and saw the union as the working men's Liberal association for rural areas. The strike threatened that role by drawing on funds and setting off class struggle in the countryside. It also came at an embarrassing moment. The first attempt to close down the strike, in November, coincided with the run up to the December election of 1910. Nicholls had lost his seat in January 1910 and Winfrey must have feared for his in December if any of his tenuous rural middle-class support vanished. But it was not the short-term interest which really mattered: that was a symptom. It was that the Liberal Party, as represented by Winfrey and Nicholls, simply could not accept industrial unrest as part of their programme or method. As Nicholls said at the general council in 1911[92]

He was opposed to strikes, especially sectional strikes and lock-outs . . . their endeavour should be to build up the union upon the lines indicated at the first meeting; that by peaceful means they should strive to improve the conditions of the men, secure better housing and freer access to the land, with fuller and fair representation of their members upon every local governing body, and when their means and numbers permitted to have their own man in Westminster.

In fact, in that old, old phrase, 'Jam yesterday, jam tomorrow, but never jam today'.

It seems that Winfrey and Nicholls and those who supported them on the executive, felt they had won their case and that the union would return to peaceful and orderly progress along the road to a New Liberal never-never land. It was not to be so. Not surprisingly St Faiths branch voted unanimously to stay out on strike, more surprisingly perhaps, Hewitt and Day 'went public' on the split and published a letter in the *Eastern Weekly Press* attacking Winfrey and Nicholls and calling on the membership to demand a special annual meeting to reverse the decision.[93]

The executive met on 12 January to decide on its course of action. Despite having received telegrams from eight branches with about 150 names, and thus meeting the rule for the calling of a special general meeting. Winfrey moved, and was supported, that the rule had not been met and that the ordinary conference would meet, as arranged, on 25 February. As if that were not enough, Winfrey and Nicholls moved as an amendment that the 42 men still locked out at St Faiths should only get full strike pay for another two weeks, then go on to half pay. On 24 February, the day before the general meeting, Winfrey amended further a motion on those 32 still locked out, to the effect that all strike pay should cease within one week. No wonder the fruits of Liberalism were beginning to seem a little bitter to the Norfolk labourer.[94]

On Saturday 25 February the delegates of the union met in Fakenham Town Hall for their annual conference. It was a 'heated' meeting according to the *Eastern Weekly Press*, which complimented the chairman (Nicholls) on keeping disorderly scenes to a minimum.[95] The meeting was opened by Nicholls who spoke at great length, and to a relatively quiet audience, on why he carried out 'the unpleasant duty' of closing the St Faiths strike and, more generally, on his view of the union. Winfrey spoke next and, as the hostility of the audience grew, attempted to argue that the strike had been against union rules, and to try to blame the members of the St Faiths branch for starting a 'forward movement', and George Edwards for supporting them. Edwards replied with some dignity quoting from the rules and letters to prove Winfrey wrong, but it was Day who seems to have spoken for the majority of the members:

> They must fight all the time. (Hear, Hear) Their employers who kept them down on 12s and 13s a week were the worst enemies they had to face, and they must fight them. (Renewed demonstrations from supporters). . . . He believed the fighting force was in themselves. (Loud applause) He did not believe too much in fighting but when he did commence he was going to fight to the utmost. (Renewed applause) He did not believe in going cap in hand to their employers. (Hear, Hear) He had no further confidence in Mr Winfrey as one of the leaders of their union. (Loud applause and strong cries of dissent)

George Hewitt then moved what was in fact a vote of no confidence in the executive. He was supported by William Smith of Wymondham (an ILP member), Bill Holmes of Norwich (also ILP), and Walter Smith of the Cossey Branch, all working men. When the vote was taken Winfrey and Nicholls's position was defeated by 59 votes to 35.

It was a startling change. The eight branches which had supported St Faiths in calling a special general council showed considerable bitterness in their attitude to Winfrey especially, but that such a large majority of delegates should vote against the Liberal leadership was a cause of great surprise and dismay. Nicholls immediately resigned as chairman and Winfrey asked for his name to be removed from the ballot paper as treasurer; both then left the meeting. Walter Smith then asked that those who had voted to close the strike be named. This was done and as a result only one of them, Arnett, was re-elected.

The aftermath of the St Faiths strike saw considerable changes within the character of the union. The defeat, strangely, as F.E. Green wrote, helped the union first by stiffening the resolve of the membership never again to be involved in such an outcome, and second by bringing the rural union to the notice of urban workers in the labour movement.[96] Of more significance was the gradual move by the union towards an identification with both the TUC and the Labour Party.

In day-to-day terms the change in leadership seems to have had little immediate effect. The work of union building was wearying and long. James 'Jimmy' Coe, joined Edwards, and Thacker retired; the union bicycles, provided for organisers, were replaced annually, and the branches grew. Opposition continued. Petty-minded, vicious and usually directed against one man, it left George Hewitt of St Faiths unemployed for three years and Herbert Harvey of Trunch nearly four. Smallholdings were often the answer for these men but even then it often continued against sons trying to find work or daughters attempting to go into service. One girl received a letter from a prospective employer saying that if her 'father is a member of the labourers' union she should not engage her'.[97] Herbert Harvey's son remembers a childhood of persecution from school teachers and the vicar because of his father's uncompromising stand for the union.[98] These are only the heroes, most vanished after a few weeks on the union's books, often driven out of a 'place' held happily for years, or even out of a village – Men like a Mr Taylor of Carbrooke who had been dismissed for arguing about a wage reduction from 13s to 12s and 'appears to have been persistently boycotted as he has never been able to get any work since'.[99]

The seasons continued, not unchanging, just the opposite – the drought summer of 1911 when the harvest was in by the middle of August; the flood summer of 1912 when the stooks floated in

the flooded fields and the old staithes and river banks collapsed –
but always there were the seasonal battles. The winter reductions,
the laying off of casuals, bargaining for harvest, hoeing, muck-
carting, weeding and the battles over job definitions, hours and
traditional conditions. Occasionally a major change could happen
and introduce a whole new element. The introduction of sugar
beet in 1912 brought with it 150 Dutch labourers working for 25s
a week, while Norfolk men got 2s 6d a day. The Norfolk men
came out for 3s a day, only to be followed by the Dutchmen
asking for 30s a week. The dispute dragged on throughout the
beet harvest.[100]

In all this the union was unhappy. It saw itself, as the constant
debates on reform show, as a modernising force within rural
society. As such these disputes, based on traditional practices and
'irrationally' followed through, were disruptive. The union
wanted a permanent place in the governance of rural England. Its
first chance at this was the Insurance Act of 1911 which
recognised the union as an Approved Society and brought in
many new members.[101] George Edwards urged labourers in 1912
to join the union and 'kill two birds with one stone and have
nothing to do with employers societies and profit making
concerns'.[102] Edwards himself got some part in governing when
he was appointed both to the local board of the insurance scheme
and the national committee.[103]

But the real goal lay just out of reach – a trade board for
agriculture. Under the Trades Boards Act of 1911 it was possible
to fix wages, hours and conditions, as well as provide organisational recognition for unions in certain trades. This was the
union's policy from 1912 onwards, the creation of a board for
agriculture – the organised farmer and the organised farm worker
sitting down together to iron out grievances. In 1913 G.H.
Roberts, Labour MP for Norwich, brought such a Bill before
Parliament. It was given a first reading and then talked out.

6 Radicalism, the second phase: Rural labour and the wages board 1910–21

When Richard Winfrey stormed out of the special union congress of 1911, he turned to Herbert Day and accused him of 'marshalling' the forces of labour to take the union over. The ILP, he said, had 'captured', the union.[1] 'Would, oh would it were true', Day might have replied for, though there was some Labour and indeed socialist strength on the new executive, it was limited. When one turns to the villages and the branches themselves, it was more limited still.

From the late 1880s various attempts had been made by Norwich socialists to gain support in the villages, particularly those near the city. For instance in October 1886 *Commonweal* reported that propaganda meetings had been organised by the Socialist League, William Morris's group, in the villages to the north and east of Norwich.[2] This work continued in the 1890s and 1900 with the Social Democratic Federation and the ILP holding village meetings.[3]

It was, however, really only from 1903 onwards that serious propaganda work began in the villages. In the early summer of that year a group of Clarion cyclists visited Aylsham to hold a series of meetings and distribute leaflets.[4] This visit established a pattern which was to become more and more common in following years. Groups of urban working men, usually artisans, with a sprinkling of labourers, rode off on a Sunday into the villages to spread the gospel of socialism. Their efforts were given a great boost in 1906 by the election of G.H. Roberts as Labour MP for one of Norwich's two seats.

Roberts was a typographer who worked at Colman's factory and had few, if any, rural connections, however, he quickly became the labourers' spokesman. More than that his victory gave the Norfolk Labour movement, indeed the whole of the East Anglian movement, the sure and certain belief that they could win. From 1906 onwards the number of meetings held outside

Norwich increased, showing the new strength and confidence of the movement. By August 1908 Bill Holmes, who we have already met, was appointed full-time organiser for the ILP in the Eastern Counties. In an article in *Labour Leader* in that month, he claimed that the ILP had over 500 members in Norwich and that they were holding twenty meetings a week in 'Norwich and District'. Additionally, they were spreading outside the city and its immediate environs for the first time and had established branches at Lowestoft and Yarmouth.[5] The following year branches were also established in Kings Lynn and Beccles, while regular meetings were being held in Wymondham and Thetford. Help came from other areas outside Norfolk in the attempt to bring socialism to the countryside. Every year members of the ILP or supporters of the Clarion intending to go on holiday to East Anglia were urged to contact Bill Holmes and do a bit of speaking while they were there. There were plenty such since Norfolk was home to the world's first 'holiday camp', the Caistor Socialist Holiday Camp. Founded in 1906 by Fletcher Dodd, the camp, which was under canvas at Caistor near Yarmouth, provided socialists with tent accommodation, a club room and organised games and food for 21s per week.[6] In west Norfolk was Harry Lowerison's Ruskin School, a progressive boarding school run by a friend of the Clarion's, Robert Blatchford. Lowerison seems to have founded the Kings Lynn branch of the ILP and was a favourite lecturer to the socialists of East Anglia on 'Art and the Worker'.[7]

These efforts were slow to bring reward. As the list of branches shows, initial success came in semi-industrial towns like Lynn and Yarmouth, while the footholds gained in market towns like Wymondham were tenuous and often relied on one or two converts to keep the cause alive. But the question that arises is, why bother at all? Socialism is after all an urban creed, class consciousness the product of the socialisation and division of labour in factory production, and its early successes, in London and Yorkshire, supported this view. The answer is that to the early members of the ILP and the Clarion this was not self-evident at all. The tradition of agrarianism as a part of socialism was a strong one fed by many socialist tracts and writings, the most famous of which was Morris's *News from Nowhere*. To many of the pioneers socialism would be a rural phenomenon. As Keir

Hardie wrote in 1895,[8]

> (After socialism had been achieved,) the youngsters will dance
> around the May-pole, whilst our young people will dance Sir
> Roger de Coverly and the many round dances sacred to the
> memory of the village green.

The title of Blatchford's tract *Merrie England*, which the author
claimed sold over a million copies, became one of the slogans of
early socialism.[9]

> All soon once again all our happy hills and vales,
> Shall be sweet with songs and gay with pleasant tales.
> And the poets' dreams bring back all the stolen cakes and ales,
> In the land of Merrie England in the morning.
> > (To the tune of 'John Peel'!)

The rural areas were the present as well as the future. The escape
from the town, especially on a bicycle, gave the worker cyclist a
release from the town of 'now' with its slums and stunted men
and women, destroyed by the blight of industrialisation, as well as
a glimpse of the future:[10]

> Soon in our faces came a warm aromatic breeze from the sun
> wooed hayfields now sweetly smelling. O what a delightful
> change from the asphalted, noisesome, bustling streets and grim
> city walls! We were going to the country lanes fresh and
> green. . . . We felt like spirits out of prison.

In this situation work in the rural areas was not only logical but
desirable, even central, to the socialist cause.

This was added to by a further set of factors, those concerned
with the 'degeneration' of the race and urban conditions. The
eugenicist arguments about racial failure brought about by city
living were as powerful among socialists as among imperialists.[11]
Socialists, and radicals in general, seem to have turned to
'rebuilding rural England' as a solution to at least part of the
problem, rather than to the 'cult of motherhood' or other 'genetic'
solutions favoured elsewhere. From the land colonies of Carpenter
and the neo-Tolstoyans, through to land nationalisation and
allotments schemes, sections of the English socialist movement

sought to recreate a 'free peasantry, a nation's pride'. In this they were not, of course, alone. We have seen Richard Winfrey advocating this kind of scheme, and these notions even permeated sections of the Tory Party represented most notably by Rider Haggard.

Together this meant that taking the gospel of socialism to the labourer was a vital and urgent task, and from 1907–8 onwards the ILP and the Clarion seem to have devoted a good deal of energy to this task, especially in East Anglia, where there was a strong radical tradition. In a sense the real beginning of this 'campaign', for so it all but became in the next few years, was a series of articles by Bruce Glasier in *Labour Leader* called 'Towards Socialism'. These articles take as the bases of socialist society the land and agricultural production. The land is the source of all value, and ultimately of all pleasure. Socialism will be like late medieval England without the poverty and disease, the village will be recreated 'invigorated and enriched' as the centre of social life.[12]

Significantly perhaps, in the month following these articles both Bruce Glasier and his wife were speaking in Norfolk, and to some extent the message seemed to be getting through.[13] After harvest in 1908 the ILP turned its attention to the labourers with a series of market town and village meetings. At East Dereham, a group formed in the early summer continued to grow rapidly and according to one report was doing well with Saturday and evening meetings. 'The young labourers of the district flock to these meetings from the villages round about.'[14] North Walsham was also visited by a band of ILP cyclists led by Bill Holmes.[15]

As we saw above, the issue of the Labour Party was forced to the union's notice at the annual delegate meeting of 1909 when Day and Harris insisted on raising the issue of affiliation despite having lost the vote for affiliation within the executive.[16] By the time the issue was raised again, in April 1910, things were changing rapidly. First, the union's practice of holding Sunday 'camp meetings', with labour 'hymns' and 'sermons' brought them strongly into conflict with nonconformist opinion. These 'comfortable, arm chair, middle class Nonconformists', as Edwards called them,[17] represented the increasing separation between the traditional Liberalism of Norfolk and the labourer. Second, as we saw in the last chapter, there was an increasing militancy among the labourers. This did not mean an automatic rejection of Liberalism but it called into question the Liberal view of the union's role in a tangible way. Third, Edwards himself was becoming, he later claimed, increasingly disenchanted with Norfolk Liberalism and its high-handed attitudes. He felt this very strongly, in relation to the first election of 1910, when he and the other organiser were withdrawn from their union work to fight the election for the Liberals on the instructions of Winfrey. Given that he had deliberately stood as an 'independent Labour' candidate only a year before it must have been particularly galling.[18] The situation was worse still when the organisers were again withdrawn from union business for the second election of 1910 when the St Faiths dispute was at its height.[19] Finally, as the elections of 1910 show, the labourers were beginning to lose faith with Norfolk Liberalism. Through East Anglia as a whole there was a swing of 5.3 per cent to the Conservatives in the January election of 1910, and one Norfolk seat, Mid-Norfolk, went Tory.[20] This was to some extent corrected in the second election, but it is clear that the honeymoon days of 1906 were over. The reasons are not far to seek. The Liberals had promised much and delivered little. The land problem was untouched, and the increasingly important question of a minimum wage was ignored. Certainly 'free trade' was safe and social reform promised, but the latter meant little to the labourer who was excluded, either directly, as from sections of the national insurance legislation or indirectly, because of the urban view of much reform. Significantly, in the two or three years after 1910 it was Labour, in the shape of G.H. Roberts and the TUC, who fought for the farm worker in national politics.

The crunch came in 1911, as we have already seen, but what is important here is to try and at least make some assessment of how deep-rooted the fundamental change of leadership carried through after the St Faiths strike was. Certainly Winfrey and Nicholls, particularly the latter, had continuing support within the union. Even at the 1911 congress a number of branches supported them and appear to have been worried about the 'ILP take over'.[21] Yet in the aftermath of meeting only one branch, Massingham, was sufficiently worried to send in a question to the executive about the 'take over'. They, said their letter, 'strongly disapprove of Mr. Smith as Chairman and Mr. Day as Treasurer and feel they cannot be led by the independent Labour [sic].' They continued that 'many will resign their membership', but Edwards reassured the executive that he had visited the branch and all was now well.[22] It is however, important to distinguish between tacit acceptance of a new leadership which promised at least to be more vigorous than the old, and any real active commitment to the cause of Labour, let alone socialism, and it is significant that Massingham branch did in fact collapse in the following months.[23] Also there was little real attempt to contest the political control of Liberalism in the rural areas before 1914.

Against this we must set a growing commitment by the farm workers' leadership, first to the labour movement in its broadest sense of the TUC and other unions locally, especially Norwich Trades Council, second to the political wing of the labour movement, although this latter process was much slower.

The first tangible sign of a change was the appearance of Smith and Edwards on the platform of the May Day demonstration in Norwich in 1911. May Day, as organised by Norwich Trades Council was, and had been for a number of years, an unequivocally 'socialist' occasion (the main speaker in 1911 was Lansbury), and no member of the farm workers' union executive had appeared on the platform in an official capacity. In 1911 both Edwards and Smith spoke, and both denied that the union was, as Smith put it, 'in the hands of wicked socialists'. Edwards went further and said that he had been accused of letting the union fall into 'labour' hands, if that was so, it was because he believed the 'labour programme' was 'right' for rural workers.[24] From 1911 onwards no Norwich May Day passed without a farm workers' representative on the platform, and from 1913 the 'new' union banner was carried in the procession.

From the summer of 1911 onwards other signs of a growing link between the union and Labour appear. In the past the open-air Sunday meetings, camp meetings as they were called following the tradition of Primitive Methodism, had always been addressed by Liberal politicians. In July 1911 a socialist speaker, George Lansbury, appeared for the first time at a union camp meeting, when he addressed a series of them in west Norfolk. At the end of the month he was replaced by Keir Hardie.[25] Hardie finished his tour with a meeting in Fakenham town square attended by over 400 people. He argued for county council smallholding, not 'peasant proprietorship, [but] co-operative buying and selling by smallholders and complete land-nationalisation'.[26] As May Day became an institution for the labourer, so from 1911 onwards socialist speakers came to dominate the platforms of union meetings.

In the winter of 1911–12 things began to go wrong. Unemployment returned with the change in the season and both publicly and privately the union admitted that membership was falling under its impact.[27] Worse still there were a large number of wage reductions that winter which the union was unable to oppose.[28] There was even a revival of the time-honoured method of rural protest when a rick was burnt near Brandon, 'supposed to be the work of an incendiary'.[29] As the spring came on things picked up in the labour market but not in union membership. However, the new links with organised labour came to the aid of the farmworkers. In September 1912 the union applied to the parliamentary committee of the TUC for a grant to aid organising work. This was passed on to member unions and several unions including the dockers and the railwaymen made grants which kept the union going through a difficult year.

The links with the railwaymen were to become more permanent. In most rural areas the only unionised workers were the railwaymen, and their crucial local role as builders of the labour movement remains unknown. However, from 1910 onwards links were made between the National Union of Railwaymen and the farm workers' union. This link was especially important in the Lancashire strike of 1913 which was arguably won so quickly by an NUR ban on the movement of farm produce from the strike area.[30] Also from 1913 onwards the NUR and the National Agricultural Labourers' Union (as it was now called) held an annual demonstration at Briston, the curious railway town in the middle of rural Norfolk.[31] These demonstrations symbolised the gradual integration of the farm labourers into the Labour movement. Formerly they had stood apart; ill-paid and scattered, their unions of the 1870s and 1890s had had little contact with the town unions. Their localism, a powerful unifying force in a small geographical area, had also made them distrustful of national organisations. By 1913 that was changing rapidly – the farm labourer was becoming a trade unionist.

The seeds sown in 1911 by Lansbury and Hardie were also

beginning to show saplings, if not fruit. In July 1912, E.G. Hemmerde had been selected as Liberal candidate for North-West Norfolk to fight a bye-election caused by the death of Sir George White. The union supported Hemmerde but G.H. Roberts launched a lengthy attack on his candidacy at a union camp meeting saying that Edwards should have been candidate.[32] Hemmerde was elected but proved even less satisfactory in Parliament than out. He refused to support G.H. Roberts's attempts to get a minimum wage for the labourer, arguing instead for land reform as a necessary first step. In September 1912 Edwards told *Labour Leader* that the union would stand a Labour candidate against Hemmerde 'at the next election'.[33] Similarly in December 1912 E.N. Bennett, a radical of impeccable qualifications selected as parliamentary candidate for another Norfolk seat, approached the union offering help, 'financial or otherwise'. The executive discussed the matter at length and agreed to accept the offer but only if it did not imply automatic support by the union for Bennett and if the union had absolute control over any financial help.[34]

As the Liberals declined in popularity, among the executive at least, so Labour's fortunes rose. The attempt by Roberts to get a 'wages board' for agriculture in 1913 established him as the 'labourers'' MP, and he became a central figure in drawing up the ILP 'Rural Programme' in September 1913. But it was not only Roberts. From 1912 onwards the ILP in East Anglia as a whole seems to have been gaining strength. At the beginning of 1913 there were branches in Kings Lynn, Yarmouth, Stalham, Norwich, Wymondham and Lowestoft. However, each of these branches was a 'centre', according to Bill Holmes, around which labourers were organised.[35] In the spring of 1913 the union, helped by the ILP, fought both the County Council elections and some Parish Council elections. Their success was mixed. The most 'famous victory' was at Burston where Tom Higdon organised to turn out all the farmers. A similar result was gained at Costessy.[36] On the County Council Edwards was elected for Freebridge Lynn, W.B. Taylor for Saham Toney, and Day already sat.[37]

This does not mean all was quiet on the industrial front in Norfolk or in the other areas where the union was now gradually building up its strength. Edith Whetham has gone as far as to say

'strikes were endemic among farm workers in the eastern
counties'.[38] The most important ones were outside Norfolk,
especially in Lancashire, and these are well covered by Alistair
Much's[39] work, but Norfolk, in the winter of 1913, again
prepared to raise the standard of revolt. They raised it under a
new leader. In July 1913 George Edwards retired. 'I am', he
wrote, 'completely broken down and with my age I must now
leave the movement in the hands of younger men.'[40]

He was replaced by Robert Walker. Walker was the son of a
Scots ploughman who had worked on the land. He had been
appointed as an organiser in 1912 and he was a socialist. He was a
very different character from Edwards. Younger and tougher, he
seems to have had a deep dislike and distrust of the rural ruling
class, especially those of southern England. His term as secretary
was marked, especially in the early years, by difficulties between
him and Edwards, who, as president, continued to influence
union policy, and whose increasing moderation was complete
anathema to Bob Walker.

Although Edwards remained organiser for Norfolk, his influence declined from this date and that of Walker increased.
Walker was a much more militant figure who seems to have been
firmly attached to the ILP before he joined the organising staff of
the union. Perhaps symbolic of this change was the union's
decision in May 1913 to sever connections with the Land
Nationalisation Society and a few months later to affiliate to the
Labour Party. The Land Nationalisation Society, although radical,
was firmly the child of New Liberalism and the panacea of land
for all; Labour offered a fair wage now, a very different
conception.[41]

In 1913 conditions in agriculture again began to improve. A.D.
Hall's *Pilgrimage of British Farming* published in 1913 said, 'In the
first place we must recognise that the industry is at present sound
and prosperous.'[42] Norfolk was no exception, and 'land was
scarce and almost impossible to get', always a sign of prosperity.[43]
Even the County Landowners' Association and the National
Farmers' Union admitted as much in mid-1913 and complained,
for the first time for some years, of a labour shortage.[44] Wages
seem to have been stable through the winter of 1913–14, but in
the spring the executive decided to go for an increase of 2s a week
and a half day on Saturdays.[45]

However, the men had, by that time, already moved. In February 1914 wages on the Home Farm on the Sandringham Estate had been raised and the 'King's men' given a half day. Then, at the beginning of March, Mr George Brereton, a tenant of the estate, put his men on to two journeys a day, i.e. 6–11, then 1–6 for no extra money. This was often done when summer hours started but his men wanted the raise granted at Sandringham. All struck work. The strike spread quickly from Brereton's farm at Flitcham to other farms in the nearby villages of Hillingdon and Babingly. The farmers responded by bringing in blacklegs through the Federation. Ironically they came from the same villages in the Cambridgeshire Fens which had supplied men to break the St Faiths strike; indeed, according to the *Eastern Weekly Press* 'most of them served the farmers who were involved in a dispute with their men at St Faiths.'[46]

The union had won the major strike in Lancashire the previous summer and was in a confident mood, and, on 4 March, a letter was sent to all organisers recalling them to Norfolk to start a campaign for a general increase of 2s a week, bringing wages to 16s. North-west Norfolk was deliberately selected, as Walker said, 'as it is the strongest centre of the Union and the demands of the men have been more insistent here than anywhere else.'[47]

The slogan of the strike became 'the King's wages and the King's conditions', a slogan which did not always impress the farmers. As a farmer at Kings Lynn market told the *Eastern Weekly Press* the King was 'a farmer for a hobby, and could afford to be generous to his men'.[48] True or not, individual farmers quickly began to settle. This was not St Faiths, the strike was general throughout north-west Norfolk and the difficulty was stopping it spreading. The union was holding as many as twenty meetings a night in the villages explaining the strike, raising funds and paying strike pay. In the midst of it they issued a newspaper, the *Labourer*, whose purpose was to link the men of Norfolk together and give them news of the other strikes which were breaking out in East Anglia, especially in north Essex. Significantly, it carried under its title the clasped hands of brotherhood, an old and respectable symbol, but the words 'Workers of the World Unite' gave a very different and new tone.[49]

In the week that the *Labourer* appeared the farmers' resistance began to collapse. It was seed time, spring ploughing was late and

2.1   Radicalism: the wayside Bethel, the origin of much of rural radicalism. This rare picture shows the bare interior of Blo' Norton Primitive Methodist Chapel about 1900. (Norfolk Rural Life Museum, Gressenhall, Norfolk)

2.2   Radicalism: an open-air 'camp meeting'. The form of the open-air preaching meeting begun by the Primitive Methodists was widely used by the unions in both the 1870s and the 1900s. Here we see a Primitive Methodist Mission Van at Beetly, near East Dereham about 1900. (Norfolk Rural Life Museum, Gressenhall, Norfolk)

2.3 Radicalism: the friendly society. Dressed in their best the men, and one woman, of the Banham Foresters gather outside their meeting place ready to march through the village in the early 1880s. Many of the early unionists of the 1870s and 1880s cut their teeth in friendly societies. (Norfolk Rural Life Museum, Gressenhall, Norfolk)

2.4 Radicalism: the Norfolk Federal Union. A unique photograph, the only one of the Norfolk unionists of this period. It was taken in the 1870s in the sand pit at Swanton Morley to celebrate the 'victory' of George Rix in the Vestry elections of 1876. In fact Rix lost because of plural votes held by farmers although he got more individual votes. The photographs were sold at 2s each for union funds. The author had a very poor copy of this photograph from Mr Bone of Yaxham who was Rix's great-nephew. According to him the man in the centre with a beard is George Rix (it certainly looks like him from drawings made much later), the man with the sash is David Reeder and the man with the basket William Hubbard. This copy of the photo came from Mr Jolly at Gressenhall who believes it to be a friendly society meeting c. 1900. This seems unlikely because of the clothes, especially the headgear, as well as because of Mr Bone's evidence. The others in the picture are the 77 people who voted for Rix. For an account of these events see the *Eastern Weekly Press*, 22 April 1876 and 10 June 1876. Any further information would be welcome. (Norfolk Rural Life Museum, Gressenhall, Norfolk)

2.5 Radicalism: the embodiment of Norfolk radicalism. George Edwards aged 17 with his mother. Trade Union branch secretary, friendly society man, and Primitive Methodist preacher, he stood for all that was best in the old tradition of the Norfolk labourer. He was founder of the 'second' union in 1906 (see plate 2.6). (Norfolk Rural Life Museum, Gressenhall, Norfolk)

2.6 Radicalism: the new leaders. George Edwards, Thomas Thacker (far left) James Arnett (next to him) and Bill Holmes (next to Edwards in the centre) at a demonstration in the years just before the Great War. The scene of the photograph is unknown even by Mrs Mayhew of Kenninghall who gave it to the museum. (Norfolk Rural Life Museum, Gressenhall, Norfolk)

2.7, 2.8   Radicalism; the second union. Swanton Morley's 'famous sand pit' once again echoes to the sound of union oratory. The photos, which came from Mrs Rayner of Swanton Morley who attended the meeting as a girl, show George Edwards and James Arnett (with beard) addressing the founding meeting of the union in the village in the spring of 1907. See pages 92–3. (Norfolk Rural Life Museum, Gressenhall, Norfolk)

2.9   Radicalism: the 1918 General Election. In 1918 George Edwards
stood as Labour candidate for South Norfolk. He stood on a platform of a
peoples' peace 'with no annexations or indemnities' and was vilified by all,
especially the county press. He was however only narrowly defeated. Here
we see him at an election meeting at East Rudham along with most of
those who lead the union during and after the war. Left to right, George
Hewitt, the leader of the St Faith's strike of 1910, Tom Higden, the
schoolmaster at Burston, 'General' Robert Walker, the uncompromising
socialist secretary of the union from 1913, an unknown man, George
Edwards, James Arnett, one of the two executive members who supported
the St Faiths strikers, and two others who are unknown, although the man
next to Arnett looks like H. A. Day, the socialist manufacturer of Norwich
who was a firm friend to the union from its foundation. There are many
copies of this photo, which suggests that, like Plate 2.4, it may have been
sold to supporters. This one came from Edgar Wicks whose father, Bob
Wicks, was a branch secretary in south Norfolk. (Norfolk Rural Life
Museum, Gressenhall, Norfolk)

2.10   Radicalism: the post-war strikes. We cannot be sure, but this slightly 'retouched' newspaper photo seems to be of the Ringer's strike. It was probably taken on one of the 'route marches' (see page 143). Note the man on the left is still wearing his military tunic, a grim reminder of the recent past. (Norfolk Rural Life Museum Gressenhall, Norfolk)

2.11   The Great Strike: 'Old George' Edwards speaking at Fakenham during the strike. Although regarded by many as a 'moderate' by the late 1900s, he never flinched or faltered and was probably instrumental in holding the union together in the difficult years of the early 1920s. We should never forget the debt every English farmworker owes him. (Norfolk Rural Life Museum, Gressenhall, Norfolk)

2.12   The Great Strike: Wicklewood, Monday 16 April 1923. 'Close on
200 agricultural workers on strike assembled on the forecourt at
Wicklewood Workhouse on Monday and waited patiently for an interview
with the Guardians' (*Norfolk News*, 21 April 1923). This photograph shows
the men on their way to the workhouse where they demanded relief and
food. It was a deliberate attempt by the union to draw attention to the
plight of the workers as well as a response to the increasing hardship of the
strike. The elderly man with the cap standing in front of the banner on the
left is Herbert Coldham, secretary of the Deopham branch. The photo
came from Mrs Buttolph of Norwich, Mr Coldham's niece, and her
husband. (Norfolk Rural Life Museum, Gressenhall, Norfolk)

2.13   The Great Strike: Walsingham Market Square, Monday 16 April
1923, the demonstrations against Sam Peel (see page 169). 'The crowd
rushed towards him as he made his way to his cycle car, and over-ripe
fruit and pieces of orange peel were thrown at him. Mr George Edwards
. . . and other of the men's leaders appealed to the crowd to desist . . . a
clod was seen on the side of the car as it moved off . . .' (*Norfolk News*, 21
April 1923). (Norfolk Rural Life Museum, Gressenhall, Norfolk)

"Be good lads!"

prices looked like being high. With a widespread stoppage it was simply not possible to bring in enough blacklegs to run the farms. On 21 March the Earl of Leicester, the biggest landowner in north-west Norfolk, announced that he had called all his tenants together and they had agreed to an immediate rise of 1s a week, and one journey, 7–3.30, on a Saturday. Another large land-owner, Sir Ailwyn Fellowes, agreed the same.[50] Within a fortnight most men in Norfolk were back on those terms.

The strike was a major victory. It was short, gained most of its demands, and showed wide solidarity. There was the inevitable victimisation, individuals, especially branch secretaries, were refused work, and there were even some evictions. But it proved the union could fight and win. Lancashire and then Norfolk had gone for 'a forward movement' and gained the least part of their demands. No union of the farm labourers since Arch had been able to do that. They had come of age.

Also in the summer of 1914 the union became involved in what was to be perhaps its most famous dispute, and one which had very little to do with its activities until that date – the Burston School Strike. In March 1913 Tom Higdon, a schoolteacher, a socialist, branch secretary of the Burston branch (a not un-common situation as non-labourers were less easily victimised) and a member, since 1911, of the executive of the union, organised the labourers to contest the Parish Council elections in Burston in south Norfolk. The result was that all the old members of the council except one (who came bottom of the poll) were replaced by labourers or their representatives. Higdon himself came top with 31 votes.[51]

In the following months the vicar of Burston, the Reverend Charles Eland, began a campaign to get Higdon and his wife, who was mistress at the school, removed. This petty-minded series of actions bore fruit when, in April 1914, Mr Iken, assistant secretary to Norfolk Education Committee, arrived at Burston School with cheques in lieu of notice for the Higdons. The children of the school then went on strike in support of their teachers and the parents, in turn, supported the children. Because Higdon was a member of the union, and a branch secretary, it decided to support him and the school strikers by a national campaign. His own union, and that of Mrs Higdon, the National Union of Teachers, did not.

During the next three years the Burston strike and the school which the Higdons set up in the village, first in a carpenter's shop and then in a new building on the green, played a major part in the union's life. Meetings, collections and rallies were organised to pay for the school, and Burston village green saw the likes of Hardie, Snowdon, George Lansbury and Tom Mann address open-air rallies. Burston became a symbol of the tyranny of the church and village and of the fight against it. Finally in 1917 the new Strike School was opened. It still stands today, its front covered with stones presented by union branches, Clarion groups and ILP branches, a remarkable story in stone.

The outbreak of war initially had little effect on the Norfolk labourer. Although the harvest was early that year, most men were still in the fields for the first weeks of war:[52]

> we were always two or three days later than anybody else, on a big farm, . . . lot of them was finished in a fortnight and three days, but we were always three weeks and three days or a month. When the war come out, just as we started harvest . . . and so I joined up as soon as we finished harvest . . . they were calling out for volunteers them days. Several of us in the village, I should think about ten of us, went that Monday morning down to Mundesley and took the shilling. . . . You had to be twenty-one them days. When I went up they said "You aren't twenty yet" . . . "All right," I say, "I'm twenty-one." . . . Some weren't about sixteen, seventeen.

Like hundreds of other Norfolk labourers, Billy Dixon went into the 9th Battalion of the Norfolk Regiment, part of the new 24th Division. By February 1915 he was in France.

To start with there seems to have been little effect on Norfolk agriculture. There was, according to the *Eastern Weekly Press*, 'no shortage of men' at harvest although there was a shortage of horses which had been taken immediately into military service.[53] Then came winter and the slack season and so there was no real impact until the early months of 1915. Nationally, by that point, the available workforce had dropped by about 7 per cent.[54] No similar estimate exists for Norfolk, but by the beginning of 1915 the labourers began flexing their muscles, a sure sign that the labour market had moved decisively in their favour.

By the middle of February 1915 the *Press* reported that 'There is a growing agitation in some parts of Norfolk for an increase in wages of agricultural labourers.' Further, to counteract the shortage of labourers, boys were already being brought on to the land on a 'half-time' basis. The union opposed this, as Robert Walker said, 'farmers would find plenty of labour if they were prepared to pay adequate wages.'[55] But it was not only labour shortage. Prices were rising, increasing both the profits of farmers and the prices of food for the labourer. In this situation the 'King's shilling', won in the summer of 1914 for most Norfolk labourers bringing their wage to 15s a week, began to seem increasingly inadequate.

In the next three weeks Walker began what must have been the most difficult campaign of his career. At meeting after meeting the demand was raised for 18s a week as a basic wage for the labourers. In response the union on 20 February sent a letter to the Farmers' Federation saying that if 18s were not granted they would call out all union members in Norfolk.[56] Walker was opposed to the war and seems to have had no compunction whatsoever about calling the strike; he seems to have seen the war and the labour shortage as a God-given opportunity of raising wages, which indeed it was.[57] Others felt differently, especially Edwards. Although nominally retired he appears to have approached the Earl of Leicester and arranged a meeting between the union, Leicester and the Farmers' Federation. It was an historic occasion as it represented *de facto* recognition of the union by the Federation at least. At the meeting 18s per week was conceded, and Edwards and the *Eastern Weekly Press* were delighted at this triumph of common sense and patriotism.[58]

Walker seems to have been less sure about this triumph, a feeling which was increased when it was clear that many Norfolk farmers were not going to pay 18s. As a result in March and April a number of local strikes broke out in about a dozen Norfolk villages.[59] On 30 April negotiation over 18s broke down in Swanton Morley. Strike notices were sent out and on Monday 10 May over 200 men in the Swanton area came out on strike. The Federation responded by preparing to bring in blacklegs by 'building huts' in the village. Walker was elated. Replying to criticism he said, 'Instead of weakening the Union it was the finest thing they could have had to strengthen it. They were backed by the whole of the trade union movement.'[60] Supported or not they won, and won easily. The strike lasted less than a week, the men got 18s a week which was also backdated, and, perhaps for the first time ever, there was no victimisation. All the men were taken back except one who had found work elsewhere.[61]

But there were other problems on the horizon. The government responded to the labour shortage of the war period by releasing boys from school, by encouraging women on to the land and by the use of soldiers.[62] The union resisted, as far as it was able, all these measures. Elsewhere in England this resistance was little more than token, in Norfolk there was some success, particularly in relation to the use of soldiers. In the early summer of 1915 the Board of Agriculture arranged with the War Department that soldiers with agricultural experience could be released for key periods of the farming year. The first batches arrived in Norfolk for haysel 1915 and were paid 4s a day if finding their own keep and 2s 6d if the farmer boarded them – higher wages than the civilian workers got. In July this was increased to 6s 6d and 4s 6d respectively.[63]

This higher rate of pay, coupled with the belief that soldiers were potential scabs and strike breakers, led to a good deal of bad feeling which came to a head at Little Massingham in June 1915 when soldiers were actually used to break a local strike over piece rates for beet hoeing.[64] The following week there was a brawl between soldiers and labourers outside a recruiting meeting in the nearby village of Great Massingham, started when John Taylor, a gardener, shouted to those going to the meeting, 'Why should I join the Army? If I was of military age I should not join and I should not advise you to join.'[65] The bad feeling was still there a year later when a farmer from West Barsham wrote in the press 'there exists a little ill-feeling amongst village folk. In one extreme case a man gave notice because he had to work with a soldier.'[66]

As a result of this 'ill-feeling' farmers in Norfolk seem to have been reluctant to use soldiers but turned to other sources. 'Volunteers' met with little more success. The Rev. J. Cough McCormick organised 'camps' of volunteers from public schools to help at harvest at Weasenham and Colkirk. However at Colkirk the scheme collapsed 'owing to a local strike'.[67] More usual was resort to the 'surplus labour' within the villages, women and children. From late 1914 onwards women were

encouraged into the workforce. However the appeals by the War
Agriculture Committee met with little success. At the end of 1915
it was admitted 'women are very little employed in Norfolk'
except in the Fens and Marsh.[68] Certainly, as the war progressed, the Women's Land Army sent numbers of middle-
class women and girls into the county, but there remained a deep
antipathy among working men and women to land work for
women. This was partly historical, a belief that women kept
down wages dating back to the days of the gang system, but it
was also connected to the growing notion that 'respectable'
women did not work, and that work on the land was particularly
ill fitted to women. This came out when George Edwards
appealed, at the beginning of 1916, for more working women to
take up land work. His appeal got short shrift from some sections.
A letter from 'A Working Woman' ended, after accusing Edwards
of being in the pay of the landlords,[69]

> I think it would be fairer if you had included the middle class
> and rich men's daughters. If our lives are at stake so are theirs,
> and some of them have never done a useful day's work in their
> lives.

Similarly 'A Working Man', wrote that the 'sacrifices made by the
rich . . . have been of a purely vicarious nature', and to urge
working people to give more was an insult.[70] Nevertheless a
'Ladies Committee', composed almost entirely of titled women,
was set up to recruit women between 16 and 60 who would work
on the land. Figures are difficult to come by on a county basis but
they claimed to have placed 1,700 women in work in Norfolk.[71]

Boy labour was different. As the pre-war school log books
show, many country lads were only too willing to leave school at
the earliest opportunity and saw little relevance in the school
curriculum to their future. Additionally, there was a long
tradition of boys working at harvest from the age of 8 or 9
onwards. In this situation, it was relatively easy to get boys to
leave school early under the exemption scheme.

The union, and the Labour representatives on the County
Education Committee, which issued exemption certificates,
protested strongly. Bob Walker summed it all up at the annual
National Union of Railwaymen and National Agricultural

Labourers' Unions annual demonstration in 1915:[72]

> When they saw the squires, the parsons and the manufacturers
> taking their children from schools and sending them into the
> fields, they would consider the question of taking their own
> little mites to the field.

Despite such protests boy labour was extensively, and willingly,
employed. In the first six months of 1915, 666 exemption
certificates were granted by the Education Committee, and that
kind of number continued to be released throughout the war.[73]
Taddy Wright of Knapton was one:

> The Norfolk Education let us go you see, and I suppose he [the
> blacksmith] put in a grant for us, asked for us. Course I always
> used to mind horses, I loved horses, I weren't scared of anything
> then. . . . Then I went back to Gimmingham [school] after the
> War, and I might just have well stopped at home. They
> couldn't do anything with us, they used to put us in the infant
> room, we'd learnt too much off the soldiers.

In January 1916 the exemption scheme was extended to girls over
12 'to look after younger children who would otherwise
undertake outdoor work'.[74]

All these measures could not, however, conceal a shortage of
labour, real or perceived, which was rapidly strengthening the
position of the labourer in the labour market. As Bob Walker said
at the special conference of the union in January 1917, called to
discuss wages for the coming year, 'Never before had the
agricultural labourers . . . got such a hold or control on their
economic position.'[75] This was increasingly recognised both by
the government and by the farmers. In March 1917, for instance,
both the Farmers' Federation and the Board of Trade were
involved in discussions over a strike at Dereham, and from then
on the government intervened more and more to keep production
going.

However, it was at national level that the great change was to
come. The harvest of 1916 was seriously down. Wet weather the
previous autumn, plus the declining number of labourers available
meant that farmers had planted less in 1915 than they had in 1914.

There was also a fall in the number of animals raised, and the continuing shortage of horses commandeered to military service made the middle-term prospects gloomy.[76] In this situation home produced supplies of cereal were threatened for the first time. Worse still the U-boat campaign was now threatening the four-fifths of breadstuffs consumed in the United Kingdom but produced overseas.[77]

This pushed the government into action. It had long been decided that whatever forms food control should take bread should be excepted. As Beveridge wrote, 'whatever else was allowed to be in short supply, whether for human or for animal consumption, there should be a sufficiency of breadstuffs to meet in full all demands for them without rationing.'[78] The supply of bread became, from late 1916 onwards, 'the dominant note in British Food Control'.[79]

The part of this policy which directly concerns us here was the attempt to increase home-grown cereal production. In January 1917 a Ministry of Food was created, followed shortly by a new Food Production Department of the Ministry of Agriculture.[80] As a direct result of these moves, arguably the first direct interference by central government in agricultural production, a sub-committee of the Reconstruction Committee was appointed under Lord Selbourne, 'To consider and report upon the methods of effecting an increase in the home-grown food supplies, having regard to the need of such increase in the interest of national security.'[81] The Selbourne Committee did for the labourer what 50 years of trade union agitation had failed to do – it guaranteed a national minimum wage and a fixed working week. The committee recommended a fixed wage as a national minimum to be set by a wages board based on the trades boards of the pre-war era. The board was to consist of representatives of the workers and the farmers as well as appointed members from government. In addition the report suggested a guaranteed minimum price for wheat and oats, though not barley.[82]

Although badly mauled by both Houses of Parliament, the Selbourne Report came to fruition in the Corn Production Act of August 1917. It guaranteed a minimum price of 60s a quarter for wheat and 38s 6s for oats. It also gave a national minimum wage of 25s per week to labourers with extra for stockmen, horsemen and shepherds. This later arrangement was largely to be negotiated by the local committees, constructed on the same basis as the national committees, who would then report to the national board.[83]

Although the Act embodied most of the union's pre-war aspirations – indeed in all but detail it was identical to the proposal put by G.H. Roberts in 1913 – it was not greeted with universal delight. The main problem, in the first instance, was the 25s minimum wage. Although this would mean a raise of 2s 6s–5s per week in Norfolk and other parts of East Anglia, it was well below what was already being paid elsewhere, especially in the north and Scotland. Further, when the local boards met for the first time in October 1917, Norfolk, because of its superior organisation among both farmers and workers, met first. They set a county wage of 30s which the national board then took as its base. This meant that in some areas of England and Scotland where wages were already above this the local boards were useless from the start.[84]

In Norfolk though it was a minor triumph. From the middle of 1916 the union had gained effective recognition by the farmers' organisations and from that date onwards meetings had been held to fix county rates. As late as July 1917 the Norfolk farmers had refused to pay more than 25s as a maximum for the county and so the award of 30s was a vindication of the union's position.

The great importance of the wages board, in the medium term at least, was psychological. A national minimum wage, enforced by the law and negotiated by the labourers' union, gave the union a tremendous fillip. Similarly the negotiation of hours and piecework rates, as well as some protection over tied cottages, added up to a charter for the labourer. As F.E. Green wrote in 1920, 'When the Corn Production Act was passed, not only was it lawful to be a trade unionist, but it really became an injunction upon every labourer.'[85] In this situation union membership grew rapidly. Although figures are difficult to come by, and generally not exact, it seems that nationally membership increased from approximately 7,100 in 1916 to 127,000 in 1919. In the same period Norfolk membership went up from about 6,500 to over 21,000.[86]

For the union itself, perhaps rather than the men of Norfolk, the change was still greater, in a symbolic sense at least. Since the days of Arch various labourers' unions had sought recognition

from the farmers and from the government. They had internalis-
ed, like most of the British labour movement, an ideal of
organisation and respectability based more on a Smilesian ethic of
improvement than on any actual notion of how best to constitute
a fighting working-class organisation. This version of the labour
world, which was codified by the Webbs, saw trade unions as
having a permanent and important stake in industry and
government. The ultimate end was a London head office, with a
full-time general secretary and organising staff from which
discussions with the organised employer and government could
be conducted in a reasonable manner. As F.E. Green, a life-long
middle-class supporter of the labourers' cause wrote in 1920,
when it appeared that the wages board would last for ever,[87]

> The setting up of the Agricultural Wages Board coincident with
> the growing confidence amongst the workers that they could
> improve their conditions by organisation and negotiation no
> doubt accounted for the weapon of the strike being laid aside
> for the time being.

In this, of course, the labourers' union was no different from the
majority of other unions in the period. As Keith Middlemass has
noted in his work on the Lloyd George coalition, there was a
distinct growth of corporatism which included the trade union
movement as a whole in this version of the state from the signing
of the treasury agreement onwards.[88] Yet, for the labourer it was
perhaps less appropriate than any other group of workers.

At the passing of the Corn Production Act, at its renewal in
1920 in a different form, and at its final repeal in 1921 the voice of
organised labour stressed, time and again, the impossibility of
organising the farm labourer into trades unions. Thus, they
argued the labourers were like those other 'inferior' groups of
workers, married women and children, who needed special
protection.[89] While, as I have stressed throughout this book, this
is true in some respects, in others it showed a willingness to place
the considerations of ideology above the real ability of the
labourer to exercise industrial muscle. The wages board guaranteed a wage, hours of work and the rate for the job. It gave some
job security and limited protection from eviction. On the other
hand, it removed from the labourer, because of the union's

acquiescence in its structure as well as the union's own rule book, the most effective weapon the labourer possessed – the lightning strike or walk-off. Structural conflict of the kind outlined in Chapter 2 may have been unpleasant and its outcome could never be guaranteed, but with local knowledge of the labour market and the state of the crops, a labourer could often win real victories.

In 1918 these changes were symbolised by the move of the union's headquarters from Fakenham to London, to the 'imposing offices in Grays Inn Road (worth about £9,000)'.[90] From the date of the move all executive meetings were held in London and the minutes are typed. Truly the end of an era![91] Even this move seems to have upset some at the time since two members of the executive, one of them Edwards, proposed that the headquarters should be in a 'central provincial town'.[92]

After 1918, for three years at least, the union's yardstick ceased to be Norfolk, but life in Norfolk continued, and by and large continued well. Wages continued to rise with each meeting of the local wages board, and up until 1919 so did local membership. Farming as a whole prospered under the impact of the war and land prices rose. As R.R. Enfield wrote in 1924,[93]

> As for the British farmer, though it is true he did not go about
> beating his drum with quite the abandon of the rest of the
> business community, he was, it must be admitted, doing very
> well . . . and for one brief space he found himself, perhaps to
> his surprise, with very little to complain about.

Although the wages board 'worked' at one level, and it did as long as farming as a whole was prospering, great political changes were taking place within the union as a whole. The slow emergence of Labour was greatly speeded up by the war. The union, perhaps surprisingly, was not so divided by the war. If any objected to it on socialist grounds, as Walter Smith and Bill Holmes certainly did, they kept that part of their politics away from union concerns, at least until 1917 or 1918. Edwards, on the other hand, actively supported the war until 1916 when conscription, that anathema to the Liberal conscience, turned him, at first slowly, then more and more rapidly in favour of a declaration of war aims and a negotiated peace. More serious was the position of G.H. Roberts. He, like Edwards, supported the war from the start but went further and joined G.N. Barnes in the Ministry of Labour. In 1917 he found himself disowned by the Norwich ILP and, in 1918, he took the coupon and stood as 'National Labour'. He was elected but it was a short-lived triumph. He was unseated in 1922 by Herbert Witard, a pacifist, the same man who had moved his expulsion from the ILP.

Burston also played its part. The committee formed to raise money, build, and then run the Strike School represented a popular socialist alliance which stretched across the country. The stones presented as a mark of support to the school building show just how wide support was from union branches, ILP branches, Clarion groups and other socialist and Labour movement bodies. For Norfolk more important were the large number of socialist speakers who came to the village and the school and then went on to speak in the countryside around. They ensured that even in the depths of the war Norfolk was probably more effectively propagandised by socialists than any other rural area of England.

But change is seldom cataclysmic and identifiable with one event. The St Faiths strike shattered Liberal credibility in the labourers' union, but it was not until 1917 that Labour could formally replace it. Similarly the growth of rural Labour during the war and after was a slow process and not one which is easily traced. Bob Walker was willing to support strike action in wartime, probably the only national general secretary of a union to do so. There can also be little doubt that there was anti-government feeling by 1916 especially over the use of women and boy labour, as well as using soldiers and German prisoners at crucial times. Again Walker and the union opposed the government on all these categories of worker. Rising food prices also affected the labourer, perhaps more so, ironically, than the urban worker, since essential food supplies in particular were moved directly to the towns and then sent back to the countryside.

From the beginning of 1917 onwards Walker became increasingly militant in his demands to the Wages board, and this industrial militancy soon moved to the political field. At the annual NUR/NALU demonstration at Briston in 1917 he said[94]

the real war will begin when the soldiers return, a war against poverty. . . . If Russia could rise, how long would it be before the working classes call on the Government who now conscript their bodies to conscript the wealth of the country as well.

A month later he restated that position and added 'he had been an absolute and convinced socialist for twenty years, and he was proud of it . . . if the Socialists had had power there would have been no war.'[95] Russia affected Walker then, perhaps gave him hope as it did to so many. More striking is the fact that the press, which was pro-war, could find no opposition at these meetings to Walker's point of view. The Norfolk labourer had not become a Bolshevik, but nor was he a rabid jingo any more than he had been in 1900. This was confirmed by the Annual Council at Fakenham in 1918 which voted 'that every official of the Union work for a people's peace'.[96]

All this made the general election of 1918 a priority for the union. They had been prepared before the war, in theory at least, to support 'labour' candidates, now they were determined to put them up. The major problem was lack of organisation. The ILP had a strong base in Norwich, despite the defection of Roberts to the National Government, and some support left in Yarmouth, Kings Lynn and Wymondham, but there seems to have been no formal Labour organisation anywhere in the country. As a direct result of the election the first rural party came into being at Wymondham in the first week of August 1918. It was founded by Edwin Gooch and selected Edwards as its candidate. Edwards stood on the Labour platform of a negotiated peace and the establishment of a League of Nations.[97] Elsewhere in the county, based largely on the remnants of ILP support, Walker stood at Kings Lynn and W. MacConnell at Yarmouth. In addition W.B. Taylor stood for East Norfolk and Noel Buxton for North Norfolk. These last two were not formally Labour but were supported by the union.[98]

They met with unrelieved hostility from the press, both Liberal and Conservative, and some hostility from the electorate, especially in Norwich where Herbert Witard was physically attacked. However, their results were creditable, especially at Kings Lynn where Walker was defeated by just over 300 votes. More important was the establishment of a Labour presence in the countryside capable of organising and winning votes. This was shown in the local elections at the end of March 1919 when the

Norfolk News said, 'it is probable that more sweeping changes have been made [in the local councils] than at any time since their creation.'[99] In these elections, at both parish and district level, Labour won seats in Yarmouth, Kings Lynn, North Walsham, Oulton Broad, Wells-next-the-Sea and Terrington St Clement.[100]

During the next two years Labour established its place in rural Norfolk. Constituency parties appeared in east and north Norfolk in 1919 and the Kings Lynn party was put on a formal footing in the same year. Others followed. But it was not on the constituency parties that real strength was based but on village branches. Here the model had to be that of the 1870s, and George Rix's inspired linking of the union to the Liberal Party at village level, so that a permanent triad – Liberal-union-chapel – was established among the Norfolk poor. To do this needed an active and credible local leadership and a programme for the rural poor.

Ultimately Labour had neither. Their 'rural' programme was a farce, and the few outstanding local leaders produced went unsupported. Instead energy went into the constituency parties which became, or were suposed to become, well oiled electoral machines, and much of the oil was ex-Liberal. Time and again in the lists of names attached to these early constituency meetings one comes across those who ten years before figured on the same lists for the Liberal Party. Not that these were not good and dedicated party workers, many of whom were genuinely disenchanted with Liberalism's failure, but they brought with them the bag and baggage of that discredited creed at precisely the moment when the labourers were at least looking for a new one. The result, eventually, was political stagnation and defeat.[101]

In 1919 it did not look like that. The Labour Party seems to have been growing very rapidly, and growing, more importantly, in the country towns and villages. It was a secret growth, for, like the union itself, to join with the Labour Party could be seen as a reason for dismissal for a labourer. From the start, however, the Labour Party was a much more working-class organisation than the Liberal Party had been. There were, it is true, some notable middle-class supporters like Dr De Vere-Pearson of Mundesley sanatorium who helped form many branches in the North Norfolk constituency, but in general terms the party was founded and supported by farm labourers and other workers, especially railwaymen, in the rural areas.

The other group involved was the aggressively working-class ex-servicemen's organisation, the National Federation of Discharged and Demobilised Sailors and Soldiers. From late 1918 onwards this group, led by A.W. Votier, a boot and shoe maker, ex-SDF member and former sergeant in the Machine Gun Corps, carried out a mass agitation based on pensions and unemployment among ex-servicemen. However, they went much further than that. First, they carried out an aggressive campaign against the government sponsored and 'officer run' Comrades of the Great War, as in May 1919 when the Federation disrupted a Comrades meeting with shouts about army discipline and attacks on the 'officer class' who ran the Comrades. The meeting collapsed when Votier got on the platform and 'harangued the meeting on socialism'.[102] Similar disruptions took place in Kings Lynn and East Dereham. Second, the Federation saw the creation of a socialist state as one of their main aims, they demanded the wholesale nationalisation of industry and land, the right to work and full wages for the unemployed. These concerns led them into close contact with the emerging Labour Party in Norfolk and indeed gave it much of its early fire.[103]

The Federation, the Labourers' Union and the NUR formed a strong base on which to build a Labour Party in Norfolk, and by the early 1920s Labour seems to have assumed the place previously taken by the Liberal Party at least among union men. As Bert Hazell said,[104]

> When I became a Union man I automatically became a Labour man, and when I was fifteen [1922] I took out my first membership card of the Labour Party, and I never bothered about the other parties, I got immersed in the Labour movement, right from the earliest. The others were just nuisances.

In 1920 there came a chance to test this strength when a bye-election was called in South Norfolk. In the previous months Labour had made a number of gains in the County Council elections and in Parish Council elections in the area. Things looked good for Labour and George Edwards stood as candidate and was returned, admittedly against a split Liberal vote. However, it was a 'famous victory'. Labour had proved that it could organise for and win a parliamentary seat in a rural area. The Labour Party had come of age in Norfolk.

Ten years after St Faiths and Sir Richard Winfrey's cry that 'the socialists had taken over' the labourers' union finally showed that that was, on the surface at least now true. Norfolk Liberalism was in a shambles, divided locally, as it was nationally, into those who did and those who did not support the Lloyd George coalition. The party's 'left', and substantial sections of its centre had defected to Labour including the Earl of Kimberly, the foremost Liberal peer in the county. Labour, on the other hand was going from strength to strength. Edwards's election saw the beginning of a massive rural propaganda drive culminating in the summer of 1921 when there seem to have been meetings every night of the week throughout Norfolk. Like George Rix in the 1870s and 1880s the new generation of radical labourers carried the banner to village greens, club rooms and public houses. Their success was mixed. In some places, like Wells-next-the-Sea, the audience was in hundreds, at other places like Saxthorpe, attendances were minute, and forced cries of despair. 'The lack of interest shown in the Labour movement was deplorable in the extreme.'[105]

That report from Saxthorpe could be seen as a grim warning. Gradually in the next year or so the post-war millitancy and optimism in the Labour movement collapsed in the face of agricultural depression, unemployment and division. Agriculture itself was about to enter a period of decline worse than that of the 1870s and 1880s, and many of the gains and hopes were to be swept away.

That things were about to change was clear to very few. Despite signs of a fall in world wheat prices in the winter of 1920, and the first real unemployment in rural areas, the attitude as the year turned is perhaps best summed up by F.E. Green, writing, I would guess in June or July of 1920:[106]

What the farm labourer has won in better conditions he will never relinquish. Landlords may go; the inefficient farmer may go; and if neither landlord nor farmer will cultivate the land, he, the peasant, will remain to reap what he has sown.

Green's was to be an hopelessly optimistic vision.

On 11 June 1921 the *Norfolk News* carried the word that in
London great things had happened. For many months at least a
section of the farmers had been agitating for the repeal or, better
still, the modification of the Agriculture Act, and now, in the first
week of June, on the eve of haysel, they got repeal. The Act had
protected the labourer against the vagaries of the market price of
agricultural products and guaranteed a minimum wage. Now this
was all gone. As George Edwards said, it was 'the greatest
betrayal of the agricultural industry that any government has ever
been guilty of'.[1]

In the next 2–3 weeks, in response to repeal, the union mounted
a campaign throughout Norfolk to explain what repeal meant and
to mobilise opposition against it.[2] In this it was supported by the
Labour Party's decision, at its conference in Brighton at the end of
June, to oppose repeal and to reintroduce at least the wages
boards, if Labour were returned to power.[3] The campaign in the
county drew both Labour and the union together in a series of
meetings bigger than any since the war. In the first week of July
the union organised between fifteen and twenty meetings in the
north of the county alone, some of them attended by over 300
people.[4]

The farmers' response was mixed. Certainly, a section believed
that by reducing the major cost of production, which they argued
was wages, they could still compete and make a profit in a free
market. Others were less sure.[5] All were agreed on two
things – wages must be reduced *now*, even before the end of the
wages board, and that there should be no future mechanism for
imposing minimum wages. 'They had absolutely made up their
minds', said J.F. Wright, the county secretary of the NFU, 'that
they were not going to tolerate the interference of a central body
in London.'[6] In the second week of July 1921 the farmers
withdrew from the local wages board, effectively making it

useless since no real compulsion could be brought as all knew that the boards were going to cease having legal force on 1 October.[7]

Although the NFU returned to the wages board nationally and locally at the end of July, there was no compromise apparent. The government had decided that the county wages boards should be replaced by conciliation committees structured in much the same way, but not backed by statutory powers to fix a minimum wage. The union, quite wrongly, initially saw this as a victory. Walker, with uncharacteristic lack of foresight, said he was now, 'very much happier' with the situation since conciliation committee rulings would be 'implied terms of contract' for the country.[8] This ignored two major problems. First, the NFU did not see the committees in that way at all. As Henry Overman, the Norfolk president said, 'no control should be reimposed in respect of wages after the abolition of Part 1 of the Agriculture Act'.[9] Second, and more ominous, a section of the farmers clearly was prepared to ignore both the conciliation committees and their own union if necessary. This view was put forward in the Farmers' Column of the *Norfolk News* on 30 July 1921. Triumphantly it greeted the end of the wages board, 'the union's boasted powers . . . have become nought beside the value of the Wages Board', and, the column went on 'nor is it likely that any substitute will be able to enforce demands beyond the capacity of the land'.[10]

The situation might have been different if agriculture as a whole were more prosperous but during 1921 things went from bad to worse. As Edith Whetham has written,[11]

the index of agricultural prices in England and Wales reached a peak of just over three times the pre-war level in September 1920, drifted downwards during the winter and fell precipitously from the Spring of 1921 for eighteen months; by the end of 1922, it stood at 157, a fall of almost one half of the peak level within two years.

In Norwich Market this movement expressed itself as shown in Table 5.

With this huge drop in prices of cereal crops there can be no doubt that the farmers of Norfolk, as in the rest of England, suffered badly. At the top of the farming 'ladder', the suffering

TABLE 5   Prices of main cereal crops, Norwich Market, 1919–22 in Quarters[12]

Year	Wheat	Barley	Oats
Sept. 1919	£3 13s 6d	£3 17s 10d	£3 4s 7d
Sept. 1920	£4 11s 10d	£4 0s 7d	£2 16s 1d
Sept. 1921	£2 18s 6d	£3 5s 11d	£1 11s 1d
Sept. 1922	£2 15s 6d	£2 2s 1d	£1 8s 8d

was such as to draw little sympathy – an end to tennis parties, a decline in field sports, and a drop in a standard of living greatly raised by high wartime prices:[13]

> It has died away – the old bluff, hospitable life of the countryside – like a summer's day . . . the economic depression had caused me to hang up my hunting-crop early, and, except for occasional afternoons alone beside my own hedges, my gun.

Few labourers would have seen it that way.

In the middle, and at the bottom of the farming ladder, things were worse. The rent still had to be paid, families fed, and there was no knowing what the future held. Every year from 1919 to 1923 crops sold cheaper than the costs of production since seed corn and fertiliser had to be bought at a high rate while crops were sold at a lower one. Uncertainty ruled the day. But at all levels the response was the same, what economic historians describe as 'reducing the cost of the factors of production' – laying down to grass, 'sucking' the land and, above all, dismissing men and introducing machines or working with family labour. Adrian Bell in less sentimental mood saw this only too well:[14]

> 'He's sacked half the men to start with.'
>
>   'What?' I gasped. 'When?'
>
>   'This morning. That doesn't look very flourishing, does it?'
>
>   'But how does he think he's going to do a farm of that size if he doesn't keep the men on?'
>
>   'He says we are behind the times, paying a lot away in

wages. He has engines and a couple of tractors; he's going to do all the cultivation with them, he thinks.'

On smaller farms the dismissal of men was not always accompanied by their replacement by machines, either because the machines were too expensive or because their efficiency on a small unit was by no means clear. In these cases there was increasing use made of family labour. Occasionally this practice extended to non-farming occupations being used to directly subsidise the farm. Harold Hicks's mother, for instance, put three boys into one room and let the others to bed and breakfast guests, taking advantage of the farm's location near the popular resort of Mudesley.[15]

More usual though was the farmer himself, or his children, taking over the duties formerly carried out by hired men. This also happened on the Hicks's farm, a relatively small unit on which old Mr Hicks already worked alongside his men:[16]

At about that time, when I left school [1924] he had to give up this Mr Mason because he couldn't keep him any longer you see. So I had the job, within the next year or so, of looking after the horses you see . . . [there was] me and my father and my uncle . . . then about year after Wally [brother] left school and he started to help as well.

When Mr Hicks came to farm in 1919 he had employed three men full-time, and casual workers at harvest.

The demand for labour was further reduced by a reduction in farming standards ('sucking' as it was known) and by laying down to grass. As in the 1880s land was put down to permanent grass and seldom, in Norfolk at least, used for stock or dairy cattle. What land remained in cultivation was left in the rotation too long and rapidly deteriorated as labour costs were cut.[17]

'Where's the farm?'
'Up on the North coast, two-forty acres, used to grow fourteen coombe of barley.'
'Now I suppose they thresh all day and take half a wagon-load to the barn, leaving two or three tons of dock and carlick seeds on the fields, to help next year's crop?'

These reductions in the demand for labour, which were to continue right through the 1920s and into the early 1930s, made a situation which was already looking grim very much worse. In the winter of 1920–1 the first signs of serious unemployment in the rural areas began to appear. At the end of December 1920 there was unemployed rioting in Norwich when shop windows were broken and the police were called to prevent looting,[18] signs that Norfolk's capital, so often the resort of the unemployed labourer in the past, no longer offered any real hope. In the first week of January 1921 Norwich City Council called an emergency meeting on unemployment which heard that between the second week in December and the first in January the number of unemployed had risen from 1,520 to 2,435. Worse still these were not the humble paupers of the past. The deputy chief constable, Mr Hodges, said that 'Certain members of the unemployed' were 'determined to use direct action' to raise the scale of relief payments. Mrs Clarkson of the relief committee was more worried still, she feared riot, she said 'worse than any foreign war', and went on that it was not 'the older men among the unemployed, but the younger' who were causing trouble, and 'most of them were discharged soldiers'.[19]

In the rural areas things were perhaps not so bad. The *Norfolk News* correspondent in Swaffam claimed that there was 'no unemployment' in his area, while it was also reported that there were, 'not many' at Aylsham.[20] However, elsewhere things were looking worse. At Depwade in south Norfolk they opened the parish pits to 'raise stones' for the first time since before the war. There were 59 registered unemployed in the district, 'several' of them agricultural labourers and 'most' of them ex-servicemen.[21] There were other signs too. At the end of January the *News* reported that 'There is no lack of help on threshing days this season . . . as there are followers of the engine beyond the limited number of other years'.[22]

As spring came on the seasonal round moved in the labourer's favour and unemployment, in the country districts at least, dropped significantly. But there were worrying signs of a more serious crisis to come.[23]

I left school at Christmas 1921, I couldn't get a job roundabout. I done a few errands for the man that kept the post

office, and helped my father on the farm. . . . I helped with the
housework. Unfortunately my mother died in the May 1922,
and I still hadn't got any work. Then Payne, at Mundesley,
wanted someone to help him out with the cows and I went
down and got a job there for 10*s* a week.

Arthur Amis's experience was certainly not uncommon. In May
1922 unemployment around Aylsham was said to be 'acute'[24] and
the highways committee of the Rural District Council set up an
unemployment committee so that 'work [could] be found for the
unemployed on the By-roads [sic] in the District'.[25] It was agreed
to employ married men first at £2 per week and to give single
men three days work a week at the same daily rate.[26] Even in July
things had not improved and the highways committee received a
deputation of unemployed and agreed to 'reopen' Ingworth gravel
pits.[27]

As the winter of 1921 came on things got dramatically worse.
With the repeal of the Agriculture Act in July, and the worsening
prospects for agriculture, more and more men were laid off. On
the eve of harvest, usually the time of fullest employment, the
Norfolk County Council vagrancy committee reported an
increase of over 500 male casuals as compared to the same period
two years before;[28] while the farming column of the *Norfolk News*
wrote[29]

There are able men looking for a harvest that have small chance
of obtaining one; men too, who would gladly take a smaller
sum than that forced by [national] agreement. We seem to be
working towards a time when no extra hands will be taken for
harvest.

By the end of October the problem was acute, and not just in
Aylsham. In October and November every Rural District Council
in Norfolk seems to have set up some form of committee, like
that at Aylsham, specifically to deal with the problems of
unemployment. The only complete figures I have been able to
find are for Depwade RDC in south Norfolk and those form the
basis of Figure 4. The movement is clear. Starting fairly low in
October unemployment shot up to a high point in January 1922,
dropping from mid-March to full employment at harvest 1922.

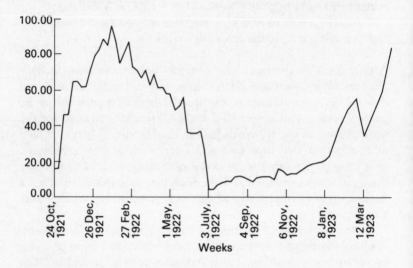

Figure 4   Unemployment payments, Depwade union, south
Norfolk, October 1921–April 1923 in £s per week

There is no reason to suspect that these figures were substantially·
different elsewhere in the country. Indeed in some areas they may
have been worse. St Faiths RDC, for instance, applied in
November 1921, to be classed as a 'special area' in order to qualify
for government aid from the Unemployed Grants Committee. In
all they asked for £2,600 for road works, drainage and
afforestation.[30] Erpingham RDC also applied for this status. Here,
a grant was also made by the Board of Guardians of £1,000 for the
'provision of work for unemployed persons' on the grounds that
it would be an 'estimated gross relief to the Poor Rate'.[31] Aylsham
received a UGC loan in March 1922 'to widen roads and remove
dangerous corners'.[32]

Few of the men interviewed for this book did not spend at least
part of the winters of 1920–1 or 1921–2 without work and it left a
bitter and lasting impression. 'Billa' Dixon returned from Flanders
to an ill-paid job in a saw mill where he was sacked for leading a
strike. From 1919 to the summer of 1923 he was a casual worker,

spending the winters as 'second corn' in a threshing crew and the summers working where he could get it.[33]

> Course they was having their own way, the farmers was then . . . they were putting us just anywhere . . . they wouldn't have cared whether you lived or died. An course them days there was a lot of unemployment, them days. When you worked on a farm like, there was always one or two people what was unemployed looking over the gate where you worked.

By February 1922 Depwade had 227 unemployed men working on the roads and in the pits, 61 on drainage schemes and 26 repainting the workhouse – all 'looking over the gate'.[34]

Parish work was irregular, badly paid and open to all kinds of abuse. Married men got preference but, despite attempts by the union to improve conditions, they were always paid less than labourers in regular work. At Depwade in October 1921 work in the pits and on the roads was paid at 2s per week less than agricultural labourers. The rate was the same at St Faiths, while Forehoe simply said wages were not to exceed those of labourers.[35] Only Erpingham, where there was a strong Labour presence on the RDC, paid the same wages as agricultural labourers.[36] The situation was made much worse in these overwhelmingly rural areas by the fact the agricultural labourers were excluded from the provisions of the Insurance Act, putting still further strains on local machinery.

Even when a rate of pay was laid down it was often not paid. Frederick Wigby wrote of working on a council drainage scheme in central Norfolk in the late 1920s,[37]

> The foreman, a hard unrelenting man, wanted his pound of flesh. . . . At the time he was living in digs at a public house in the town. Each night he expected men from his gang to keep him supplied with beer. Anyone such as Ernie and I who lived out of town, were expected to give him a packet of twenty cigarettes a'piece on Saturday morning. . . . There were no trade unions and such like to fight your battles for you. . . . No cigarettes or beer meant no work on Mondays, it was as simple as that.

Even then the work was not regular. Drainage work, especially on peaty soil, simply stopped when the weather got too cold, or too wet – two weeks before Christmas in Frederick Wigby's case. Then it was back to the dole, unless you were a labourer, when it

"THE UNLAID GHOST."

Organised Farmer: Let's work together, m'lad, never mind joining a Union; don't waste your money, I'll . . . .

Non-Union Man: Gawd! What's that thing behind you? (*To Ghost*) What 'yer want? Who *are* you?

Ghost of Serf: I am the Ghost of one-time slavery. *I cannot rest.* Do you want me back again? *YOU* CALLED ME !

Figure 5   A cartoon from *The Landworker*, 1922. The spectre of the past is raised by the farmer and by Sam Peel's 'company' union. See pages 139–44. (Museum of English Rural Life, Reading)

was the Guardians or resort to traditional methods. Wigby and his mate Ernie tried 'stealing' and selling wood but 'cutting up and selling logs in the country, was like sending coals to Newcastle'.[38] So they gathered holly, took it to Norwich, 'and after "totting" it around the town for the next day or two, made a shilling each out of the deal'.[39]

When such work failed the labourer had to turn to the Guardians or to charity. In Blofield Union, expenditure on out relief went up from an average of £8 a week in the winter of 1918, to an average of £24 a week in the winter of 1921.[40] 'Parish pay' was bad enough, private charity was often worse. Not only was it less, but it was not infrequently made personally humiliating, as at Thetford in December 1921 where the unemployed were paid in tokens exchangeable at certain tradesmen's shops with the stern warning that 'no luxuries will be allowed'.[41]

In the autumn of 1921, with conditions deteriorating rapidly, the union, for the first time for five years, came face to face with its own weakness. As we have seen winter was always a bad time. Work was short, even in the best years, and wage reductions were usual before the wages board had brought wages under government control. With the end of the board in October 1921 this protection vanished. Even before the end of the board, the union had been forced to accept a reduction in Norfolk from 46s per week to 42s, then on 17 September 1921, the Norfolk National Farmers' Union announced that it was going to press for a reduction to 39s from the first meeting of the conciliation committee, the voluntary replacement for the local wages board. Worse still the announcement said this wage was only to run to the end of December when the situation would have to be reviewed.[42] The union executive met two days later in London and accepted the reduction but added 'we do not agree to any reduction below 39/- per week, and no increase in hours'.[43]

Faced with the possibility of a winter strike against a background of rising unemployment there was little else they could do, but things were about to take a dramatic turn for the worse. On the 5 October Sam Peel, for the union, accepted not 39s but 36s a week.[44] It was the first sign of a split within the union's ranks which was to hamper seriously its work in Norfolk in the next eighteen months. Just how serious the situation was was shown also at the beginning of October by the entrance on to

the scene of a completely unpredictable factor, Mr Womack
William Ringer. On 23 September Ringer mounted his granary
steps, having called all his men together, as he did to make any
important announcement. He informed his men that from that
day their wages would be reduced to 30s per week, that being the
price of a coomb of wheat that week at Norwich Market.[45] He
then issued each man with a printed notice.[46]

TAKE NOTICE – All hands on the farm will receive in wages
from the first of October 1921 the price of a coomb of wheat
[18 stone] taken [sic] for the month of September [to] rise and
fall as the markets go the first of the month. The working hours
to be from 7 a.m. to 3 p.m. If all agreed no further notice need
be taken. If not, take a weeks notice from 23rd September 1921.

In a way the dispute at Ringer's prefigured the next two or three
years in Norfolk. Ringer was a traditionalist and a paternalist – in
short 'a good master'. His workers were well housed, regularly
employed and received extra payments on the birth of children.
He even imported medical services on to his farm when his own
daughter nearly died of a tonsil infection, to operate on all his
men's children.[47] Nor was his workforce unionised, with a few
exceptions. Jack Sadler said of his father who was out on strike for
49 weeks:[48]

I don't think my father was in the union, not until the strike
came. . . . I don't think he thought there was any need for it.
He'd got a job and a good master . . . there was a lot of them
thought that.

Even when the strike was under way this powerful influence
continued:[49]

If Mr Ringer wanted anything done he'd go to one of them tell
them to go and get a load of straw or this and that then come
back out on strike again. They always stood on the corner at
Titchwell, the Chalk Pit Corner we called it, and when my
father got there he [Ringer] said "Well come on together", and
walked up the street, and they all went bar three others and my
father. . . . Mr Ringer came back to these four and said "You

got some rotten B——s in your union as well as I have in
mine . . ." and of course when the strike was over he didn't
take them four back.

This points to the other, inevitable, side of paternalism. Ringer
was 'a good master' but he was also harsh when his law was
broken. He owned all the cottages in his villages and single men
were 'lodged' on the married ones with 'never a by your leave'.
He forbad the keeping of animals by any of his workers depriving
them of some little independence. He owned the lease of the pub
and was a major figure on the school governors, and like all
paternalists of the old school he linked religious and secular power
by standing at the church door to make sure his men attended. In
Titchwell, in particular, there was no room to move outside
Womack William Ringer's all-pervading influence.

In this situation what followed was unlikely. Non-unionised or
not, all his men refused his terms, even when, as the *Norfolk News*
put it,[50]

> He would undertake to find them all the flour they wanted at
> 2s 6d a stone, and what meat they required at 1s 2d per lb. for
> the best joints and 9d per lb. for other joints, as he considered
> tradesmen were profiteering and charging more for meat than
> they should.

This almost eighteenth-century approach was met by the
traditional response from the labourers in the form of a song.
Written by Fred Sewell, one of the strikers from Sedgeford, it
goes to the tune of 'The Church is One Foundation':[51]

We are the boys from Ringer's who refused thirty bob a week,
He said he'd sell us coal cheap and flour and milk and meat
We do not want his charity we want a living wage,
So that our little children may live to a good old age.

And so you find us and our friends, we mean to stand for right,
We have the best of leaders to help us in our fight
And when we ask you to support us, as your time may come
    soon,
Then you'll remember us friends, who you forgot so soon.

The nights are cold and dreary, but still we carry on
If needs be for a twelve month, we do not care how long.
But when the job is finished, and victory we have won,
All you who did support us, will join in the glad well done.

By the middle of October 161 men, the vast majority of Ringer's considerable workforce, were out on strike, plus some 25 men from the farm of another farmer, Mr Hancock of Burnham Norton. Hancock was a much smaller farmer who does not always seem to have got on with Ringer[52] but on this occasion he supported him. By the beginning of December, those few who remained at work had joined the strike taking the total up to over 200.

The result was predictable. Ringer was a member, despite his belief in dealing directly with his men and his objections to workers' unions of both the National Farmers' Union and the Farmers' Federation. The latter organisation's sole reason for existence was the provision of blackleg labour and in mid-November ten strike breakers were brought on to Ringer's farm to carry out essential winter ploughing and threshing. One old man wrote[53]

During the strike labour was drafted in from Yarmouth by train to Docking, thence by a farm lorry, ex-army, a Pierce Arrow, to a barn at Titchwell and Brancaster Field House and Town Farm Brancaster and Sedgeford, beds and cooking utensils provided by the Farmers' Federation.

After a time the locals were hostile to the "Black Legs" as the foreign labour was called and police protection was brought in, they occupied the riding stables at Titchwell to guard the farmhouse and those working on the land, as horses were being detached from what they were doing, in tumbrils or plough, and turned adrift bolting for home.

During barley sowing one policeman would stand at each end of the field and one would escort the man driving the pair of horses and the drill.

When threshing a corn stack instead of three men on the corn stack, the usual procedure, there were six blacklegs and four policemen took up positions on the ground around them for

protection. . . . . All this I saw when twelve years old, as a
strikers son. [Punctuation as original]

The importation of strike breakers (from Cambridgeshire as well
as Yarmouth), and the necessity of police protection for them,
heightened the temper of the dispute and from mid-December
onwards violence threatened on a number of occasions. There was
also a determined campaign by the Norfolk labour movement as a
whole to gain support for the men. This took the form of 'route
marches' as the press called them, by the strikers, their wives and
children and their supporters. Starting at Sedgeford, the most
southerly of the villages in dispute, they marched north ending at
Titchwell where Ringer's farmhouse stood.[54]
    The strikers also received considerable support from the
national labour movement, especially the *Daily Herald*. At
Christmas 1921 the *Herald* and other labour movement organisations got together a party for the strikers' children which George
Lansbury attended as Father Christmas, a 'get-up' which 'almost
succeeded in ending my earthly career by suffocation'.[55] After the
party Lansbury talked, in his own words, 'an unconscionable
time' about 'what the Movement stands for'. He ended optimist-
ically, 'I am certain that the women and men of Norfolk will not
be broken either by [Ringer] or anyone else.'[56]
    But it was not to be. For a start the strike was fought at the
wrong time of year. October saw the end of summer work, the
eight weeks after harvest were probably the quietest of the
farming year. Despite this, the unity and the solidarity of the men
on strike was remarkable. On 12s a week strike pay they never
faltered even though many had been non-unionised at the
beginning of the dispute. Yet that was not enough. With rising
unemployment, blackleg labour could be found fairly easily,
outside the area at least. In Norfolk itself attempts were made to
recruit from the unemployed on a more permanent basis but
without success. The Board of Guardians at Gayton, for instance,
attempted to force unemployed workers to go to Ringer's farm,
and there were other cases of men turning up, sent by guardians,
and turning back when they discovered the true situation.[57] Even
Ringer's advertisement's in the press for '300 agricultural
workers . . . immediately; permanently' seems to have drawn no
response.[58]

However, enough labour was found to keep the farm going, and that was enough. Threshing, for instance, was largely done by contract labour from off the farm and needed only a few workers provided by the farmer to feed the engine and stack. Ploughing was more difficult but winter ploughing was unusual, except for barley, and could be left to the spring. With a large force of police to protect them, which they had, a few men could work even a large farm in the winter. Ultimately though, it was events away from Ringer's that led to defeat, and it is to them that we must now turn.

In 1918, as we saw, the union had moved its headquarters to London. At one level this was a realistic and sensible recognition of its increasing national importance, but at another it took away from Norfolk its special status. More importantly it took away the figure of Robert Walker who, until that time, had been a considerable local figure, although national secretary, and had spent much of his time in Norfolk. In place of the headquarters at Fakenham, and Walker, Norfolk got a county committee increasingly dominated by the figure of Sam Peel. Peel came from Wells-next-the-Sea and was an ex-labourer. He had been active in Liberal politics before the war but seems to have been a Labour supporter by 1918. By the early 1920s he was Labour County Councillor for Wells, a JP and a member of the Norfolk wages board. In 1921 he became head of the union side on the conciliation committee.

Sam Peel was in all respects a moderate. Like George Edwards, but lacking his resolve, he was in an older mould of union leader. He was, for instance, a strong nonconformist and had consistently opposed strike action in the years after the war. But Peel spoke for Norfolk. Like old George Rix fifty years earlier he was a man of the county and after the move to London seems to have spoken for a considerable federalist feeling in the county.

But he spoke for a more powerful feeling than that – he spoke also for the old idea of an agricultural interest. There was, and indeed is, a strong belief in large areas of rural England that agriculture is a separate and unified whole, with different and often opposed interests to those of other sectors. The classic case here is, of course, cheap food. The urban working class demands cheap food and is supported by the labour movement. Cheap food means low farm prices, low farm prices, it is then argued, mean low farm wages. There is a unity, therefore, of agriculture to keep food prices high – or so it is argued by those who see agriculture as an 'interest'. This argument was especially strong in times of crisis and sometimes found institutional expression. Lord Winchelsea's short-lived 'National Agricultural Union' of the early 1890s sought to bring landowners, farmers and labourers together in a defence of their 'common interests' against industrial capital. The union failed but the ideology remained strong and with the crisis of 1921 it began to reassert itself.

The immediate reasons for this are obvious. Despite initial enthusiasm for the repeal of the Agriculture Act among some sections of farmers, it quickly became clear that any reduction in wages, as a major cost of production, was simply going to be wiped out by continuing decline in market prices. For instance both the *Farmer and Stock Breeder*, and the *Mark Lane Express* (probably the most important of the farmer's papers) welcomed repeal in the summer of 1921.

However, as prices continued to fall in the spring of 1922 when, according to normal expectations, they should have risen, attitudes began to change. First, the farmers, and to a lesser extent the landowners, began to realise that the old cry of a depressed and oppressed agriculture was taking on a new and real force. As Newby *et al.* say in the introduction to their study of the modern farmer, 'farming to the farmer is . . . a constant battle against the meddling of an ignorant, but intimidatingly large, urban majority of the population.'[59] In this situation the argument that agriculture was 'misunderstood' and being singled out by the government for especially hard treatment got more and more support. In January 1922 J.F. Wright, County Secretary of the NFU, told a meeting in Swaffham Corn Hall that 'all the extravagant predictions about a farm wage crisis in Norfolk' had come to nought because it was not 'a "wage crisis" but a crisis of the industry'. This crisis could only be met by a 'unity of the agricultural interest' in the face of the government.[60] The 'unity' position was made clearer still in February 1922 at the Diss branch of the NFU when Henry Mutimer said, 'The one panacea was that the labourer must see that our interests are his interests'.[61]

This appeal to the labourers to join in the unity of agriculture constituted the second phase of the farmers' response, and it found a willing listener in Sam Peel. On 25 February Peel, on behalf of the Norfolk committee of the union, accepted a reduction to 30s a week for ordinary labourers.[62] The national executive and other

CUTTING DOWN EXPENSES.

Farmer: Cold this morning, Jarvis! Where's your overcoat?
Jarvis: No overcoat for me this winter, Mr. Smith. Seems I ain't done paying for that there motor of yours yet.

Figure 6   As the winter of 1922 dragged on and wage reductions continued the mood of the farmworkers grew more bitter. A cartoon from *The Landworker* in the winter of 1922. (Museum of English Rural Life, Reading)

sections of the Norfolk leadership were horrified. Not only was the whole basis of the long, and increasingly bitter, Ringer's dispute the argument that 30*s* was not a living wage, but also national and local policy was set on strike action to resist a reduction to 30*s*. Further, a ballot taken at the beginning of February in Norfolk showed a majority of 7 to 1 in favour of strike action to prevent a reduction to 30*s*.[63]

However, Peel's position, and indeed local support, was much more substantial than these figures were to suggest. For a start as early as October 1921 Peel was prepared to accept a reduction to 36*s* where national policy was for no less than 39*s*. It is clear that in this case Peel 'agreed' with the local NFU but was overruled by head office.[64] Thus even before the Ringer's dispute there were signs of a split between the local committee and the national executive. This split, which was increasingly seen in terms of moderation, localism and unity of agriculture (Peel) *vs* socialism, centralism and class war (Walker) assumed more and more importance in the next nine months and was instrumental in debilitating the union up to the eve of the 'great strike' in 1923.

The split came into the open with Peel's acceptance of 30*s* in February 1922. Immediately the national executive condemned Peel's action, and that of the other members of the Norfolk Conciliation Committee, and called upon them to resign. In this they were supported by a substantial section of the Norfolk 'rank-and-file' in the form of branch resolutions, and by other sections of the Norfolk leadership, most notably George Hewitt of St Faiths. Hewitt, the leader of the 1910 strike and a confirmed socialist, said,[65]

> I know what our members' feeling is and that their vote was 7 to 1 against accepting 30/- . . . . I doubt whether our members will accept it and whether our members on the Conciliation Committee will be able to lead the men with them.

However, faced with an agreement by the local committee the national executive could do little. Both their internal structure and the government structure laid down for the conciliation committees put total power, in this respect, into the hands of the local representatives.

In the short term though it was disastrous for the men out at

Ringer's. By the end of February Ringer seems to have had about 100 blacklegs on his farms, most of them from outside west Norfolk. As a result he was 'adamant in his determination not to reinstate all the men'.[66] In particular he refused to take back the small group led by Bob Wagg and Jack Sadler who he regarded as the leading trouble-makers.[67] On 17 March 1923, at Ringer's farm in Titchwell, an agreement was reached[68]

1. Messrs. Ringer agree to observe the wages as fixed by the Norfolk Conciliation Committee.
2. Messrs. Ringer agree to reinstate as many of their former employees as they are able to find work for and preference will be given to regular men. When it is necessary to increase the staffs on the farms every effort will be made to give priority to former employees who desire re-employment by the firm.
3. In consequence of this undertaking the Union representatives agree to declare the strike at an end on this day 25th March 1922.

A month after the end of the strike 102 men formerly employed by Ringer were still on the union books, three months after the end of the strike 31 were still on the books. It was not until November 1922, eight months after the end of the strike and thirteen months after it began, that the last name, that of Mr Neale of Barnham Norton, was taken from the list of those receiving strike pay.[69]

It is not difficult to imagine how some of the Norfolk leadership and indeed membership must have felt in this situation. Take George Hewitt for example. Although Hewitt was now a Labour JP and a respectable smallholder, as well as a member of the union executive, it was barely ten years since he had led the St Faiths strike. The outcome at Ringer's must have looked very similar, and Hewitt, who had been on the union's books for two and a half years after St Faiths, knew only too well the humiliation and bitterness, as well as the victimisation, that followed in the wake of a lost battle. Significantly, it was Hewitt who was to replace Peel as the Norfolk 'leader' of the farm workers.

However, there were many who did feel differently. If the

Ringer's strike, and the humiliation of the defeat in the conciliation committee, stiffened the resolve of Hewitt and Walker, it sapped that of others and Sam Peel's arguments appealed to them. As the spring of 1922 passed the split between these two groups within the union began to widen.

In the wake of the Ringer's defeat, and the acceptance of the farmers' 30s per week, the Norfolk county committee was forced to resign and seek re-election on a new, reorganised county system. Interestingly, and perhaps surprisingly, Peel, and his main supporter W.B. Taylor of Swanton Morley, were both re-elected.[70] Even three months later Peel and Taylor were elected to serve as delegates from Norfolk to the union's biennial conference, with Peel receiving the highest number of votes given to any delegate.[71] However, Peel was replaced as chairman of the conciliation committee by George Hewitt, and Bob Wagg, one of the Ringer's strikers, was also elected.[72]

The stage was set for an open confrontation of the two wings of the union in Norfolk, and that confrontation came at the biennial conference in London at the beginning of June 1922. Peel and Taylor came to the conference as aggrieved men. Supported by some of the Norfolk delegates, especially the then young Edwin Gooch, they presented a case in which Norfolk, that most democratic and radical of counties, had been forced by the London-based executive to act as scape-goats and then summarily dismissed. As W.B. Taylor put it, 'the principle of democratic government had been infringed by the Executive Comittee'.

Peel and Gooch both defended the action of the Norfolk conciliation committee's acceptance of 30s, and Taylor argued that the union, 'must recognise the times through which the agricultural industry was passing'.[73] Peel and Gooch also both urged support for a policy of moderation, and using the Conciliation Committees. As Gooch said, 'Better terms could be got by conciliation than by a strike policy.'[74]

But the militants had their support and spokesmen too, and despite the attempts of the president, Walter Smith MP, who was a moderate, to have the issues shelved, they spoke strongly in support of the so called 'strike policy'. Not surprisingly Robert Walker was perhaps the strongest opponent of the moderates. He said quite simply that while it was union policy he would work through the committees but, 'if the Union at any time decided

the Conciliation Committees were a farce and a failure they would
have no greater supporter than him.'[75] Bill Holmes took a similar
line and pointed out that despite Peel's support, the executive had
received many branch resolutions calling for action against Peel
and the Norfolk committee including twenty-eight from within
the county itself.[76] One of these resolutions in fact appeared in the
Land Worker as a letter. It ended: 'Our representatives have not
gained one point in favour of the men they represented. Every
time they made an agreement it was in favour of the farmers.'[77]

The issue was not put to a vote, but at some point in that
conference Sam Peel must have made a crucial decision. During
the course of the afternoon he (and Gooch) withdrew their names
from the ballot for the executive. Holmes and Hewitt were both
elected. In view of what followed in the next three or four weeks
it seems likely that Peel had thought he could swing part of the
conference to his view and split the union and then thought better
of it. On the last weekend of June, Sam Peel announced that he
was to be president of a new agricultural labourers' union – the
National Union of Land Workers.[78]

The union was founded by Harry Lovell, who had been
assistant secretary of the NUAW, and J. Purchase, Hertfordshire
organiser of the union. Their objects were laid out in a statement
published on the same weekend that Peel announced he was to be
president. The crucial notion behind the new union was the
foundation of a National Agricultural Party, 'based on the
principle of political co-operation by the sectional interests within
the industry as opposed to alliance with the Labour Party'.[79] As
Lovell wrote in the *Darlington Times*, 'The old political creed must
go, and the new creed for the countryside must be agriculture for
the agriculturalist.'[80] Peel himself stated the case for a 'new union'
clearly in the *Norfolk News* at the beginning of July 1922. It is
worth quoting at length since it represents a cogent presentation
of the 'united agriculture' policy which Peel, and his union, stood
for:[81]

the next step in the agricultural industry is that all those whose
interests are affected should meet together instead of perpetuat-
ing the present spririt of antagonism between the various parties
in the industry and by exchange of the facts, as they are seen
and realised by each section, be led to form such a policy as will

give the land worker a security of employment and a real living
wage, as well as the farmer and landlord what is their rightful
share. . . . The new union has been formed with the ideal in
view that co-operation and the spirit of goodwill shall replace
that of antagonism and suspicion.

There can be little doubt that Peel spoke for a large section of the
farm workers. His position was well known before he left the
union, and by his own admission he had talked to Lovell and
Purchase as early as May 1922 about splitting away. In these
circumstances the strength of opposition to Peel in Norfolk is
very striking indeed. It was led by, of all people, George
Edwards. For some years Edwards had seemed increasingly out of
step with the union leadership, especially Robert Walker. He was
a Labour MP, but still in some respects a Liberal, like so many of
his generation. Yet Peel's action and his insistence that agriculture
was a 'special' interest seems to have raised in Edwards the ghosts
of his own childhood, which, interestingly, he had just written
about in his autobiography.

At the beginning of July, at an open-air meeting on the
Buttland at Aylsham, all his power and anger seem to return. He
spoke of his childhood in the 1860s, of the bitterness caused by the
failure of Arch's union and of Lord Winchelsea's attempt to form
a united agriculture organisation in the 1890s:[82]

> The labourers had their views on the wages question, they
> claimed the right to obtain the highest value for the labour they
> gave; that was their starting point. But the farmer took the
> opposite view and was bound to do so. . . . He had to buy
> labour, and he had to buy it as he did everything else, at the
> very cheapest rate he could. There must come a conflict. Where
> was there a common interest and how are the two classes to
> have one common object as long as this position existed, so
> long as our social system remained as it was today?

In speaking for himself, and from his own experience, Edwards
spoke for a large section of the Norfolk labourers. Peel had been
able to call up the bonds between master and man, the
fact – which was undeniable – that agriculture was suffering
badly, and even Norfolk localism. With the exception of the

latter, which Edwards could appeal to at least as strongly, 'old George' presented the other side, the years of low wages, bad food and housing and the personal humiliation which characterised so much of labouring life. By raising his own ghosts he raised those of thousands of Norfolk labourers.

But it could not be that simple. After harvest in 1922 the farmers pressed for a further reduction to 25s for a 54-hour week.[83] The reformed Norfolk committee seem to have been unwilling, or unable, with the exception of Edwards, to oppose the reduction. Again it was winter, and Ringer's must have been constantly in mind. Further, in Norfolk at least, Peel's shadow loomed large – there was always the possibility that he was right and that the Norfolk labourer was unwilling to strike in the face of a crippled agriculture – that remained untested. Further, although Walker and the national executive were committed to strike action in defence of 30s, indeed they were committed to direct action to raise wages to 40s, they seem to have been unwilling to intervene in Norfolk again while the situation looked so fluid.[84]

It was Peel's moment of triumph. Although his union had practically no membership in Norfolk, and never was to have, his principles seem to have carried the day. At the end of December, at a United Agriculture meeting in Norwich Corn Hall, Peel proposed that the National Union of Land Workers 'shall be recognised as the official negotiating body on behalf of the agriculture labourers' section'.[85] Although the meeting had no formal power it was convened by, and supported by, the County Landowners' Association and the National Farmers' Union. More than that the motion was seconded by Henry Overman, one of the most important figures in the Norfolk NFU.

As the old year turned Peel's campaign must have looked near success. It was after all 'sensible'. Only pressure from all sections of agriculture, it was argued, could effect a change in government policy which would bring back prosperity. Given the depression and still high, if falling, unemployment, it was by no means certain that Peel's call would fall on deaf ears – after all it 'fitted' with the whole ideology of country life as 'different' from that of the class-ridden and antagonistic society of urban England. Peel promised the old days back, the days of an organic society when master and man respected each other, when wages were properly bargained for but were fair, when the sun always shone on the 'fair field full of folk'.

To thousands in Norfolk though, the 'old days' looked different. Like Edwards they remembered the insecurity of employment afforded by 'dry weather masters' and the weaknesses of a system of bargaining based on a deal, especially in winter. The older men, and there must have been many, could remember the collapse of Arch's union in 1896 and the hard fight that followed. To these the golden age was not the day before yesterday but yesterday itself – the period of the wages board, of a guaranteed working week and a guaranteed county wage. The board was the rock upon which they had built their church – only the Labour Party would return it, only with its return could the labourer expect a fair wage.

From the standpoint of Labour, the payment of a living wage comes before every other claim. It comes before not only the farmer's profit, but also the money lender's interest, the landlord's rent and the middleman's toll on the product of agriculture. The argument that the farmer cannot afford to pay, even if it were true, would be neither here nor there.

G.D.H. Cole, 'Stand Behind the Rural Workers' 1923[1]

Compared with 1921–2 the winter of 1922–3 was not that bad. Nevertheless, there can be little doubt that there was now a long-term unemployment problem in rural Norfolk. Additionally the general prospects of agriculture had, if anything got worse. Prices were low after harvest in 1922 and the price of malting barley, vitally important in west Norfolk, fell badly.[2]

In this situation tension inevitably increased. Farmers, after two bad years, looked at an apparently unendingly bleak future while the labourers, sensing some easing of their plight, seem to have regained confidence in their position. But, most important of all were the demands, made increasingly strident from December 1922 onwards, for further reductions in wages to meet the further drop in market prices. As *The Times's* agricultural correspondent wrote in March 1923,[3]

When I visited Norfolk and adjoining counties last autumn evidences of coming trouble were clearly discernible . . . it was recognised then . . . that the gross proceeds from the harvest of 1922 would be wholly insufficient to allow of a bare living wage to all, employed and employers, who had a right to expect such a reward for their part in the common enterprise.

In this situation there was an increasing sense of desperation on both sides. The farmers believed that only by forcing the plight of

To NORFOLK FARM WORKERS.

The Farmers have no quarrel with

YOU

Concessions have been offered in

YOUR INTERESTS.

NO REDUCTION OF WAGES.

2 extra hours asked for the 25/-

(20 minutes extra per day)

THIS IS ALL **YOU** ARE EXPECTED TO
CONTRIBUTE TOWARDS THE INDUSTRY'S
PLIGHT.

THINK IT OVER!

Before you decide to support an upheaval in

AGRICULTURE.

Farmers agree to offer facilities for Saturday Half-day.

NO SEEDTIME MEANS
NO HARVEST.

Roberts & Co., Printers, Ten Bell Lane, Norwich.

Figure 7 The stick and carrot. A NFU leaflet issued during the
1923 strike combines the appeal to the 'unity of agriculture' and
the open threat of further unemployment. (Museum of English
Rural Life, Reading)

agriculture before the government could any real aid be expected; the labourers felt that only by an effective stand against reductions could the union survive, not only in Norfolk but nationally. With Peel's union to one side and the farmers to the other, they could only go forward.

In mid-January at a Norfolk NFU executive meeting, J.F. Wright, the county secretary said 'it was a well known fact that 25s a week was impossible with the income of the industry'.[4] The following day Peel, 'on behalf of the labourer' agreed saying that the 'wage that is being paid is an uneconomic wage and that wages made up a 'disproportionate' part of farmers' expenditure'.[5] This 'disproportionate charge' had fallen, on a base of 100 in 1919 to 68 by the winter of 1922, a good deal faster than the fall in the cost of living. It should also be remembered that labourers' wages were, on average 45–50 per cent lower than those of industrial workers to begin with.[6]

It was the final straw. In a sense there was nothing left to lose. In common with other unions, membership of the NUAW had been falling in the early 1920s; Peel could still break the union with his appeals to unity and nobody, even the farmers, believed that 25s, let alone less, approached a living wage. In February 1923 the union withdrew from the conciliation committee. As H.E. Durham, a national executive member, said at a meeting in Norwich at the end of February,[7]

the Conciliation Committee had set its own face on the farmers side. . . . They recognised that the Conciliation Committee was of no use, and should be ignored. Scrap the committee and have no more to do with them.

At the beginning of March there were two last, desperate attempts to avoid a strike. Wright, for the farmers' side requested a meeting but all that was offered was 24s 9d for 54 hours, a reduction of 3s for an increase of 4 hours. It was rejected.[8] The following week the final card was played. Believing still in the 'special relationship' between agriculture and the Conservative Party, and thinking that the continued collapse of prices and the threat of a dispute might change the situation, the NFU persuaded the NUAW to go on a joint delegation to Bonar Law, the Prime Minister.

If either side had any hopes they were quickly dashed. Bonar Law informed them,[9]

> I do not see what can be done, or what you could expect the Government to do . . . it comes to this: is the industry to be self-supporting or is it not? . . . If there were any way we would like to help you, but it seems to me that agriculture must live on an economic basis.

As for a wages board, or any interference in the wages question, they 'existed in good times. That is the difference.' And so the farmers returned to the shires, to the heartland of Tory England, holding true to the absurd belief that 'their' party cared for agriculture, and turned their eyes towards Norfolk where a set-piece battle was about to be fought.

In fact, by then that battle had started. On 10 March some farmers, acting at the urging of Mr G.H. Mutimer, the chairman of the conciliation committee, had sent out one week's notice of a reduction to 5½d an hour for a week of 54 hours. By 17 March James Lunnon, the union's organising secretary, had set up a strike headquarters. The place chosen had its significance. It was the Keir Hardie Memorial Hall in Bridewell Alley, a small flint building bought by the Norwich ILP and turned into a working men's club. There, under a steel engraving of John Wesley preaching, Jimmy Lunnon began to organise the biggest farm labourers' strike since 1873, and the last strike of national significance which the NUAW was to lead.

Initially the situation was confused. The union instructed only men who had been reduced to come out which produced some strange anomalies:[10]

> When it came to the strike and he said that I am knocking you down from 25s to a pound, and he came to me and he said, "What are you doing?" I said, "Well, if you knock me down anything at all I shall be out on strike, because I belong to the union." "I know that," he said. And after eventually arguing a little bit he said, "If I don't pay I've got to have somebody milk the cows, so I'd better pay you."

As Arthur Amis was the only union man on his farm, he was put in the strange position of keeping his full wage while the non-unionists, who stayed at work, were reduced.

This situation was duplicated throughout the Trunch district, where Arthur Amis lived, in the first weeks of the strike. Herbert Harvey told the *Norfolk News* on Sunday 18 March,[11]

> The men have come out on the larger farms where they have received notice . . . but a good many employers took no action, and the men, of course, are in those cases remaining at work.

This situation, especially in the first weeks of the strike, was extremely common. An *Eastern Daily Press* reporter spoke to a team-man working near North Walsham who told him[12]

> We are all working on this farm. . . . We had notice that our wages were to be chopped to 5½d an hour and that we would have to work 54 hours a week. Of course, we didn't like it and were not going to do it, so master said he was not going to be dictated by them other farmers and he withdrew the notice. We are having our sixpence an hour for 50 hours. What I say is if one master can pay the 25s, why can't the others? And surely 50 hours is enough for anybody to work.

The early sending out of notices, and the consequent uneven response to the strike call in the first weeks of March paled into insignificance in the face of another factor – the weather. The Ringer's strike, like earlier disastrous strikes, had been fought in winter; it was now spring. More than that it was an exceptional one. As *The Times* said at the beginning of March.[13]

> The men's attitude stiffened under the influence of the weather. Two fine days (Friday and Saturday) and a drying east wind have followed six wet weeks, in which it has been possible to do very little on the land. Work is much behind.

This was to be a crucial factor. Spring ploughing was well behind even before the strike started and the farmers' slogan of 'no seedtime – no harvest' (see p. 155) was double-edged. If the worst really came to the worst the labourer had parish doles; the farmer had a lot further to fall.

It was decided, on 17 March, that if the farmers did not increase their basic offer, which stood at 24s for 50 hours, all union members in Norfolk would leave work starting on 24 March.[14] On the 24th both sides met again at the Bishop's Palace in Norwich at the urging of the Bishop. No agreement was reached and on the 24th a call went out for a 'general strike' of all Norfolk labourers.

The response was mixed and the result of a complex set of relations. First, there can be no doubt that the union overestimated its power in some areas of the county,[15] and membership had been falling as Table 6 shows. Especially in the south of the

TABLE 6   Union membership, national and Norfolk, 1918–23

	Norfolk membership	National membership
1918	11,000★	53,086
1919	21,000★	126,911
1920	16,982	102,884
1921	15,000★	103,526
1922	11,000★	46,695
1923	10,100	37,714

The figures marked ★ are my estimates as no county figures exist except for the years 1914, 1915, 1920 and 1923. The only year which might be seriously out, given national trends, is 1921, but, as we have seen this was an especially bad year in the county.

county, except in the immediate vicinity of Diss and Burston, hundreds seem to have left the union and then, as a result, refused to come out on strike. However, by the end of March even south Norfolk seems to have been affected. On the 31st the *Norfolk News* said, under the headline, 'South Norfolk. Strike Extending', 'A correspondent who went round those villages on Thursday found most men at work, but on Tuesday the stoppage appeared complete.'[16]

But there were other reasons for the unevenness of response to the strike call. For a start even after the county emergency committee called for a general stoppage on 24 March, large numbers of workers seemed to have believed (or indeed wanted to believe) that this did not apply if the reduction in wages had not been made. This confusion seems to have been shared by the leadership whose statements on precisely who should come out were often unclear. Indeed even according to Jimmy Lunnon's report on the dispute, written after the event, it appears that at most there was only a period of two weeks when all men should have been out, and these two weeks did indeed see the highest number 'on the union books', 7,102 men, or about a quarter of the Norfolk farm workforce.[17]

This situation was made worse by the undoubted fact that large numbers of farmers did not reduce their men's wages. Early on in the strike it was said that whole areas on the western boundary of the county, in the marshes and fens, were unaffected:[18]

> The dispute has scarcely touched the Marshland district. Here the farming is so different from 'Norfolk' farming that it appears to be another county altogether. . . . The wages paid in Marshland are generally above those given in the surrounding districts; and, added to this, the majority of the labourers are small holders as well.

Even in the districts that the *Norfolk News* would have recognised as 'Norfolk', sending out of reduction notices was by no means universal. At the top end of the scale Joynson Hicks, then Postmaster-General, did not reduce wages on his Norfolk estates nor did the Labour Peer, the Earl of Kimberly.[19] These were clearly political decisions. More usual, even among large farmers, was a simple refusal to implement cuts either because they genuinely thought them unfair or, more usually, because they could not afford a strike. As J.E. Goodley said to the Kings Lynn branch of the NFU during the first week of the strike,[20]

> He must say that most of the present trouble came from those farmers who had not carried out the original decision of the Farmer's Union. . . . There were far too many farmers sitting on the fence, waiting to see which way things were going.

This seems to have been especially true on the smaller farms, though by no means restricted to them. On small farms the relationship between master and man was especially close. As the *Norfolk News* said, 'they have been on their jobs so many years, and have such an understanding with their employers, that they dislike to cause any ill-feeling.'[21] In this situation many farmers simply went on paying the old rate and the men, union or non-union, stayed at work. As the bonds of county transcended those of nation, and even area those of county, so the farm remained the centre of the labourer's world.

A final problem was that of the animals. To a cowman, a shepherd or a team-man no animal in his care was anything but his 'own'. Horse brasses and plumes, for instance, to beloved rural idyllicists were almost inevitably the property of the team-man who took them with him from job to job to decorate 'his' team. Preparation for showing of animals and ploughing matches was done by the men, not by the farmers. In many cases identification was total. To ask a man who had spent hours of his time and part of his meagre wage on the loving care of animals, to walk off and leave them, perhaps unmilked or worse, uncared for, was to ask a great deal. In the first weeks of the strike the union recognised this and added still further to the confusion of 'in' or 'out'. As Herbert Harvey, secretary of the Trunch branch said,[22]

Where all the labour has left the farm . . . if the farmer likes to approach any of the men and make arrangements for feeding of the stock, the Union are not going to tell the men they must not do so. We are not out to do anything in the least unfair or improper.

An even more formal arrangement was made in Kelling where, because the milk from one farm was supplied to the Sanitorium, Jimmy Lunnon allowed the men back for milking; while, in another case[23]

A small farmer with two cows said if he was allowed to have his men back he was prepared to give the milk from one of the cows for distribution amongst the needy families of the immediate district. Mr. Lunnon said it had been suggested to the farmer that the milk from the one cow should be placed at the disposal of the lock-out Committee, adding, humorously, that the red flag should be placed on the cow's tail.

This easy attitude, which characterised the first week of the strike, seems to have given all involved a curious sense of unreality. Most labourers on strike looked upon it all as an unwanted holiday. The sun shone, but when the garden was dug there was little to do:[24]

> Very few of the labourers who have come out were to be seen
> abroad. . . . One of them had been out for a walk with his wife
> and little boy. They were picking primroses. The man looked
> as if he hardly knew how to use his unwanted leisure. He
> looked uncomfortable and ill at ease.

Similarly the farmers seem to have treated the whole thing as a kind of aberration, believing that the men would quickly go back and they could simply get on with the spring ploughing.

However, from the second week onwards attitudes began to change. Although the call for 'all out' met with a mixed response, about a quarter of Norfolk's farm labourers did come out, and, perhaps more importantly, came out in a restricted geographical area. For example, both the *Norfolk News* and the *Eastern Daily Press* give the figure of 90 per cent of men out in north and north-east Norfolk, and certainly in some areas of west and central Norfolk the figure may well have been similar.

In this situation the farmers' initial confidence began to falter, and as the weather continued fine blacklegs were introduced into the area. These were at first carefully described by both the press and the NFU as 'volunteers' or 'helpers'. The vast majority of these first strike breakers were middle-class.[25] The agricultural colleges sent many, most of whom were farmers' sons, while many more 'came' through appeals in the *Farmer and Stock Breeder* and the *Mark Lane Express*. In other cases sons and daughters of farmers in Norfolk abandoned the tennis parties and other recreations suited to the life of the youthful county gentry and took to the plough tail. Of one of these the *Norfolk News* said, apparently without any sense of irony,[26]

> She is not only a splendid rider to hounds, but can do various
> kinds of agricultural work – ploughing, drilling, milking. She
> is the daughter of a farmer and has a riding school.

Miss Groom of Stiffkey in Norfolk worked her father's farm during the strike,[27]

> You see we'd always had our own ponies and so we could deal with horses and it was like when I worked in the war, you know, you really felt you were doing some good . . . when you feel you're doing something that's necessary you are happy aren't you?

It was this sense of increasing solidarity among the farmers, both in Norfolk and outside, that cheered J.F. Wright, the county secretary, as the strike dragged on:[28]

> Farmers throughout Norfolk are becoming strongly united, . . . and those who had required their men to work 54 hours are dropping to 52 . . . while those who have been paying 25s for 50 hours are agreeing to fall in line with 52 hours.

In the face of 'volunteer' labour, and the introduction of ordinary blacklegs through the Farmers' Federation, the union stepped up picketing. Initially this took the form of 'route marches', as the press called them, moving out from a village, around the lanes, looking for men at work:[29]

> we went round turned a lot of them out once . . . all over the shop, and got locked up, one or two of us did went round all over the place, Southrepps, Northrepps . . . soon as they heard us and the bugle they soon stopped work . . . me and a chap, there was an old bloke, he was carting the mangols, he'd got the horse coming back against the mangol hill. We asked him what he meant being there and he said, "I don't work here really, I'm just here to lend a hand." We out with the horses and shot the load up. A load of sheep pens and all we shot up.

The bugle came from Trunch:[30]

> There was a lot weren't in the union, that's what the trouble was, was so many outside. When the first strike came after the war, a lot of men weren't in the union. . . . So as soon as we got the strike on, ours was the headquarters at Trunch, we met

N. D. 13.

National Union of Agricultural Workers.

Hardie Memorial Hall,

Norwich.

March 19th, 1923.

DEAR SIR AND BROTHER,

As you will have seen by the papers we did not reach a settlement with the employers last Saturday, and we meet again next Saturday.

Therefore this week we have to go full steam ahead. Every man on affected farms must be out, and on no circumstances must members make separate bargains, however good, as every man at work weakens our position.

The week-end meetings were an enormous success, and gave a great send-off to our fight this week.

Will Secretaries and members generally read carefully the circulars that have been sent out as these give all details for the conduct of the dispute, and kindly remember that our success depends very largely upon the way in which instructions are carried out.

Cycle Scouts. Please arrange for the organisation of all your cyclists, both for special picket work, and also for a daily visit to other branches. This interchange of visits will do a lot of good.

Dispute Fund. Get collecting boxes made and go round to every person in our villages. Collections should also be made at all public meetings, and the proceeds, after paying expenses, sent to Mr. Gooch, the treasurer, or to myself.

New Members. The Executive Committee has decided to allow non-unionists, who join up and come out with us, half-pay. That is, men who join now will receive 6 - per week or 1 - per day. Members upon half-pay must be placed on a separate lock-out sheet.

Colours. Where it is desired to use colours to brighten things up, such colours should be Red and Green.

Demonstrations. Please arrange demonstrations for next week-end. It is probable a central demonstration will be held in Norwich on Sunday.

Now brothers, keep together at all costs. Be determined in this fight for bare justice, and victory must crown our united efforts.

Yours, with best wishes,

JAMES LUNNON.

The Caxton Press (I.C. Printers), Maddermarket, Norwich.

Figure 8   The invention of the flying picket? The instructions sent out by Jimmie Lunnon at the start of the Great Strike. Within ten days the pickets were out of his control in parts of Norfolk. (Museum of English Rural Life, Reading)

there, nine o'clock of the mornings, one of them had an old
trumpet you know, from the war, blew up give them call all
around. Up would come the bikes, Gimmingham, Paston,
Knapton; Trunch Hill was full of bicycles. Off we'd go,
"Where we going to?" "We'll go to Southrepps, Thorpe,
Roughton, all round." "Right, when we get to Southrepps, you
chaps that lives, like Paston, anybodys like working a horse on
the land." Pulled up on the bikes, way they'd go half-a-dozen
across, cut the reins through . . . shoot the cart up and turn the
horse off, and they could go where they liked. . . . We didn't
go in the same village and do that if they were working, put the
strangers there, then we done it when we go where we weren't
known.

'Up would come the bikes . . .' a phrase which could sum up a
great deal about the later part of the strike. Bicycles were much
cheaper after the war and many if not most younger labourers had
them. Right from the beginning of the strike they were formed,
on union instructions, into 'cycle scouts' which gave the pickets
much-needed mobility (see page 164).

By the second and third weeks of the strike, effective picketing
in many areas of Norfolk was making the situation increasingly
difficult for the farmers. J.F. Wright published a letter from a
farmer in the Aylsham district (not far from Trunch!) during the
third week of the strike.[31]

Can't something be done . . . to protect the men from this
intimidation by large gangs of strikers? The local police are
doing what they can, but seem unable to stop it. On my farm
there are 14 men out on strike and there are 22 horses (including
colts) standing idle. No Barley is sown. The men began to
come back on Saturday, but they have left again because they
are afraid to stay.

The self-confident tone of the farmers, as reported in the press, as
well as the cocky assurance of the national farmers' papers, began
to change.[32] On 7 April the executive committee of the Norfolk
NFU met in Norwich to a barrage of complaints about
picketing:[33]

'I am spending £60 in labour and getting nothing for it,' was the complaint. 'The men are all working in the yards and cannot get out on the farm. I have applied for police protection, but can't get it.'

There was, of course, an element of hysteria in these reports as shown by the constant insistence, from the second week on, that it was all the work of outside agitators.[34] However, the basis was there, at least as far as the effectiveness of picketing went. The confidential report of the Chief Constable of Norfolk sent to the Home Office on 11 April says[35]

Up to Easter Monday as long as I had a Constable on a farm or following a gang, the men abstained from going on the farms. But they now changed their methods. They arranged gangs of anything from 30 to 300 men who would collect at some point from villages 5 to 10 miles away and then raid farms, taking no notice of a Constable who might be present, and fetched out men from work. . . . As they came from a distance neither the farmers, labourers, or Police, had any idea who the strikers were and it was impossible for one or two Constables to prevent such large numbers going on the farms.

The response was to draft more police into the county, and to appeal for more blackleg labour. By 14 April over 600 extra police were on duty in the county including men from the Metropolitan force, the West Riding and Hertfordshire. Also, on Monday 9 April the NFU put out a 'wireless broadcast appeal . . . for farmers' sons and farm pupils to come to the assistance of Norfolk farmers'. The impartial power of public broadcasting brought over 100 men to Norfolk by Friday.[36] Most significant of all, by 14 April the first cases against strikers had been heard at Petty Sessions.

The situation in Norfolk at this point was complex and worth examining in more detail. The first thing is that in some very real sense a section of the rank and file had taken over the day-to-day running of the strike. Although the union originally organised the cycle scouts from Norwich, by the third week they were deeply worried about what was happening in the county. As early as 27

March, Lunnon, the 'chief firebrand' according to the Chief Constable,[37] had sent instructions to strikers ordering them not to enter fields, but to remain on the roads or other public places. But Edwin Gooch complained on 14 April, 'action on the part of certain men which has been brought to notice has been absolutely spontaneous on their part'.[38]

It should be stressed that we are talking about a section of the rank and file. First they were 'younger men', as the Chief Constable put it, as indeed had been their rick-burning ancestors of 90 years earlier. More significantly a number of them, like 'Billa' Dixon of Trunch, were ex-soldiers. The military precision of the route marches, the use of bugles, frequent mention of medal ribbons and khaki greatcoats in the press, all point to this. So does the fact that meetings and marches often began and ended not just on village greens but specifically at war memorials. A description from the first week of the strike will serve as an example:[39]

Gathering from the various villages, they made the War
Memorial clock tower at Gaywood their rallying point, and like
a regiment of soldiers they marched into the town.

These men were very different from the older labourers. The continuity of village life had been broken for them, as had the promises of the coalition government. Many had seen two winters unemployment and had little respect for the farmers who they believed had 'done well out of the war' and were now starving their men to keep up profits. The *Mark Lane Express* reported one striker shouting as they left a field after stopping farm pupils at work. 'This is a revolution; we fought for the land and we are going to have it'; while a local leader is reported as saying, 'You have been soldiers; you know how to fight'.[40]

This situation was made worse by the employment of middle-class volunteers as blacklegs. The volunteers were usually young and conspicuously 'gentry'. They had not fought in the war and were outsiders. At least an ordinary blackleg, say an unemployed Yarmouth fisherman, as many were, could be understood. He was out of work and Yarmouth had always provided the Farmers' Federation with labour. Nor if you 'fetched him one' did he appeal to police or class for protection. You might not like scabs, but they inhabited the same world as you. The ill-feeling in this situation can be illustrated by an incident on the farm of Mr E.H. Ringer at Rougham. A farm pupil called Eric Hockley from Hatfield Broad Oak in Essex was working with a team of horses alongside his employer. A group of strikers came into the field and ordered him to unyoke the team:[41]

> 'They swore at me and called us blacklegs, telling us we were taking bread out of their mouths. I undid the horses, and as I was bending down to do this, one of them hit me with a stick across my back; another struck me a blow with his fist in my ear.'

Ringer continued the story,

> One of them asked Hockley, 'Where were you in 1914?' He replied 'I am not 18 now.' One of the strikers then said, 'We have been through five years of war. You made your pile in the war and we are going to have it now.'

All the feelings of this section of the farmworkers are there – the war, profiteering and the intense dislike, even hatred, of sections of the rural ruling class, which were becoming the language of the strike, now increasingly referred to as the 'Norfolk farm war' in the national press.

As picketing by the 'cycle scouts' continued and more police were brought in to the county, not only did bad feeling increase, but so did the number of arrests. By the end of the strike upwards of 200 summonses had been issued in the Walsingham Petty Sessional District alone.[42] These were mostly for trespass or minor assault and were dealt with summarily.

This increased tension still further. For generations the labourer had seen game law offences dealt with by a bench composed of game-preserving landowners – now he saw strike cases judged by those who the strike was against. One old worker spoke about the demonstrations against the magistrates at North Walsham, and in particular against E.G. Cubbit, an especially unpopular local farmers' leader. It is impossible on the page to indicate the strength of feeling in this man's voice as he spoke fifty years after the end of the strike:[43]

There was always somebody up to court, every court day, we all used to go up there then. And old Squire Cubbit, he was the head magistrate. I've seen him coming in there and eggs hitting him everywhere. Yes, they used to throw them – course he was an old farmer, he was an old humbug. We used to pelt him. A lot of them had to pay for it.

But the real hatred was reserved for the man who a year earlier had been Norfolk's hero but was now a traitor – Sam Peel. The strike was the end for him and his union. He had publicly supported the proposed reduction in wages and what little support he actually had gained evaporated. While he stayed within the union, even as a fierce critic, he could rely on support. Once he had moved outside and worse still, allied himself with the farmers and landowners, he was completely rejected.

The extent of this rejection was clear when at the beginning of the third week of the strike he took his place as a JP on the Walsingham bench to try a group of strikers charged with trespass and assault. Among them were two ex-soldiers, one of whom wore his Mons Star in court. At the end of the hearing Peel was stoned and 'covered' in rotten fruit and vegetables by an angry crowd. Despite appeals from George Edwards he was eventually only got away from the court house under the protection of a 'cordon' of police, including some from Norwich.[44]

That Walsingham court had another significance since it marked the adoption by the union leadership of a new tactic. The union was advised that a JP 'sat' for the whole of a county, though by custom he or she was attached to a particular bench. It was therefore decided to move sympathetic JPs from bench to bench whenever strike cases were to be heard. This was done for the first time at Walsingham on 16 April.

As the court opened 'on the stroke of ten o'clock', ten 'visiting' justices arrived to sit on the bench. The Walsingham justices, after a mild protest agreed to let them sit, and it is significant that the level of fines, even for those found guilty, was well below the £2 or 14 days given out elsewhere in the county earlier in the strike. No one among the fifteen defendants was fined more than 5s and a number of charges were either dropped or dismissed.[45]

Encouraged by this success, the union sent George Hewitt to North Walsham the following day. There was one strike case

involving two farm labourers and their wives. As Hewitt arrived
E.G. Cubbit rose and said that 'under the circumstances' he was
adjourning the court until Friday, and despite protests from the
union lawyers, the court was adjourned. On the Friday Cubbitt
appeared with a letter from the Lord Chancellor which while it
'urged' Hewitt not to sit, said that it would not be 'proper', 'That
the case pending before the Bench should for that reason be left
undisposed of.' In this situation a compromise was worked out
whereby in return for Hewitt and the three others who had come
with him not sitting, Cubbit, who was an active farmers' leader,
and Colonel Petre, whose men were out on strike, agreed also not
to sit.[46]

But there was another reason for compromise. As W.B. Taylor
said at the magistrates' meeting,[47]

> The county stood on the edge of what he hoped and believed
> might prove to be a complete and just settlement of the
> controversy. Any action likely to jeopardise or prejudice that
> must be carefully considered.

And, indeed, settlement was in sight.

There can be little doubt that from both sides the situation in
Norfolk was getting out of hand. For the farmers' side the season
was relentlessly changing. If the strike did not end soon their
losses would be enormous. Rent and rates still had to be paid as
did interest on capital. Seed corn and fertilisers had been bought.
Even if there were no outgoings in terms of wages, other costs
would not simply go away and if work was not resumed there
would be nothing at all to sell in the autumn. In the face of this
their much-vaunted solidarity was collapsing. All over the county
individual farmers were making bargains with their men, and
although the workers' side said that no man should go back for
less than 30s, many hundreds clearly were.[48]

In this situation the strike was increasingly confined to certain
key areas in the west, on the big farms, and in the north-east,
where the union was strongly organised. In these areas violence
was increasing and the struggle was taking a much more serious
turn which neither side particularly wanted.

For the union the situation was little better. For a start the strike seemed to have little hope of bringing about the return of the wages boards, increasingly the leadership's universal panacea. Bonar Law and the rest of the government constantly made that clear. On the other hand the strike was crippling financially. Reserve funds were falling rapidly and, despite TUC support, and especially the support of the NUR, it is clear that by mid-April the union was facing bankruptcy.[49]

On the ground things were, if anything, worse. Men were going back where the masters paid 25s for 50 hours which was seriously damaging the union's credibility at local level. On the other hand those who were 'sticking out' seem to have been less and less under the direct control of the leadership. Even where union JPs sat on the bench, for instance, they constantly referred to their own condemnation of trespass and violence against blacklegs.[50]

Further, real hardship was becoming apparent in some areas. Although there were few women farm workers in Norfolk by 1923, the support of women was vital. No strike could succeed if wives, mothers and daughters, who were the ones who had to beg credit from shopkeepers and eke out strike pay, were not wholeheartedly involved in its support. After four weeks this problem was becoming acute. Credit was running out and strike pay was inadequate. Worse than that, evictions had started in some parts of west Norfolk, including some on the farm of Womack William Ringer.[51]

On the 16 April a deputation of over 200 labourers on strike arrived at Wicklewood workhouse in central Norfolk demanding relief for themselves and their families, and it was agreed to investigate with special meetings set up in all villages in the district.[52] A week earlier the British Legion had made a grant of £500 to their Norfolk branch for the aid of Norfolk members. It was decided to contact all local branches to find out cases of distress and issue help in the form 'food tickets only on local tradesmen'.[53]

By mid-April, what to the leadership of both sides had started off as a set-piece battle which would bring the problems of agriculture before the government, had taken on a more serious turn. Relations on the land were at the lowest ebb since the 1870s, real distress was beginning to appear, and, at county level attitudes were hardening. Then, like some knight on a white horse, flourishing the lance of moderation, a saviour appeared in the unlikely shape of J. Ramsey MacDonald.

Walker's report on the strike spelt it out:[54]

> Two abortive conferences were held in the Shire Hall, Norwich, with Mr. Gosling in the chair. Following this breakdown of negotiations a delegate conference was held at Norwich on Wednesday April 18th, when a decision was reached to accept 26/- per week for 50 hours. The evening prior however to this, on the 17th, Mr. MacDonald having succeeded in bringing about a settlement in the Building Trade Dispute it was suggested in several quarters that MacDonald should be approached with regard to our dispute.

That evening, Walker saw MacDonald at the House of Commons. MacDonald moved quickly. When Walker returned from Norwich he found a meeting had been arranged with Gosling, from the Ministry of Agriculture, and 'representatives of the farmers'.

That evening a provisional agreement was reached and Walker, in his own words 'hurried off to Norfolk next morning',[55] to place the agreement before the emergency committee. The agreement was brief,[56]

> That the terms of the settlement of the present dispute shall be, – That a wage of 25/- shall be paid for a guaranteed fifty hours' week, and any more hours worked in excess of fifty up to four per week shall be paid for at the rate of 6d. per hour, after which work will be paid for at overtime rates, the hours to be so arranged as to secure a weekly half holiday.

This text was discussed in Norwich on 20 April and since there was 'no serious opposition'[57] the Norfolk committee agreed to the terms. The one exception was raised by George Hewitt. With his own experience of a three-year lock-out in mind, he insisted that the clause 'There is to be no victimisation' was added.[58] There was also a 'hidden agenda' for the farmers' side in that the government had come up with some 'aid' to agriculture. This included rate reductions, government aid on surfacing unclassified rural roads (thus reducing local rates); aid to milk producers; a tax of 10s on the import of malting barley and a merchandise marks bill. These concessions were vital to the farmers but, as the 'confidential' *Norfolk County National Farmers Union Gazette* said,[59]

> Had your representatives not agreed to pass part of the relief above mentioned to the workers, it would have been very probable that the concessions in question would have been indefinitely delayed, if not lost, since public opinion and feeling of the House of Commons would have indubitably shifted to the side of the men. The sympathy and help of other counties would have been alienated because the Norfolk refusal would have jeopardised any relief which they would have otherwise obtained.

There were other hidden agendas which were more serious. The agreement, signed on 21 April in Norwich, was apparently simple but contained a vital clause, that on victimisation. As the men went back to work on 23 April it rapidly became clear that the farmers had a quite different view of victimisation from that of the men. The farmers argued that many of their number had to 'reorganise and readjust their business' in view of the strike and, as a result, many men could not be taken back 'immediately'. Their argument was that as long as a man was not actually replaced no victimisation had taken place.[60]

On their side the union argued that 'no victimisation' meant that all men employed at the beginning of the strike should be reinstated immediately and consequently instructed their members not to return to work unless all their fellows got their jobs back.[61] Inevitably, the farmers used this moment as an excuse to settle scores or 'weed out' the 'trouble makers':[62]

> Some of the cases were pretty hard. I can well recall one case, because he was a local preacher, a chap named Quantrill, and he had eleven kiddies, and he worked for a local preacher. They were both on the same circuit, they both preached from the same plan. . . . Of course, being a local preacher, he could encourage the men, he could speak, and speak very competent-ly. A result was that when the strike was over, Thurston said to Jack Quantrill, "Jack, you and I part company," his boss, "and what's more you won't get another job within a ten-mile

radius" . . . and he didn't, and John Quantrill had to cycle
about 14 miles to work each way in a sand quarry.

These kinds of cases, without the historical irony of one chapel
man sacking another, were repeated time and again throughout
Norfolk:[63]

> Tom Allen was one got the sack after the strike, him and
> Arthur Wright and George Brown . . . who were team-men,
> they were the three sacked. We went and met in the morning
> we should have gone back to work and they were the only
> three that really spoke I suppose, and as they spoke he said, "I
> shan't want you, and I shan't want you . . ." and that was it,
> we said, "If you don't want them, you don't want us", and we
> walked out . . . until they got a job we wouldn't go back again.

A week after the official end of the strike there were still over
2,300 men on the union's books and so, not surprisingly, they
turned to MacDonald. To their shock Lunnon and Walker, who
went with a delegation from the NFU to see Britain's next Prime
Minister, found that 'he quite frankly agreed with the farmers as
to their interpretation of the word "victimisation" '.[64]

The national executive pondered briefly and decided that they
would have to accept MacDonald's ruling. In Norfolk some men
stayed out until their fellows got work elsewhere or until, driven
by desperation, they drifted back to work. Two poems, probably
by the same Fred Sewell of Sedgeford who wrote the strike songs
during the Ringer's dispute, were pinned on the parish notice-
board in Ringstead where the men stuck out for several weeks:[65]

> No work, no pay
> No milk today
> He dose [sic] his work
> By night and day.
>
> No straw, no hay
> No extra pay.
> A policeman guards him
> By night and day.

> I am a Ringstead striker
> I used to work in the field.
> It grieves the farmer dearly
> To think I will not yield.
> I'll fight for the taking back of all men
> Until the very end.
> If rich men lose their Blessed goods
> So much the worse for them.

And so the 'great strike' ended. It was not a famous victory but nor was it the defeat that Jimmy Lunnon, and those who have written since thought it was – it stopped the rot and it saved the union. Without it Peel might have led the farmworker down the rosy path to the damnation that was the United Agricultural Party. Even in February 1923 in the run-up to the strike, the NFU was discreetly advising its members to have nothing to do with Peel since he represented nobody.[66] A defeat in 1923 would certainly have given Peel's union a good deal of credence and maybe broken the NUAW. Further, 25s for 50 hours represented a real gain of 2s per week since for the first time it gave the labourer a guaranteed working week with overtime. Only once more were the labourers of Norfolk to have to take a wage cut, and that in the worst times of the early 1930s when wages had risen again anyway.

In the short term the outcome of the 'great strike' gave the labourer confidence. That summer there was a rash of harvest strikes, the first for some years. But above all it stopped the rot. As 'Billa' Dixon said,[67]

That was the turn of the tide, after that we went back, and we asked for, the farmers had had enough, they got chopped over the strike, we asked for another 5s, and we got it, and went on. . . . Then more went into the union, and it got hold then up to where we are today. They were the start them days, getting the wages, and we had to do it on nothing.

9 The long term

The Norfolk strike, as Howard Newby has noted, was a watershed in the union's history.[1] It 'proved' to the executive, with one or two exceptions, that strike action, although unfortunately necessary on occasions, did not work. As James Lunnon wrote at the end of his report on the strike, 'One feels that on the 25/- settlement we are humiliated.'[2] By 1923 Lunnon, Edwards, and many others saw the only alternative as state action, a direct link with those Liberal grandees who had founded the union in 1906. Even in 1976 Reg Bottini, then general secretary of the union could write,[3]

> There is one more lesson we must draw from the history of our Union. The last great strike in Norfolk in 1923 was called to oppose wage cuts. . . . The principal result of that strike was the 1924 Agricultural Wages Act. . . . Our 1974 and 1976 biennial conferences overwhelmingly defeated motions seeking to abolish the Agricultural Wages Board. The delegates recognised that whatever faults the Board has shown . . . there is no alternative for such a scattered labour force as agricultural workers to a centralised body fixing national rates below which no farm worker may legally be paid.

That this policy dominated the union after 1923 was no coincidence. Walker resigned as general secretary in 1928 and was replaced by Bill Holmes. He was followed in 1945 by Alf Dann, who had worked in the union's legal department during the 1923 strike. The president of the union from 1928 until 1964 was Edwin Gooch, erstwhile supporter of Sam Peel, and a leading moderate during the early 1920s. His successor was Bert Hazell, who has already figured in these pages as a founder of Wymondham Labour Party and an activist in the 1923 strike.

But it was more than that. As attendance at any biennial of the union quickly shows, Norfolk has remained a dominant force in the union. Even in the post-Second World War period, a large number of executive members, and perhaps more importantly, organisers, came from Norfolk and had experienced the 1923 strike. Their interpretation of the strike's outcome was vital to union policy up to the early 1970s.

Particularly important was Edwin Gooch who, as Newby says, virtually rebuilt the policy of the union after 1928 over the head of the older and more militant Bill Holmes. There is an uneasy sense about the period of Gooch's power that the policies of Peel triumphed by the back door.[4]

> during the 1930s [Gooch] convinced his Executive that the farm workers' interests were not necessarily identical with those of the industrial worker. He was also brave enough to lead his Union into the political wilderness which the break with the Labour policy implied. Thereafter Gooch sought common cause with the NFU on agricultural policy matters.

This, of course, was not simply a product of Gooch's real abilities. The Labour Party showed less and less interest in the rural areas after restoring the wages board in 1924. Such rural policy as the party had became more and more tokenistic, consisting of little more than a rehearsal of old promises on the tied cottage and, until the early 1950s, phrases about the 'land' and the 'people'. More than that the rural areas themselves underwent fundamental changes. The number of men on the land continued to decline, even in Norfolk. Increased mechanisation and the use of agricultural contractors for many operations meant that the workforce, even on the huge farms of west Norfolk, got smaller and smaller.

Additionally, especially after the war, ever larger numbers of urban dwellers moved into rural areas. As permanent residents in the small commuter estates which sprang up in any village within twenty miles of a town large enough to support a substantial number of white-collar workers, or as 'weekenders' in any property over 50 years old, they came to represent the majority of inhabitants in many villages. Thus the labourer was marginalised, he became a stranger in his own land.[5]

But the 'long term' goes back, as well as forward, from 1923, and from that history a number of threads need to be drawn. The first concerns change. Rural England, as I noted at the beginning of this study, is defined ideologically as 'changeless'. To some extent, in the nineteenth century at least, a technological history supports this. Under horse agriculture, and before the widespread adoption of the reaper binder, the processes of arable agriculture looked remarkably similar for a period of several hundred years. Yet this is nonsensical once any detailed work is done.

The Norfolk farm worker's position in society was constantly changing. The end of paternalism, the growth of casualisation and the eventual decline and end of that system mark the great changes. Within that, shorter-term movements of wages and prices, even of the season of the year altered the rural world. These changes have, to some extent, been detailed in this study.

Second, and as a result of these changes, so the world view of the labourer changed. Time and space have meant that the early years of the nineteenth century have got short shrift in this study, but from the 1840s and 1850s onwards we can see the emergence of a cultural and political response to those changes which has some coherence. I have divided that response into two periods 1860–1900 and 1900–23. The first period was characterised by a local consciousness based on the village and small town. The chapels, friendly societies, trades unions and radical organisations of that period, although they had national links, were local in their base, consciousness and organisation. This localist approach had real strengths which most historians, of labour in particular, have ignored. It was flexible and manageable, but above all it was intensely democratic. The organisations thrown up, be they chapels or union branches, involved, potentially at least, all the members in real processes of control.

The second period, from approximately 1900 onwards, saw this change. As English society as a whole 'nationalised',[6] the chapel, the Liberal Party and the trade union movement looked more and more to a world beyond the village and the county town. In this process the labourer sought a home first in the labour movement and then, via that movement, in national government through a national minimum wage and a national agricultural policy. There is, perhaps, a third period, that since the permanent establishment of the wages board in 1924 which saw a growth, institutionally at least, of some sort of 'agricultural consciousness' in which national policy was less and less that of 'labour' and more and more that of 'industry'. It is this period that Howard Newby addresses so well.[7]

The third thread which needs picking up lies behind this chronology – that of the consistency of conflict. Certainly until the early 1920s, with or without the wages board, conflict was all but endemic on the farms of Norfolk. This conflict was localised, often to only one farm, and personalised into master and man. Its subject was equally local – doing or not doing a particular job in a particular way, the price of hoeing an especially heavy field or harvesting a laid crop – but it was no less intense for that. In fact the opposite was often the case. Without the mediation of the 'union chap', tempers were lost and violence followed.

This kind of conflict ended with the permanent establishment of the wages board and its general acceptance by both the farmers and the labourers. But it was not only the board. The self-improved and respectable labourers who made up the village leadership in both periods of unionisation had little time for this kind of spontaneous action. In the same way that Rix or Edwards attacked smoking and drinking and urged reading and improvement, so they sought to improve industrial relations. As we saw above from the first, the union rules attempted to prevent local disputes and they frequently refused to support strikes or lock-outs of this kind.

This leads to a more complex question which centres around the division within the poor, frequently noted by historians as well as contemporaries, between the rough and the respectable. Evidence here is difficult to come by. It is certain that the 'old' leadership, crucially those of the period of up to c.1900 were 'respectable' in that they were frequently chapel members, teetotal or temperance and so on. It is also clear that at local level this tradition continued strong. Most of the men interviewed for this study who had held union office were, or had been, temperance advocates, and had been or were chapel members. Several of them also made implicit distinctions between rough and respectable, on the question of drink particularly.

It is less clear whether this respectable model of leadership continued into the twentieth century. As I noted above the links between the chapel and the union were much less close after 1900.

This meant, crucially, that the union seldom met in the village chapel, moving its allegiance instead to the village pub:[8]

> there was always the meetings when we had the pub, we never charged nothing for union's meetings, no. The union couldn't afford it . . . we used to give them a gallon of beer, we'd didn't get nothing, but we got the customer. Last meeting of the year we'd give them a bottle of rum . . . and they'd mix that with the beer.

Old George Rix would not have approved!

Even if there was a continuity of the chapel culture in the leadership, as the union grew it inevitably drew in some of the 'rough' working class from the villages. This seems to have been especially true after the Great War when the union reached its peak and when many of its members were ex-soldiers. It is clear from the accounts of picketing during the 1923 strike that parts of this section of the membership were out of the control of the more respectable leadership.

During the fifty or so years after 1870 the farm labourers of Norfolk developed a remarkable radical and trade union movement. It was the product of specific and economic forces which were perhaps not duplicated elsewhere – Norfolk, as any Norfolk person will tell you, is always different. Yet the study of that movement is revealing in many ways. Crucially it gives the lie to the timeless and stupid figure of Hodge. George Rix was about as far from that character as it is possible to be, as were George Hewitt or Herbert Harvey. Men of their time and their locality, they educated themselves and their fellows in the expectation of a better life now, as well as preaching salvation in the hereafter.

Other elements also seek comparison elsewhere. The 'local' model of trades unionism which Rix and others advocated in the 1870s has a curiously modern feel to it, with its criticism of the leadership and paid officials, and its insistence on the rights of the rank-and-file. It is too easy, as I said above, to dismiss this as backwardness. The fact was that what we now call 'in-plant bargaining', if by rough and ready means, was remarkably effective at times. Perhaps the time has come to re-think our labour history outside the academic blinkers of a 'modernisation theory' essentially dating from the Webbs. It is, after all, possible that the kind of nationalised and centralised unions, so beloved of most labour historians, were not only inefficient for the labour in the 1870s and 1880s, but downright inappropriate.

One continuity remains, that of exploitation. The word is difficult even to write. Revisionist history, like revisionist economics and revisionist unemployment policy, will no doubt prove in time that such a thing does not exist and never has existed. Those historians who continue to insist on its centrality to the history of the poor will thus, as in the late 1940s and 1950s, be relegated to some kind of cold war Aunt Sally stall where those who have objective minds can hurl clods at them. If so, so be it. History is a political discipline, as Hayek argued long ago, and what we think of the past of our institutions fundamentally shapes the way we view them now.[9]

The centrality of agricultural production remains with us, and must do for the foreseeable future, and so with the anonymous balladeer who first wrote these words down in the seventeenth century I say,

Come all you jolly ploughmen, of courage stout and bold,
That labours all the winter in stormy winds and cold.
To fill our field with plenty, our farmyards to renew,
That bread may not be wanting, behold the painful plough.

For Samson was the strongest man, and Solomon was wise,
Alexander for to conquer was all his daily prize.
King David he was valiant, and many thousands slew,
Yet none of these great heroes could live without the plough.

Notes

Introduction

1 Raymond Williams, *The Country and the City* (London 1973); Martin J. Wiener, *English Culture and the Decline of the Industrial Spirit 1850–1980* (Cambridge 1981).

2 For a very limited discussion of these problems see Alun Howkins, 'Television History: Bread or Blood', *History Workshop Journal*, no. 12, 1981.

3 E.P. Thompson, *The Making of the English Working Class* (Harmondsworth 1968), p. 916.

4 E.J. Hobsbawm and George Rude, *Captain Swing* (London 1969); A. Charlesworth, *Social Protest in Rural Society, the Spatial Diffusion of the Captain Swing Disturbances of 1830–31* (Norwich 1979); Roger Wells, 'The Development of the English Rural Proletariat and Social Protest, 1700–1850', *Journal of Peasant Studies*, VI, 2. See the subsequent debate between Wells and A. Charlesworth in the same journal. Heated and not always entirely lacking in light.

5 See Chapter 4 below.

6 W. Hasbach, *A History of the English Agricultural Labourer* (London, new ed, 1908).

7 Gareth Stedman Jones, *Outcast London* (Oxford 1971).

8 Geoffrey Crossick, *An Artisan Elite in Victorian Society* (London 1978); Robert Q. Gray, *The Labour Aristocracy in Victorian Edinburgh* (Oxford 1976).

9 Reg Groves, *Sharpen the Sickle*, NUAAW Edition (London 1949).

10 See below, pp. 1–14 and 39–56.

11 See below, pp. 14 ff.

12 Raphael Samuel (ed.), *Village Life and Labour* (London 1975).

13 For two perceptive discussions of this aspect of oral history see Louisa Passerini, 'Work, Ideology and Consensus under Italian Fascism', *History Workshop Journal*, no. 8; Alessandro Portelli, 'The Peculiarities of Oral History', *ibid.*, no. 12.

14 See Chapters 5–7 below.

15 R.W. Johnson, 'The Nationalisation of English Rural Politics, Norfolk South West, 1945–70', *Parliamentary Affairs*, XXVI, winter 1972–3, p. 53.

1 The land and the people

1 P.J. Perry (ed.), *British Agriculture 1875–1914* (London 1973), pp. xi–xii.

2 Perry, *ibid.*, *passim.*
3 P.J. Perry, *British Farming in the Great Depression* (Newton Abbot 1974), p. 56.
4 *PP 1881, XVII, Royal Commission on Agriculture, England*, p. 734.
5 C.S. Read, 'Agriculture in Norfolk', in W. White, *Norfolk Directory* (London 1883), pp. 26 ff.
6 *PP 1895, XVII, Royal Commission on Agriculture, England Report of Mr R. Henry Rew on the County of Norfolk*, p. 340.
7 *Ibid.*, p. 347.
8 F.M.L. Thompson, *English Landed Society in the Nineteenth Century* (London 1963), p. 304.
9 *Ibid.*, p. 320.
10 F.M.L. Thompson, 'The Land Market in the Nineteenth Century' in W.E. Minchinton (ed.), *Essays in Agrarian History*, vol. II (Newton Abbot 1968), p. 49.
11 Thompson, *Landed Society, op. cit.*, pp. 304–5.
12 Michael Home, *Winter Harvest* (London 1967), p. 114.
13 *Ibid.*, p. 22.
14 John Lowerson, 'Breakdown or Reinforcement? The Social and Political Role of the Late Victorian Gentry in the South East', in M.D.G. Wanklyn (ed.), *Landownership and Power in the Regions* (Wolverhampton 1979), p. 131.
15 Home, *Winter Harvest, op. cit.*, p. 120.
16 Lt-Col. D.C. Pedder, *Where Men Decay: A Survey of Present Rural Conditions* (London 1908), p. 121.
17 *PP 1874 LXXII, Return of Owners of Land 1873*, pt 1, n.p. but under Norfolk.
18 P.J. Perry, 'Where was the Great Agricultural Depression?', in P.J. Perry (ed.), *op. cit.*, pp. 129–49.
19 *Ibid.*, pp. 136, 139, 142.
20 Perry suggests this explanation for Cheshire and Lancashire. Perry, *ibid.*, p. 139.
21 H. Rider Haggard, *A Farmer's Year, being his Commonplace Book for 1898* (London 1899), p. 33.
22 *PP 1895, op. cit.*, p. 362.
23 *PP 1895, op. cit.*, p. 348.
24 Perry, *op. cit.*, p. xxiii.
25 *PP 1895, op. cit.*, p. 422.
26 *Ibid.*, p. 421.
27 *Ibid.*
28 *Ibid.*, p. 359.
29 B.R. Mitchell and Phyllis Deane, *Abstract of British Historical Statistics* (Cambridge 1962), p. 78.
30 *Ibid.*
31 *PP 1895, op. cit.*, p. 355.
32 Roland E. Prothero (later Lord Ernle), *English Farming Past and Present* (London 1912), p. 382.
33 Haggard, *Farmer's Year, op. cit.*, p. 169.

34 'The Profits of Wheat Growing', *Estates Magazine*, vol. 5, no. 8, July 1905, p. 300.

35 Prothero, *op. cit.*, p. 382.

36 Haggard, *Rural England* (London 1902), vol. II, p. 453.

37 *Ibid.*, p. 457.

38 Ministry of Agriculture and Fisheries, *Report on the Sugar Beet Industry at Home and Abroad* (Economic Series No. 27), (London 1931).

39 *Ibid.*, p. 82.

40 Data from census reports.

41 E.J.T. Collins, 'Harvest Technology and Labour Supply in Britain' (unpublished Ph.D. Thesis, Nottingham University, 1970), for example pp. 6–9; D. Morgan, 'The Place of Harvesters in Nineteenth Century Village Life' in Raphael Samuel (ed.), *Village Life and Labour* (London 1975), pp. 29–38.

42 *PP 1867, XVII, Sixth Report of the Children's Employment Commission*, p. 175.

43 This figure is very approximate. It was arrived at by taking contemporary estimates of the numbers employed per 100 acres on Norfolk farms and then subtracting this number from the total population of labourers on the 1841 census.

44 For an account of a childhood in this period in central Norfolk see, George Edwards, *From Crow Scaring to Westminster* (London 1922).

45 For a discussion of this see, *PP 1906 XCVI, Report on the Decline in the Agricultural Population*.

46 Anne Digby, *Pauper Palaces* (London 1978), pp. 100–5.

47 *PP 1867, op. cit.*, p. 186.

48 Mitchell and Deane, *op. cit.*, p. 60.

49 *PP 1893–94 XXXV, Royal Commission on Labour, The Agricultural Labourer*, Summary Report, p. 9.

50 *Ibid.*, 'Report by Mr Arthur Wilson Fox upon the Poor Law Union of Swaffam', p. 67.

51 See Collins, *op. cit.*, esp. pp. 35 ff.

52 *Ibid.*, p. 200.

53 *Ibid.*, pp. 234–5.

54 *Ibid.*

55 *PP 1895, op. cit.*, pp. 363–4.

56 Collins, *op. cit.*, p. 89.

57 *PP 1905 XCVII, Second Report of Mr Wilson Fox on the Wages, Earnings and Conditions of Employment of Agricultural Labourers in the U.K.*, p. 237.

58 Haggard, *Farmer's Year, op. cit.*, p. 460.

59 Edith H. Whetham, *The Agrarian History of England and Wales*, vol. VIII, 1914–1939 (Cambridge 1978), p. 71.

60 *Eastern Weekly Press* (hereafter *EWP*), 24 April 1915, p. 3.

61 *Ibid.*, 14 June 1915, p. 2.

62 P.E.Dewey, 'Government Provision of Farm Labour in England and Wales 1914–18' *Agricultural History Review*, vol 27, pt II, p. 121.

63 For examples see, B.J. Armstrong, *A Norfolk Diary* (ed. Herbert B. Armstrong), (London 1949) on harvest festivals. Also Digby, *op. cit.*, Chapter 11, although there are problems of dating here. The *EWP* and the *Norfolk News* provide a great deal of material on Christmas charity. See also Chapter 2 below.

2   Structural conflict and the farmworker

1 Prothero (Ernle), *op. cit.*, p. 406.
2 Howard Newby, 'The Deferential Dialectic', *Comparative Studies in Society and History*, vol. 17, no. 2, pp. 155–8. Also his fine study, *The Deferential Worker*. Penguin ed. (1975).
3 Interview AJH/Jack Leeder, Knapton, Norfolk, team-man. Tape in author's possession.
4 NUAAW Archive, EC Minutes, 24 February 1911, University of Reading, Museum of English Rural Life.
5 *Ibid.*
6 Interview AJH/Jack Sadler, Titchwell, Norfolk, roadman, formerly labourer. Tape in author's possession.
7 Interview AJH/Jack Leeder, *op. cit.*
8 NUAAW Archive, *op. cit.*, EC Minutes, 24 April 1911, min. 6.
9 *EWP*, 10 November 1906, p. 6.
10 *Ibid.*, 9 December 1899, p. 8.
11 *Ibid.*, 4 October 1913, p. 8.
12 NUAAW Archive, *op. cit.*, EC Minutes, 29 July 1911.
13 *Norfolk News* (hereafter *NN*), 10 November 1900, p. 5
14 NUAAW Archive, *op. cit.*, EC Minutes, 24 November 1911; 24 February 1911.
15 *PP 1900 LXXXIII*, *op. cit.*, pp. 587–92.
16 *NN*, 20 October 1900, p. 5.
17 *Ibid.*, 20 June 1900, p. 7.
18 NUAAW Archive, *op. cit.*, EC Minutes, 6 June 1910.
19 Howard Newby, 'The Low Earnings of Agricultural Workers: a Sociological Approach', *Journal of Agricultural Economics*, vol. XXIII, no. 1, p. 415.
20 *Ibid.*, p. 417.
21 Howard Newby, 'Deference and the Agricultural Worker', *Sociological Review*, vol. 23, no. 1, p. 56.
22 Interview AJH/Bert Hazel, Wymondham, Norfolk, team-man. Tape in author's possession.
23 *Ibid.*
24 Interview Jack Leeder, *op. cit.*
25 Rider Haggard, *Farmer's Year*, *op. cit.*, p. 57.
26 F.E. Green, *A History of the English Agricultural Labourer* (London 1920), p. 4.
27 Interview Sadler, *op. cit.*

28 *PP 1902 CXX, Census of England and Wales: County of Norfolk*, p. 507.
29 *NRO*, Labour Books, Barnham Brom Area; *ibid.*, Labour Books, Ditchingham/Hempnall Area.
30 Interview Jack Leeder, *op. cit.*
31 Adrian Bell, *Corduroy* (London 1936) p. 36.
32 Interview AJH/Mrs Moy, Yaxham, Norfolk, teacher, f. team-man. Tape in author's possession.
33 Interview AJH/William 'Billa' Dixon, Trunch, Norfolk, labourer. Tape in author's possession.
34 See for example, the strikes fought by the NNALU and NALU in the winter of 1890–1.
35 *LG*, February 1895, p. 37; November 1896, p. 325; February 1902, p. 16; February 1909, p. 60.
36 Interview AJH/Charlie Barber, Great Fransham, Norfolk, team-man. Tape in author's possession.
37 Interview Dixon, *op. cit.*
38 Interview Trevor Lummis/Sidney Watts, fisherman, Happisburgh, Norfolk. Tape deposited at University of Essex. I am grateful to Trevor Lummis for letting me use this material.
39 Interview AJH/Harold Hicks, Trunch, Norfolk, farmer. Tape in author's possession.
40 Interview Jack Leeder, *op. cit.*
41 Interview AJH/William 'Billa' Lee, Paston, Norfolk, labourer. Tape in author's possession.
42 *PP 1919 IX, Wages and Conditions in Agriculture*, Report on Investigators – Norfolk, E.W. Moss-Blundell, p. 435.
43 Interview Jack Leeder, *op. cit.*
44 *NN*, 21 July 1900, p. 8.
45 Interview Barber, *op. cit.*
46 See *EWP*, 11 August 1900, p. 3; and *ibid.*, 23 June 1900, p. 3.
47 Interview Barber, *op. cit.*
48 Interview Dixon, *op. cit.*
49 *EWP*, 11 August 1900, p. 3.
50 *LG*, October 1906, p. 293.
51 Interview Lee, *op. cit.*
52 Home, *Winter Harvest, op. cit.*, ch. 8 *passim*.
53 Interview AJH/'Taddy' Wright, Knapton, Norfolk, labourer. Tape in author's possession.
54 Interview AJH/George Harvey, Gimmingham, Norfolk, small-holder. Tape in author's possession.
55 Alun Howkins, 'Economic Crime and Class Law: Poaching and the Game Laws, 1840–1880', in Sandra E. Burman and Barbara Harrell Bond (eds), *The Imposition of Law* (New York 1979).
56 *Ibid.*, pp. 285–6.
57 See George Edwards, *op. cit.*, pp. 15 ff.; 'The King of the Norfolk Poachers', *I Walked by Night* (ed. L. Rider Haggard), (Ipswich 1974), pp. 43–5.

58 *NN*, 20 January 1900, p. 11.
59 *Ibid.*, 10 February 1900, p. 5.
60 *Ibid.*, 15 January 1921, p. 7.
61 Home, *Winter Harvest, op. cit.*, pp. 84–6; Michael Home, *Autumn Fields* (London 1944), pp. 180 and 190.
62 Interview Hicks, *op. cit.*
63 *NN*, 12 May 1900, p. 8.
64 *NN*, 24 February 1900, p. 8.
65 Interview Dixon, *op. cit.*
66 Interview Dixon, *op. cit.*
67 *Ibid.*
68 For the ramifications of these arguments see, Eileen and Stephen Yeo (eds), *Popular Culture and Class Conflict 1590–1914* (Brighton 1981).
69 Howkins, *op. cit.*, in Yeo (eds), *Ibid.*, p. 286.
70 Newby, 'Differential Dialectic', *op. cit.*, G. Stedman Jones, *Outcast London* (Penguin edn 1976), ch. 13.
71 See David Roberts, *Paternalism in Early Victorian England* (London 1979).
72 Norfolk Federation of Women's Institutes, *Within Living Memory* (Ipswich 1972), p. 77.
73 Interview Harvey, *op. cit.*
74 Interview Sadler, *op. cit.*
75 Interview Lee, *op. cit.*
76 Interview Sadler, *op. cit.*
77 Interview Sadler, *op. cit.*
78 Interview AJH/Arthur Amis, Trunch, Norfolk, cowman. Tape in author's possession.
79 NUAAW Archive, *op. cit.*, EC Minutes, 10 October 1908.
80 Interview Jack Leeder, *op. cit.*

3   Radicalism, the first phase: The chapel

1 Ira D. Sankey, *Sacred Songs and Solo's* (n.d. but c. 1870 Cheap Edition), Hymn no. 1.
2 *Ibid.*, 'Daniel's Band', Hymn no. 7.
3 Donald Davie, *A Gathered Church: The Literature of the English Dissenting Interest 1780–1830* (London 1978), p. 66.
4 C.B. Jewson, *Jacobin City, A Portrait of Norwich 1788–1802* (Glasgow 1975), p. 137.
5 This was the national response. A. Everitt, *The Pattern of Rural Dissent; The Nineteenth Century* (Leicester 1872); Clyde Binfield, *So Down to Prayers, Studies in English Nonconformity 1780–1820* (London 1977).
6 Cyril Jolly, *The Spreading Flame. The Coming of Methodism to Norfolk 1751–1811* (Gressenhall, n.d. but 1973), p. 3.
7 *Ibid.*, pp. 80–7.

8 Digby, *op. cit.*, pp. 29–30, R.A.C. Parker, *Coke of Norfolk: A Financial and Agricultural Study* (Oxford 1975), pp. 147–52.
9 Digby, *op. cit.*, p. 6.
10 *Ibid.*
11 From the signing of Tom Brown, born in Norfolk, *c.* 1902. The ballad was printed first in the 1830s and there are several versions in the Madden Collection.
12 E.P. Thompson, 'The Moral Economy of the English Crowd in the Eighteenth Century', *Past and Present*, no. 50; John Walter and Keith Wrightson, 'Dearth and the Social Order in Early Modern England', *Past and Present*, no. 71.
13 Bryan R. Wilson, 'An Analysis of Sect Development', in Bryan R. Wilson (ed.), *Patterns of Sectarianism* (London 1967), p. 31.
14 A.D. Gilbert, *Religion and Society in Industrial England* (London 1976), p. 89.
15 H.B. Kendall, *The History of the Primitive Methodist Church* (London 1911), vol. I, chs I–V.
16 *Ibid.*, p. 131.
17 W.R. Ward (ed.), *The Early Correspondence of Jabez Bunting 1820–29*, Camden Fourth Series, vol. 11 (London 1972), pp. 196, 203.
18 George Borrow, *Lavengro*, Everyman Edition (London 1906), pp. 156–8.
19 Robert Key, *The Gospel Among the Masses* (London 1872), p. 16.
20 *Ibid.*, p. 18.
21 Augustus Jessopp, *Arcady for Better or Worse* (London n.d. but 1886), pp. 77–8.
22 Gilbert, *op. cit.*, p. 90.
23 Sankey, *op. cit.*, Hymn no. 1.
24 Eugene Weber, *Peasants into Frenchmen* (London 1979), p. 222.
25 Nigel Adrian Scotland, 'The Role of Methodism in the Origin and Development of the Revolt of the Field in Lincolnshire, Norfolk and Suffolk, 1872–96', unpublished Ph.D. thesis, University of Aberdeen 1975, pp. 83 ff.
26 *Swanton Morley Methodist Chapel 1868–1968 Centenary Booklet* (East Dereham 1968) p. 5.
27 Cyril Jolly, *History of the East Dereham Methodist Circuit* (Wymondham 1955), p. 20.
28 *EWP*, 11 July 1974, p. 1.
29 Frank Tice, *The History of Methodism in Cambridge* (London 1966), p. 70.
30 Samuel Smith, 'Anecdotes and Facts of Primitive Methodism', in *Primitive Methodist Itinerant Preacher* (1872).
31 Hugh Bourne's Journal quoted in William Antliff, *The Life of Hugh Bourne* (new edition, London 1892), p. 180.
32 Kendall, *op. cit.*, vol. I, pp. 469–76.
33 *Ibid.*, vol. II, pp. 507–20.
34 E.J. Hobsbawm, *Primitive Rebels* (Manchester 1959), pp. 135–40; E.P. Thompson, *The Making of the English Working Class*, Penguin

edn (Harmondsworth 1968), p. 921.

35 *EWP*, 14 December 1872, p. 1 for a group of examples.

36 East Dereham Primitive Methodist Circuit Quarterly Meeting Minutes. MS in the possession of Cyril Jolly. I am grateful to Mr Jolly for letting me see these minutes.

37 *Ibid.*

38 Wilson, *op. cit.*, p. 23.

39 The phrase is H. Richard Niebuhr's. See his *The Social Sources of Denominationalism*, pb. ed. (Cleveland, Ohio 1957).

40 J.C. Buckmaster (ed.) *A Village Politician. The Life Story of John Buckly* (London 1897), p. 39.

41 *Ibid.*, p. 40. On language see also Joseph Ritson, *The Romance of Primitive Methodism* (London 1909), p. 178.

42 *EWP*, 22 June 1872, p. 6.

43 George Edwards, *op. cit.*, p. 32.

44 *Ibid.*, p. 34.

45 *Ibid.*, p. 48.

46 *Ibid.*, p. 36.

47 Rev. William C. Tonks, *Victory in the Villages. The History of the Brinkworth Circuit* (Aberdare 1907), p. 81.

48 Binfield, *op. cit.*, chs 4 and 5; Patricia Hollis (ed.), *Pressure from Without* (London 1974), chs 8 and 9.

49 Armstrong, *op. cit.*, p. 172.

50 *Ibid.*, 178–9.

51 *EWP*, 21 March 1874, p. 6.

52 Armstrong, *op. cit.*, pp. 187–8.

53 *EWP*, 14 April 1877, p. 4.

54 Interview AJH/Mr Moy, Yaxham, Norfolk, labourer.

55 *EWP*, 3 June 1882, p. 1.

56 *Ibid.*, 22 May 1875, p. 5.

57 *Ibid.*, 7 April 1906, p. 6.

58 *Ibid.*, 21 April 1906, p. 4.

59 See E.P. Thompson, *The Making of the English Working Class*, *op. cit.*, p. 391.

60 Jessopp, *op. cit.*, p. 77.

61 Interview AJH/Bert Hazel, Wymondham, Norfolk, team-man. Tape in author's possession.

62 Tonks, *op. cit.*, p. 22.

63 F. Clifford, *The Agricultural Lock Out of 1874* (Edinburgh and London 1875), p. 370.

64 *EWP*, 14 April 1906, p. 5.

65 *Ibid.*, 4 January 1890, p. 1.

66 *Ibid.*, 25 June 1892, p. 1.

67 Niebuhr, *op. cit.*, p. 28.

68 Max Weber, *The Protestant Ethic and the Spirit of Capitalism* (London 1930).

69 Wilson, *op. cit.*, *passim*.

70 Binfield, *op. cit.*, ch. 8.

71 *Eastern Weekly Leader* (hereafter *EWL*), 14 September 1895, p. 10.
72 K.S. Inglis, *Churches and the Working Class in Victorian England* (London 1963), pp. 287–304; Kenneth Young, *Chapel* (London 1972), pp. 22–3.
73 Kendall, *op. cit.*, vol. II, pp. 510–11.
74 *EWP*, 6 April 1907, p. 6.
75 *Ibid.*, 9 November 1901, p. 9.
76 *Ibid.*, 29 June 1907, p. 6.
77 'Sons of Labour' written by Robert Green of Sheringham, Norfolk. The tune used like so many is a gospel one, in this case 'Hark the Gospel News is Sounding'.

4 Radicalism, the first phase: The local unions 1872–96

1 Quoted in, Josiah Sage, *The Memoirs of Josiah Sage* (London 1951), p. 18.
2 Joseph Arch, *Joseph Arch: The Story of his Life, Told by Himself* (London 1898), pp. 58–61.
3 *Ibid.*, pp. 60–1.
4 F. Clifford, *The Agricultural Lock-Out of 1874* (Edinburgh and London 1875); W. Hasbach, *A History of the English Agricultural Labourer* (new edn, London 1966), original London 1908.
5 S. Webb and B. Webb, *The History of Trade Unionism* (London 1950).
6 R. Arnold, 'The "Revolt of the Field" in Kent, 1872–92', *Past and Present* no. 64; J.P.D. Dunbabin, *Rural Discontent in Nineteenth Century Britain* (London 1974); Ian Carter, *Farm Life in Northeast Scotland, 1840–1914, The Poor Man's Country* (Edinburgh 1979).
7 Pamela Horn, 'Labour Organisations', in G.E. Mingay (ed.), *The Victorian Countryside*, vol. 2 (London 1981), p. 583.
8 Arch, *op. cit.*, p. 283, see also *English Labourer's Chronicle* (hereafter *ELC*) (1878), especially 20 April 1878, p. 5; *ibid.*, 7, 27 April 1878, p. 7.
9 J.J. Hissey, *A Tour in a Phaeton through the Eastern Counties* (London 1889), p. 59 ff.
10 R.S. Joby, *Forgotten Railways of East Anglia* (Newton Abbot, 1977).
11 *Jarrold's Illustrated Guide to Cromer and Neighbourhood* (Norwich, n.d. but ? 1894), pp. 7–8.
12 L. Marion Springhall, *Labouring Life in Norfolk Villages 1834–1914* (London 1936), ch. XI, *passim*.
13 Interview AJH/Percy Brown, Aylsham, Norfolk, Chimney sweep. Tape in author's possession.
14 See *Kelly's Directory of Norfolk* (London 1896); W. White, *Norfolk Directory* (London 1883).

15 *Kelly's, op. cit.*, p. 100.
16 *EWP*, 30 March 1872, p. 5; 6 April 1872, p. 1.
17 Rex Stedman, 'Vox Populi: The Norfolk Newspaper Press 1760–1900', unpublished FLA thesis 1971, p. 282.
18 *NN*, 11 September 1897, p. 10.
19 *Ibid.*
20 Stedman, *op. cit.*, p. 284.
21 *EWP*, 13 April 1872, p. 1.
22 Springhall, *op. cit.*, pp. 80–1. On Fakenham see also L. Marion Springhall, 'The Norfolk Agricultural Labourer, 1834–1884. A study in Social and Economic History', unpublished PhD thesis, London University 1935, pp. 101 ff. On Dereham see Chapter 4 above.
23 *Ibid.*
24 *EWP*, 1 June 1872, p. 7.
25 Figures supplied by John Cook of UEA. I am grateful to John for letting me see these figures.
26 *Ibid.*
27 J.P.D. Dunbabin, *Rural Discontent, op. cit.*, pp. 62–9.
28 J.P.D. Dunbabin, 'The Incidence and Organisation of Agricultural Trades Unionism in the 1870's', *Agricultural History Review*, vol. 16 (1968).
29 *EWP, ibid.*, 1 June 1872, p. 7.
30 *Ibid.*, 11 January 1873, p. 4.
31 *Ibid.*, 1 June 1872, p. 7.
32 *Ibid.*, 2 January 1875, p. 1; 24 April 1874, p. 1.
33 For example, David Jones, 'Thomas Campbell Foster and the rural labourer; incendiarism in East Anglia in the 1840s', *Social History*, no. 1, January 1976; John Archer, 'The Myth and Reality of the Norfolk Incendiary, 1830–1870', unpublished paper given at the East Anglian History Workshop meeting, Essex, December 1976.
34 The preceding pages are based on material mostly from the local press in the period 1870–1910.
35 *EWP*, 14 September 1872, p. 1.
36 *EWP*, 23 November 1872, p. 1 (my estimate).
37 *EWP*, 21 June 1879, p. 1.
38 *Ibid.*
39 Dunbabin, *Rural Discontent, op. cit.*, pp. 80–1.
40 Dunbabin, *ibid.*, p. 79.
41 *Ibid.*, 119, see also J.P.D. Dunbabin, 'The "Revolt of the Field": The Agricultural Labourers' Movement in the 1870s', *Past and Present*, no. 26, pp. 90–3.
42 See Ch. 5 of A. Howkins, 'The Great Momentous Time: Radicalism and the Norfolk Farm Labourer 1870–1923', unpublished PhD thesis, University of Essex, 1983. It is hoped this material will appear shortly as an article.
43 *EWP*, 5 June 1875, p. 1.
44 *Ibid.*, 21 October 1876, p. 1.
45 *Ibid.*, 16 June 1877, p. 1.

46 See for example, *EWP*, 9 March 1878, p. 1; *ibid.*, 16 March 1978, p. 1; *ELC*, 16 March 1878, p. 6.
47 *EWP*, 23 March 1878, p. 1.
48 *ELC*, 20 April 1878, p. 5.
49 *EWP*, 5 October 1878, p. 1.
50 *Ibid.*, 19 October 1878, p. 1.
51 *Ibid.*, 8 February 1879, p. 1.
52 *Ibid.*, 22 February 1879, p. 1.
53 *Ibid.*, 16 March 1889, p. 8.
54 Dunbabin, *Rural Discontent*, p. 82, argues the revival was the result of the dock strike.
55 Edwards, *op. cit.*, pp. 54–5; *EWP*, 23 November 1889, p. 1.
56 *EWP*, 30 November 1889, p. 1.
57 *Ibid.*
58 *Ibid.*, 4 January 1890, p. 1; see also 11 June 1892, p. 1, letter from Edward James accusing Rix of being anti-strike.
59 *EWP*, 1 February 1890, p. 1.
60 Edwards, *op. cit.*, p. 56.
61 *Ibid.*, p. 57.
62 *PP 1895*, *op. cit.*, p. 365.
63 *PP 1893–4*, *op. cit.*
64 *EWP*, 3 January 1891, p. 1; 10 January 1891, p. 1.
65 *Ibid.*, 3 January 1891, p. 1.
66 *Ibid.*, 7 February 1891, pp. 1–2.
67 *Ibid.*, 7 May 1892, p. 1.
68 *Ibid.*, 16 April 1892, p. 1.
69 *Ibid.*, 20 October 1894, p. 1.
70 *Ibid.*, 6 January 1894, p. 1.
71 Edwards, *op. cit.*, p. 66.
72 See Cawston and Shipdham, *EWP*, 1 August 1894, p. 1.
73 *Ibid.*, 4 May 1895.
74 *Eastern Weekly Leader*, 8 February 1896, p. 2.

5 Radicalism, the second phase: The second union

1 *Norwich Mercury* (hereafter *NM*), 12 May 1900, p. 7.
2 *Ibid.*
3 Haggard, *Farmer's Year*, *op. cit.*, pp. 421–2, 459–69; *EWP*, 15 May 1899, p. 1.
4 *EWP*, 25 March 1899, p. 5.
5 *Ibid.*, 9 December 1899, p. 6.
6 *Ibid.*, 4 November 1899, p. 1.
7 *Ibid.*, 23 June 1900, p. 3.
8 *Ibid.*, 11 August 1900, p. 3.

9 Sir Richard Winfrey, *Leaves from My Life* (Kings Lynn 1936), p. 43.
10 *Ibid.*, p. 107; *EWP*, 23 June 1900, p. 3.
11 *Ibid.*, 14 July 1900, p. 4.
12 *Ibid.*
13 See Sir Richard Winfrey, *Great Men and Others I have Met* (Northampton 1943), pp. 95–7.
14 *EWP*, 23 June 1900, p. 3.
15 Edwards, *op. cit.*, p. 95.
16 *NM*, 12 May 1900, p. 7.
17 See *EWP*, 29 March 1902, p. 1 and 16 August 1902, p. 1.
18 Edwards, *op. cit.*, p. 96.
19 *Ibid.*, p. 95.
20 *EWP*, 12 April 1902, p. 6.
21 *Ibid.*, 12 April 1902, p. 6.
22 Rev. A.H. Baverstock, *The Failure of the Church in the Villages* (London 1913), p. 5.
23 *EWP*, 8 November 1902, p. 11; *NN*, 31 March 1900, p. 5.
24 *LG*, February 1903, p. 52; *ibid.*, March 1903, p. 80.
25 *EWP*, 6 December 1902, p. 6.
26 *LG*, October 1904, p. 290.
27 *Ibid.*, July 1906, p. 195.
28 *EWP*, 25 October 1902, p. 4.
29 *Ibid.* This issue of the paper refers to 'scores of simultaneous meetings'.
30 Henry Pelling, *Social Geography of British Elections, 1885–1910* (London 1967).
31 Winfrey, *Leaves, op. cit.*, p. 35.
32 *EWP*, 20 January 1906, p. 1.
33 *Ibid.*, 3 February 1906, p. 6.
34 *Ibid.*
35 R.H. Mottram, *Bowler Hat: A Last Glance at the Old Country Banking* (London 1940), pp. 159–60.
36 *EWP*, 20 January 1906, p. 6.
37 Edwards, *op. cit.*, p. 98.
38 *EWP*, 28 July 1906, p. 6.
39 Interview Nick Mansfield/Tom Barker, Erpingham, Norfolk, Labourer. Tape in Norfolk Museum of Rural Life, Gressenhall, Norfolk. I am grateful to Nick Mansfield for making this tape available.
40 Winfrey, *Great Man, op. cit.*, pp. 95–7, Joyce Bellamy and John Saville, *Dictionary of Labour Biography*, vol. 5 (London 1978), pp. 163–5.
41 *Cox's County Who's Who Series. Norfolk, Suffolk and Cambridgeshire 1912* (London 1912), entry under Day.
42 *EWP*, 13 December 1902, p. 3.
43 *Ibid.*, 28 July 1906, p. 3.
44 *Ibid.*

45 *Ibid.*
46 *Ibid.*
47 *Ibid.*
48 *Ibid.*
49 *Ibid.*, 22 September 1906, p. 6.
50 Executive Committee of the Eastern Counties Agricultural Labourers and Small Holders' Union Minutes (hereafter EC Mins), Museum of English Rural Life, University of Reading, Meeting, 27 April 1907.
51 *Ibid.*, 12 October 1907.
52 *Ibid.*, 16 April 1912.
53 *Ibid.*, 12 November 1906.
54 Eastern Counties Agricultural Labourers and Small Holders' Union Minute Book, St Faiths Branch (hereafter St Faiths Mins), Museum of English Rural Life, University of Reading, Meeting, 5 September 1906.
55 Interview AJH/Walter Pardon, Knapton, Norfolk, carpenter. Tape in author's possession.
56 Interview Mrs Rayner, Swanton Morley, Norfolk, father teamman/smallholder. Tape in author's possession.
57 Edwards, *op. cit.*, pp. 116–18; *EWL*, 9 February 1895, p. 5.
58 Interview C. Jolly, Gressenhall, Norfolk, father labourer. Tape in author's possession.
59 Interview Mrs Rayner, *op. cit.*
60 *Ibid.*
61 The complete text is in National Agricultural Labourers and Rural Workers' Union, *Song Book* (Norwich n.d. but *c.* 1919), pp. 8–9. Copy in Norfolk and Norwich Record Office (hereafter NNRO). Walter Pardon of Knapton, a fine traditional singer, knows this song and two others included in the song book.
62 *Ibid.*, p. 13. This song was also used by Arch's union.
63 Interview Mrs Rayner, *op. cit.*
64 Interview AJH/Charlie Barber, Gressenhall, Norfolk, team-man. Tape in author's possession.
65 EC Mins, 24–25 April 1908; 10 October 1900, for example.
66 *Ibid.*, 25 April 1908; 2 May 1908.
67 St Faiths Mins, 28 December 1908.
68 EC Mins, 10 October 1908.
69 *EWP*, 9 May 1908, p. 3.
70 *Ibid.*, 26 March 1910, p. 2.
71 *Ibid.*
72 EC Mins for those months.
73 Groves, *op. cit.*, p. 101.
74 St Faiths Mins, 29 April 1910.
75 EC Mins, 20 May 1910.
76 *EWP*, 28 May 1910, p. 3.
77 EC Mins, 5 May 1910. Edwards's letter was written in the 1st week of May.

78 *EWP*, 28 May 1910, p. 5.
79 *Ibid.*
80 *Ibid.*
81 *Ibid.*, 4 June 1910, p. 5.
82 *Ibid.*
83 Green, *op. cit.*, p. 179.
84 *EWP*, 23 July 1910, p. 2.
85 *Ibid.*, 27 August 1910, p. 3.
86 *Ibid.*
87 *Ibid.*, 24 September 1910, p. 6.
88 EC Mins, 19 November 1910.
89 Letter dated 13 December 1910, in EC Mins.
90 EC Mins, 28 December 1910.
91 *EWP*, 14 January 1911, p. 5.
92 *Ibid.*, 4 March 1911, p. 8.
93 *Ibid.*, 7 January 1911, p. 5.
94 EC Mins, 12 January 1911 and 24 February 1911.
95 For what follows see *EWP*, 4 March 1911 and Edwards, *op. cit.*, pp. 166 ff.
96 Green, *op. cit.*, p. 182.
97 *EWP*, 16 July 1910, p. 6.
98 Interview AJH/George Harvey, Gimmingham, Norfolk, small-holder. Tape in author's possession.
99 EC Mins, 23 April 1911.
100 *EWP*, 9 October 1912, p. 5; 16 November 1912, p. 10.
101 Green, *op. cit.*, p. 182.
102 *EWP*, 26 June 1912, p. 5.
103 *Ibid.*, 11 May 1912, p. 6.

6   Radicalism, the second phase: Rural labour and the wages board 1910–21

1 *EWP*, 4 March 1911, p. 4.
2 *Commonweal*, 23 October 1886, p. 237. I am grateful to Anna Davin for this reference.
3 Groves. *op. cit.*, pp. 98 ff.
4 *EWP*, 9 May 1903, p. 3.
5 *Labour Leader* (hereafter *LL*), 31 August 1906, p. 230.
6 *Ibid.*, 1 May 1908, p. 274 for one such account.
7 *Ibid.*, 1 March 1907, p. 636.
8 *Ibid.*, 11 May 1895, p. 169.
9 *Ibid.*, 4 May 1895, p. 2.
10 *Ibid.*, 9 March 1895, p. 3.
11 See Anna Davin, 'Imperialism and Motherhood', *History Workshop Journal*, no. 5, pp. 16–18 and 22 ff.

12 The series ran from the issue of 14 August 1908 until 9 September 1908 and took up the whole front page.
13 *LL*, 4 September 1908, p. 574.
14 *Ibid.*, 28 August 1908, p. 551.
15 *EWP*, 18 July 1908, p. 6.
16 EC Mins, 19 February 1909.
17 *EWP*, 28 August 1909, p. 6.
18 Edwards, *op. cit.*, p. 119.
19 EC Mins, 19 November 1910.
20 Pelling, *op. cit.*, p. 95.
21 *EWP*, 4 March 1911, p. 8.
22 EC Mins, 22 April 1911.
23 *Ibid.*, 29 July 1911.
24 *EWP*, 13 May 1911, p. 7.
25 *Ibid.*, 29 July 1911, p. 6.
26 *Ibid.*, 5 August 1911, p. 10.
27 See *EWP*, 7 October 1911, p. 6 and 16 December 1911, p. 4; EC Mins, 21 October 1911 and 11 April 1912.
28 EC Mins, 18 January 1912; 10 February 1912.
29 *EWP*, 24 February 1912, p. 6.
30 Groves, *op. cit.*, p. 121.
31 *EWP*, 7 July 1913, p. 10.
32 *Ibid.*, 27 July 1912, p. 3.
33 *LL*, 19 September 1912, p. 606.
34 EC Mins, 2 December 1912.
35 *LL*, 23 January 1913, p. 13.
36 *Ibid.*, 10 April 1913, p. 13.
37 *EWP*, 15 March 1913, p. 3.
38 Whetham, *op. cit.*, p. 62.
39 A.F. Much, 'Agricultural Labour in the North West c. 1870–1920', unpublished PhD thesis, University of Manchester, 1980.
40 EC Mins, 19 July 1913.
41 EC Mins, 10 May 1913.
42 A.D. Hall, *A Pilgrimage of British Farming* (London 1913), p. 431.
43 *Ibid.*, p. 84.
44 *EWP*, 16 August 1913, p. 2.
45 EC Mins, 4 March 1914.
46 *EWP*, 7 March 1914.
47 *Ibid.*, 14 March 1914, p. 4.
48 *Ibid.*
49 *The Labourer* (hereafter *TL*), 21 March 1914, p. 1.
50 *EWP*, 21 March 1914, p. 4.
51 There is a good account of the strike in Bertram Edwards, *The Burston School Strike* (London 1974). The figures quoted are on p. 16.
52 Interview AJH/Billy Dixon, Trunch, Norfolk, team-man. Tape in author's possession.
53 *EWP*, 15 August 1914, p. 2.
54 P.E. Dewey, 'Agricultural Labour Supply in England and Wales

during the First World War', *Economic History Review*, 2nd series, vol. XXVIII, no. 1, February 1975, pp. 103–4.

55 *EWP*, 6 February 1915, p. 4.
56 EC Mins, 20 February 1915.
57 Interview with Walker, *EWP*, 20 March 1915, p. 8.
58 *Ibid.*, p. 20.
59 See EC Mins, 27 February 1915; 10 April 1915; 18 May 1915.
60 *EWP*, 15 May 1915, p. 2.
61 *Ibid.*, 24 May 1915, p. 2.
62 See Dewey, 'Government Provision', *op. cit.*, *passim*.
63 *EWP*, 14 June 1915, p. 2; 17 July 1915, p. 2.
64 *Ibid.*, 26 June 1915, p. 4.
65 *Ibid.*, p. 5.
66 *Ibid.*, 1 July 1916, p. 5.
67 *Ibid.*, 23 August 1915, p. 2.
68 *Ibid.*, 18 December 1915, p. 2.
69 *Ibid.*, 15 January 1916, p. 2.
70 *Ibid.*
71 *Ibid.*
72 *Ibid.*, 14 August 1915, p. 2.
73 *Ibid.*, 10 July 1915, p. 2.
74 Interview AJH/'Taddy' Wright, Knapton, Norfolk, labourer/team-man. Tape in author's possession.
75 *Ibid.*, 10 February 1917, p. 3.
76 Whetham, *op. cit.*, pp. 89–91.
77 Sir William H. Beveridge, *British Food Control* (London 1928), pp. 88–9. See also Sir T.H. Middleton, *Food Production in War* (London 1923).
78 Beveridge, *op. cit.*, p. 82.
79 *Ibid.*, p. 83.
80 Whetham, *op. cit.*, pp. 89 ff.
81 *PP 1917–18 XVIII Reconstruction Committee: Pt. 1 of the Report of the Agricultural Policy Sub-Committee*, p. 349.
82 *Ibid.*, p. 434.
83 *PP 1917–18, I, Corn Production Bill*, p. 249 ff.
84 F.E. Green, *op. cit.*, pp. 288–9.
85 Green, *op. cit.*, pp. 259.
86 These figures are little better than approximation. In 1948 Fred Bond of the union's head office made an estimate for Reg Groves based on various materials. The problem for Bond, and for me, was that much material was lost during bombing. The Norfolk figures are accurate for 1915, 1920 and 1923, interim figures were arrived at by working out a relationship between national and Norfolk figures for these dates and projecting backwards and forwards.
87 Green, *op. cit.*, p. 298.
88 R.K. Middlemass, *Politics in Industrial Society* (London 1979).
89 See, for example, the speech by George Edwards on the repeal of the Agriculture Act, *Hansard*, 2 July 1921.

90 J.W. Robertson Scott, 'The Farm Labourer's £90,000 Nest Egg' in *The World's Work*, November 1922, p. 452.
91 The minutes are typed from 24 November 1918.
92 EC Mins, 11 May 1918.
93 R.R. Enfield, *The Agricultural Crisis 1920–23* (London 1924), p. 14.
94 *EWP*, 16 June 1917, p. 8.
95 *Ibid.*, 14 July 1917, p. 5.
96 *Ibid.*, 16 March 1918, p. 4.
97 *Ibid.*, 17 August 1918, p. 3.
98 *Ibid.*, 30 November 1918, p. 1.
99 *NN*, 28 March 1919, p. 7.
100 *Ibid.*, 12 April 1919, p. 5.
101 For an excellent example see the speech by Noel Buxton, an ex-Liberal, at Fakenham in 7 February 1920 on the subject of why he joined the Labour Party. *NN*, 14 February 1920, p. 2.
102 *NN*, 17 May 1919, p. 8.
103 See *NN*, 15 March 1919, p. 3.
104 Interview AJH/Bert Hazel, Wymondham, Norfolk, team-man. Tape in author's possession.
105 *NN*, 26 July 1919, p. 8.
106 Green, *op. cit.*, p. 331.

7 The great betrayal

1 *NN*, 11 June 1921, p. 5. For a rather thin and policy-orientated discussion of the repeal of the Act, see Edith Whetham, 'The Agriculture Act, 1920 and its Repeal – the "Great Betrayal" ', *Agricultural History Review*, vol. 22 (1974), pp. 36–49.
2 *NN*, 2 July 1921, pp. 5 and 3.
3 *Ibid.*, 23 June 1921, p. 5.
4 *Ibid.*, 2 July 1921, pp. 5 and 8
5 See report of Norfolk NFU meeting at Wymondham, *NN*, 9 July 1921, p. 2.
6 *NN*, 9 July 1921, p. 2.
7 *Ibid.*, 17 July 1921, p. 2.
8 *Ibid.*, 23 July 1921, p. 2. See also the article by Walker in the *Land Worker* (hereafter *LW*) September 1921, p. 3.
9 *NN*, 23 July 1921, p. 2.
10 *Ibid.*, 30 July 1921, p. 2.
11 Whetham, *op. cit.*, p. 142.
12 From weekly prices given in *NN*.
13 A.G. Street, *Farmers' Glory* (London 1932), see also his *The Gentleman of the Party* (London 1936), for a long-term view of the decline of agriculture.
14 Adrian Bell, *Silver Ley* (London 1936), p. 149.
15 Interview AJH/Harold Hicks, Trunch, Norfolk, farmer. Tape in

author's possession.
16 *Ibid.*
17 Henry Williamson, *The Story of a Norfolk Farm* (London 1941).
18 *NN*, 25 December 1920, p. 4.
19 *NN*, 8 January 1921, p. 6.
20 *Ibid.*, 8 January 1921, p. 8; 22 January 1921, p. 6.
21 *Ibid.*, 8 January 1921, p. 3.
22 *Ibid.*, 22 January 1921, p. 2.
23 Interview AJH/Arthur Amis, Trunch, Norfolk, cowman. Tape in author's possession.
24 *NN*, 25 May 1921, p. 8.
25 Minutes of the Aylsham Rural District Council Highways Committee, 10 May 1921, NNRO, Norwich.
26 *Ibid.*, 24 May 1921.
27 *Ibid.*, 19 July 1921.
28 *NN*, 16 July 1921, p. 5.
29 *Ibid.*, 23 July 1921, p. 2.
30 Minutes of the St Faiths Rural District Council Unemployment Committee, 21 November 1921, NNRO, Norwich.
31 Minutes of the Erpingham Board of Guardians, 13 March 1922, 10 April 1922 NNRO, Norwich.
32 Minutes, Aylsham, *op. cit.*, 28 March 1922.
33 Interview AJH/Billy Dixon, Trunch, Norfolk, team-man. Tape in author's possession.
34 Minutes, Depwade Rural District Council, 24 April 1921, NNRO, Norwich.
35 Depwade, *op. cit.*, 20 October 1921; St Faiths, *op. cit.*, 25 October 1921; Minutes of the Forehoe Rural District Council Unemployment Committee, 6 February 1922, NNRO, Norwich.
36 Erpingham, *op. cit.*, 24 October 1921.
37 Frederick C. Wigby, *Just a Country Boy* (Wymondham 1971), p. 128.
38 *Ibid.*, p. 129.
39 *Ibid.*, p. 132.
40 Minutes, Blofield Board of Guardians, 5 February 1918 and 14 February 1921, NNRO, Norwich.
41 *NN*, 3 February 1921, p. 7.
42 *Ibid.*, 17 September 1921, p. 2.
43 EC Mins, 20 September 1921.
44 *NN*, 8 October 1921, p. 5.
45 *Ibid.*
46 Copy in NUAAW Archive, Museum of English Rural Life, University of Reading.
47 Interview AJH/Jack Sadler, Titchwell, Norfolk, roadman. Tape in author's possession.
48 *Ibid.*
49 *Ibid.*
50 *NN*, 8 October 1921, p. 5.
51 Printed leaflet in private collection. Also sent to the author by an

anonymous ex-labourer in response to a letter in the *Eastern Daily Press*.
52 Interview Sadler, *op. cit.*
53 Anonymous letter to author. In author's possession.
54 *NN*, 10 December 1921, p. 5 for one example.
55 *Daily Herald* (hereafter *DH*), 30 December 1921, p. 6.
56 *Ibid.*
57 *NN*, 17 December 1921, p. 5.
58 *Eastern Daily Press* (hereafter *EDP*), 6 December 1921, p. 2.
59 Howard Newby, Colin Bell, David Rose and Peter Saunders, *Property Paternalism and Power* (London 1978), p. 16.
60 *NN*, 14 January 1922, p. 2.
61 *Ibid.*, 25 February 1922, p. 2.
62 *Ibid.*, 4 March 1922, p. 7.
63 *Ibid.*, 11 February 1922, p. 5.
64 *Ibid.*, 8 October 1921, p. 5, also *LW*, November 1921.
65 EC Mins, 23 March 1922.
66 *NN*, 11 March 1922, p. 2.
67 Interview Sadler, *op. cit.*; letter to author, in author's possession.
68 Copy in private collection.
69 EC Mins, 28 April 1922; 27 June 1922; 26 October 1922.
70 *LW*, April 1922, p. 1.
71 *NN*, 24 June 1922, p. 10.
72 *LW*, April 1922, p. 1.
73 *NN*, 24 June, p. 10.
74 *Ibid.*
75 *Ibid.*, see all EC Mins, 23 March 1922.
76 *Ibid.*
77 *LW*, April 1922, p. 16.
78 *NN*, 8 July 1922, p. 8.
79 *NN*, 1 July 1922, p. 5.
80 *Darlington Times*, 12 August 1922. In Press Cuttings Book, NUAAW Archive, Museum of English Rural Life, University of Reading.
81 *NN* 8 July 1922, p. 8.
82 *NN*, *ibid.*
83 *NN*, 21 October 1922, p. 2.
84 EC Mins, 19 September 1922.
85 *NN*, 23 December 1922, p. 2.

8 The great strike

1 The *New Leader*, 13 April 1923, p. 6.
2 *The Times* (London) (hereafter *T*), 19 March 1923, p. 18.
3 *Ibid.*
4 *NN*, 27 January 1923, p. 2.

5 *Ibid.*
6 Bellerby, *op. cit.*, p. 49.
7 *NN*, 24 February 1923, p. 2.
8 *Ibid.*, 3 March 1923, p. 2.
9 *T*, 19 March 1923, p. 18.
10 Interview AJH/Arthur Amis, Trunch, Norfolk, cowman. Tape in author's possession.
11 *NN*, 24 March 1923, p.9.
12 *EDP*, 22 March 1923, p. 9.
13 *T*, 17 March 1923, p. 10.
14 EC Mins, James Lunnon's Report on the Strike, 24 May 1923.
15 *NN*, 24 March 1923, p. 9.
16 *Ibid.*, 31 March 1923, p. 9.
17 EC Mins, Lunnon's report, *op. cit.*, also Robert Walker's report to the same meeting. For confusion see *NN*, 24 March 1923, p. 5; *ibid.*, 31 March 1923, p. 8.
18 *NN*, 24 March 1923, p. 9.
19 *Ibid.*
20 *Ibid.*
21 *Ibid.*
22 *Ibid.*
23 *Ibid.*
24 *EDP*, 22 March 1923, p. 9.
25 *NN*, 7 April 1923, p. 5.
26 *Ibid.*, p. 8.
27 Interview AJH/Miss R. Groom, Stiffkey, Norfolk, father farmer. Tape in author's possession.
28 *MLE*, 2 April 1923, p. 584.
29 Interview AJH/Herbert Neal, Paston, Norfolk, labourer. Tape in author's possession.
30 Interview AJH/Billy Dixon, Knapton, Norfolk, team-man. Tape in author's possession.
31 *NN*, 7 April 1923, p. 5.
32 See *MLE*, 9 April 1923, pp. 628–9.
33 *NN*, 14 April 1923.
34 *MLE*, 9 April 1923, p. 628.
35 CAB 24/159/02243/703, 'Strike of Agricultural Labourers in Norfolk, PRO.
36 *NN*, 14 April 1923, p. 8; CAB 24, *op. cit.*, p. 704.
37 CAB 24, *op. cit.*, p. 704.
38 *NN*, 14 April 1923, p. 8.
39 *NN*, 31 March 1923, p. 5.
40 *MLE*, 9 April 1923, p. 628.
41 *NN*, 7 April 1923, p. 5.
42 EC Mins, Lunnon's Report, *op. cit.*
43 Interview AJH/Billy Lee, Paston, Norfolk, Labourer. Tape in author's possession.
44 *NN*, 21 April 1923, p. 8.

45 *Ibid.*
46 *NN*, 28 April 1923, p. 8.
47 *NN*, 21 April 1923, p. 5.
48 *NN*, 14 April 1923, p. 8.
49 See EC Mins, Walker's report, *op. cit.*; M.J. Madden, 'The National Union of Agricultural Workers 1906–1956 (A Study of the Development and Effects of the Policies of Leadership)', unpublished B Litt thesis, Oxford, 1956, pp. 82–3.
50 *NN*, 21 April 1923, p. 5.
51 *Ibid.*, p. 8.
52 *Ibid.*, p. 9.
53 *Ibid.*, 14 April 1923, p. 8.
54 EC Mins, Walker's report, *op. cit.*
55 *Ibid.*
56 *Ibid.*
57 *NN*, 28 April 1923, p. 9.
58 EC Mins, Walker's report, *op. cit.*
59 Apart from this one copy in a private collection I can find no reference to this publication either in the standard indexes or in the NFU Archive.
60 Statement by J.F. Wright, quoted in *NN*, 28 April 1923, p. 9.
61 *NN*, 28 April 1923, p. 9.
62 Interview AJH/Bert Hazel, Wymondham, Norfolk, team-man. Tape in author's possession.
63 Interview Lee, *op. cit.*
64 EC Mins, 23 April 1923,
65 *EDP*, 23 April 1923, p. 7.
66 'We have no evidence that the NULW can provide any such practical support', NFU Minutes of Council Meetings, GPC report on NULW, Museum of English Rural Life, University of Reading.
67 Interview Dixon, *op. cit.*

9   The long term

1 Newby, *Deferential Worker, op. cit.*, pp. 226 ff.
2 EC Mins, Lunnon's report, *op. cit.*
3 *LW*, August 1976, p. 173.
4 Newby, *Deferential Worker, op. cit.*, p. 236.
5 *Ibid.*, pp. 326 ff.
6 See R.W. Johnson, 'The Nationalisation of English Rural Politics: Norfolk South West, 1945–1970', *Parliamentary Affairs*, vol. XXVI, no. 1, (Winter 1972–3).
7 See especially, *Deferential Worker, op. cit.*, pp. 368 ff., also Newby *et al.*, *Property, Paternalism and Power, op. cit.*, pp. 248 ff.
8 Interview AJH/Billy Dixon, *op. cit.*
9 F.A. Hayek (ed.), *Capitalism and the Historians* (London 1954).

Bibliography

What follows is a comprehensive bibliography of works which have had some kind of influence, no matter how indirect, on this book. It deliberately does not include many works, especially academic theses, which I have read and which were so far away from my subject as to have no influence at all.

The major sources for this book were the local press, the collection of the NUAAW at Reading, and interviews with old farm workers and farmers. It should be clear that of the local press I have relied fairly heavily on one paper, the *Eastern Weekly Press*. The reason for this is simple. As a radical/Liberal paper designed for the working man it reported, often in detail, on the unions' activities. The rest of the Norfolk press usually ignored the farm labourers except when they were being 'difficult'. I have checked the other local papers, especially the Tory *Norfolk News*, whenever anything seemed contentious. After 1919 the position changes since the *EWP* vanished in that year. From then on the *NN* became more centrist in its politics and gave more space to the doings of the labourers' union.

The Bibliography is divided into

A Manuscript sources
B Interviews
C Printed sources
D Secondary sources

Each of these sections is further subdivided as indicated.

A Manuscript Sources

1 Historical Records of the National Union of Agricultural and Allied Workers, Museum of English Rural Life, Reading.
2 Historical Records of the National Farmers' Union, Museum of English Rural Life, Reading.
3 Historical Records of the Country Landowners' Association, Museum of English Rural Life, Reading.
4 Material held in the Norwich and Norfolk Records Office, Norwich.
  Aylsham Rural District Council Highways Committee, Minutes
  Blofield Board of Guardians, Minutes

Burnham Thorpe, Buntings Endowed School, Log Book
Depwade Board of Guardians, Minutes
Depwade Rural District Council, Minutes
Edwards Papers
Erpingham Board of Guardians, Minutes
Forehoe Rural District Council, Unemployment Committee, Minutes
Henderson Papers
Labour Book, Barnham Broom Area
Labour Book, Ditchlingham/Hempnall Area
Labour Book, Hindringham
Labour Book, Reyermaston
Labour Book, Tutlington
Loddon and Clavering Rural District Council, Minutes
Norfolk County Council Agriculture Committee, Drainage Sub-Committee, Minutes
Norfolk County Council Unemployment Committee, Minutes
Runcton Holme National School, Log Book
Runhall National School, Log Book
St Faiths Rural District Council Unemployment Committee, Minutes
Swafield National School, Log Book
5 Manuscript material in private hands
East Dereham Primitive Methodist Circuit Quarterly Meeting, Minutes (in the possession of Mr C. Jolly).
Files of letters to author on farm life and 1923 strike (40 items) (in author's possession).
Scrapbook of Ringer's Strike (in private hands).
6 Manuscripts held in PRO
CAB 24 'Reports on Revolutionary and Subversive Organisations', 1919–23.

B   Interviews

All tapes held by author except those indicated★. It is intended to deposit copies in the Norfolk Rural Life Museum, Gressenhall.

Arthur Amis, b. Trunch, Norfolk, 1907, cowman.

Charlie Barber, b. 1881, Great Fransham, Norfolk, team-man/small-holder.

★Tom Barker, b. 1910 East Beckenham, Norfolk, labourer. (This interview was carried out by Nick Mansfield of the Norfolk Museums Service and is deposited at the Norfolk Rural Life Museum, Gressenhall.)

Percy Brown, b. Felmingham, Norfolk, 1903, chimney-sweep.

Arthur Clarke, b. Bacton, Norfolk, 1887, fisherman/labourer.

Billy Dixon, b. Trunch, Norfolk, 1894, labourer/team-man/gardener.

Miss Ruth Groome, b. Warham, Norfolk, 1911, farmer.

Reg Harvey, b. Gimmingham, Norfolk, 1903, smallholder.
Bert Hazel, b. Attleborough, Norfolk, 1907, team-man.
Harold Hicks, b. Swanton Abbot, Norfolk, 1909, farmer.
Billy Lee, b. Paston Green, Norfolk 1900, labourer.
Bert Leeder, b. Happisburgh, Norfolk, 1905, blacksmith.
Jack Leeder, b. Happisburgh, Norfolk, 1901, team-man.
Charles Leveridge, b. Carbrooke, Norfolk, 1893, team-man.
Percy Mann, b. Winborough, Norfolk, 1901, labourer.
Mrs Ada Moy, b. Runhall, Norfolk, 1890, school teacher,f. labourer/-
    team-man.
Mr W. Moy, b. Hindringham, Norfolk, 1890, smallholder.
Herbert Neale, b. Paston, Norfolk, 1898, labourer.
Herbert Rayner, b. Whitwell, Norfolk, 1907, team-man.
Mrs Rayner, b. Swanton Morley, Norfolk, c. 1900, f. labourer/-
    smallholder.
Jack Sadler, b. Titchwell, Norfolk, 1902, labourer/roadman.
William 'Bertie' Symonds, b. Briston, Norfolk, 1891, team-man.
*Sidney Watts, b. Happisburgh, Norfolk, 1889, fisherman. (This
    interview was carried out by Trevor Lummis and is deposited at the
    University of Essex.)
Arthur 'Taddy' Wright, b. Knapton, Norfolk, 1902, labourer.

C   Printed Sources

1 Newspapers

Commonweal (London)
Daily Herald (London)
Daylight (Norwich)
The Dereham and Fakenham Times (East Dereham)
Eastern Daily Press (Norwich)
Eastern Evening News (Norwich)
Eastern Star (Norwich)
Eastern Weekly Leader (Norwich)
Eastern Weekly Press (Norwich)
The Estates Magazine (London)
English Labourer's Chronicle (Leamington Spa)
Farmer and Stock Breeder (London)
The Labourer (Fakenham)
The Labour Gazette (London)
Labour Leader (London)
The Land Worker (London)
Mark Lane Express (London)
Morning Chronicle (London)
The New Leader (London)
New Times (Colchester)

The New Voice (London)
Norfolk Chronicle (Norwich)
Norfolk News (Norwich)
Norwich Mercury (Norwich)
People's Weekly Journal (Norwich)
Primitive Methodist Itinerant Preacher (London)
Primitive Methodist Magazine (London)
The Sword and the Shield (Norwich)
The Times (London)

2 British Parliamentary Papers

Royal Commission on Agriculture, England; Report of Mr Henry Rew on the County of Norfolk, PP 1895, XVII.

Royal Commission on the Depressed Condition of the Agricultural Interest, PP 1881, XVII.

First Report . . . on the Wages, Earnings and Condition of Employment of Agricultural Labourers in the United Kingdom, PP 1900, LXXXII.

Second Report . . . on the Wages, Earnings and Conditions of Employment in Agriculture, PP 1905, XCVII.

Report of the Departmental Committee on Agricultural Machinery, PP 1919, VIII.

The Agricultural Output of Great Britain 1908, PP 1912–13, X; 1925, PP 1927, XXV.

Sixth Report of the Children's Employment Commission, PP 1867, XVI.

Commission on the Employment of Children, Young Persons and Women in Agriculture, PP 1867–8, XVII.

Reports by Investigators on Wages and Conditions of Employment in Agriculture, PP 1919, IX.

Corn Production Bill, PP 1917–18, I.

Report of the Inter-Departmental Committee on Agricultural Tied Cottages, PP 1931–2, VI.

Report on the Decline in the Agricultural Population of Great Britain, 1881–1906, PP 1906, XCVI.

Census of England and Wales, 1841–1921.

Report of the Chief Registrar of Friendly Societies, PP 1895, XCI; PP 1907, LXXVIII; PP 1909, LXXIX; PP 1910, LXXXIII; PP 1911, LXXVI; PP 1912–13, LXXXII; PP 1916, XXIV; PP 1917–18, XXVII; PP 1918, X; PP 1919, XXXIX; PP 1920, XXXVII; PP 1921, XXVII; PP 1922, XVII; PP 1923, XIX.

First Report of Her Majesty's Commissioners for Inquiry into the Housing of the Working Classes, PP 1884–5, XXX.

Annual Report of the Inspector General of Recruiting, PP 1900, IX; PP 1902, X; PP 1903, XI; PP 1904, VIII; PP 1905, IX; PP 1906, XIV; PP 1907, IX; PP 1908, XI; PP 1909, X; PP 1910, LX; PP 1911, XLVI; PP 1912–13, LI.

Interim Report of His Majesty's Commissioners . . . into the Economic Prospects of Agriculture, PP 1919, VIII.

Royal Commission on Labour, The Agricultural Labourer, PP 1893–4, XXXV.

Royal Commission on Labour, The Agricultural Labourer, Report on the Poor Law Union of Swaffam, PP 1893–4, XXXV.

Report of the Committee appointed to inquire into the financial results of the occupation of agricultural land and the cost of living of rural workers, PP 1919, VIII.

Return of Owners of Land, PP 1874, LXXXII, Pts I and II.

Royal Commission on the Poor Laws and the Relief of Distress, PP 1910, XLVII.

Reconstruction Committee; Pt. 1 of the Report of the Agricultural Policy Sub-Committee, PP 1917–18, XVIII.

Ministry of Agriculture and Fisheries, *Report on the Sugar Beet Industry at Home and Abroad* (Economic Series no. 27), London, 1931.

3 Printed primary sources (excluding biography, autobiography and memoir)

Lord Addison, *A Policy for British Agriculture*, L.B.C. ed., London 1939.

W. Andrews, *Bygone Norfolk*, London 1898.

B.J. Armstrong, *A Norfolk Diary*, London 1948.

B.J. Armstrong (ed.), *Armstrong's Norfolk Diary. Further Passages from the Diary of the Rev. Benjamin John Armstrong*, London 1963.

H.J.D. Astley, *Memorials of Old Norfolk*, London 1908.

Viscount Astor and B. Seebohm Rowntree, *British Agriculture* (Pelican edn), Harmondsworth 1939.

R.N. Bacon, *Prize Report on the Agriculture of Norfolk*, London 1844.

A.H. Baverstock, *The English Agricultural Labourer*, London 1912.

A.H. Baverstock, *The Failure of the Church in the Villages*, London 1913.

Adrian Bell, *Corduroy*, London 1936.

Adrian Bell, *Silver Ley*, London 1936.

E.N. Bennett, *Problems of Village Life*, London 1914.

William Henry Bidwell, *The Annals of an East Anglian Bank*, Norwich 1900.

George Borrow, *Lavengro*, Everyman edn, London 1906.

Helen Dendy (afterwards Bosanquet), *Social Conditions in Provincial Towns*, London 1912.

G.F. Bosworth, *Agriculture and the Land*, London 1917.

Cloudesley Brereton, 'The Rise and Decline of Norfolk Farming', *English Review*, vol. 63, November 1936.

G.C. Brodrick, *English Land and English Landlords*, London 1881.

J. Browne, *History of Congregationalism and Memorials of the Churches in Norfolk and Suffolk*, London 1877.

J.B. Burne, *Parson and Peasant*, London 1891.

A.J. Burrows, *The Agricultural Depression*, London 1882.

James Caird, *English Agriculture in 1850–51*, London 1852.

Cambridge University Department of Agriculture, *Reports of the Farm Economics Branch* nos 1–22, Cambridge 1925–34.

Arthur Clayden, *The Revolt of the Field*, London 1874.

F. Clifford, *The Agricultural Lock Out of 1874*, Edinburgh and London 1875.

Christopher Davies, *Norfolk Broads and Rivers*, London 1883.

M.F. Davies, *Life in an English Village*, London 1909.

Dandy, *see* Bosanquet.

O. Jocelyn Dunlop, *The Farm Labourer. The History of a Modern Problem*, London 1913.

R.R. Enfield, *The Agricultural Crisis 1920–23*, London 1924.

Lord Eversley, 'The Decline in the Number of Agricultural Labourers in Britain', *Journal of the Royal Statistical Society*, LXX, 1907.

Montague Fordham, *The Rebuilding of Rural England*, London 1924.

A. Wilson Fox, 'Agricultural Wages in England and Wales during the Last Half Century', *Journal of the Royal Statistical Society*, LXVI, 1903.

John Glyde, Jun., *The Moral, Social and Religious Condition of Ipswich*, new edn, Wakefield 1971.

F.E. Green, *The Tyranny of the Countryside*, London 1913.

F.E. Green, *Can Farmers Pay Higher Wages?*, London n.d. but 1918.

F.E. Green, *A History of the English Agricultural Labourer, 1870–1920*, London 1920.

Edwin Grey, *Cottage Life in a Hertfordshire Village*, St Albans 1934.

H. Rider Haggard, *A Farmer's Year being his Commonplace Book for 1898*, London 1899.

H. Rider Haggard, *Rural England*, 2 vols, London 1902.

A.D. (later Sir Daniel) Hall, *A Pilgrimage of British Farming*, London 1913.

A.D. (later Sir Daniel) Hall, *Agriculture After the War*, London 1920.

I. Hannah, *The Heart of East Anglia*, London 1915.

H.D. Harben, *The Rural Problem*, London 1913.

H.T. Cozens Hardy, *Broad Norfolk*, Norwich 1893.

W. Hasbach, *A History of the English Agricultural Labourer*, London 1966, original edn London 1908.

C.B. Hawkins, *Norwich: a Social Survey*, London 1910.

Richard Heath, *The English Peasant*, London 1893.

J.J. Hissey, *A Tour in a Phaeton through the Eastern Counties*, London 1889.

Christopher Holdenby, *Folk of the Furrow*, London 1913.

F. Impey, *Three Acres and a Cow*, London 1886.

G.A. Jamieson, *The Present Agricultural Depression*, London 1885.

Jarrold's Illustrated Guide to Cromer and Neighbourhood, Norwich n.d. but ? 1894.

Richard Jefferies, *The Toilers of the Field*, London 1892.

Richard Jefferies, *Hodge and his Masters*, 2 vols, London 1966.

Augustus Jessopp, *Arcady for Better or Worse*, London, n.d. but 1886.

Augustus Jessopp, *The Trials of a Country Parson*, London 1890.

T.E. Kebbel, *The Agricultural Labourer*, new edn, London 1893.

Kelly's Directory of Norfolk, London 1896.

H.B. Kendall, *The History of the Primitive Methodist Church*, 2 vols, London 1911.

Labour's Appeal to the Nation, London 1923.

Labour's Appeal to the People, London 1922.

The Labour Party and the Countryside. A Statement of Policy with Regard to Agriculture and Rural Life, London, n.d. but 1922?

'A Lady Farmer', *Norfolk and the Squires, Clergy, Farmers and Labourers etc.*, Kings Lynn 1875.

The Land. The Report of the Land Enquiry Committee, Vol. 1 Rural, London 1913.

H.C. Long, *Business Aspects of Farming*, London 1925.

James Long, *Making the Most of the Land*, n.d. but c. 1912.

W. Hammond Long, 'Facets of Farm Labour and Wages, Mainly in the Eighteenth and Nineteenth Century', *Journal of the Royal Agricultural Society of England*, CXXXVI.

Primrose McConnell, *The Diary of a Working Farmer*, London 1906.

G.M. MacDermott, 'Agricultural Conditions in Norfolk', *Economic Review*, no. 24, 1914.

H.P. Mann, 'Life in an Agricultural Village in England', *Sociological Papers* 1, 1904.

William Marshall, *The Rural Economy of Norfolk*, 2 vols, London 1787.

George F. Millin, *Life in Our Village*, London 1891.

J.C. Morton, *Handbook of Farm Labour*, London 1961.

W.J. Moscrop, 'Report – The Farm – Prize Competition in Norfolk and Suffolk in 1886', *Journal of the Royal Agricultural Society of England, 2nd Series*, vol. 22.

National Agricultural Labourers' and Rural Workers' Union, *Song Book*, Norwich, n.d. but ? 1918.

A.H. Patterson, *From Hay Loft to Temple: the Story of Primitive Methodism in Yarmouth*, London 1903.

A.H. Patterson, *Man and Nature in the Broads*, London 1895.

Lt-Col. D.C. Pedder, *The Secret of Rural Depopulation*, Fabian Tracts no. 118, London 1904.

Lt-Col. D.C. Pedder, *Where Men Decay: A Survey of Present Rural Conditions*, London 1908.

Edwin A. Pratt. *The Transition in Agriculture*, London 1909.

C.S. Read, 'Recent Improvements in Norfolk Farming', *Journal of the Royal Agricultural Society of England*, XIX, 1858.

W. Richards, *Agricultural Distress*, London 1893.

J.E. Ritchie, *East Anglia: Personal Recollections and Historical Associations*, London 1883.

Joseph Ritson, *The Romance of Primitive Methodism*, London 1909.

B.S. Rowntree and M. Kendall, *How the Labourer Lives*, London 1913.

B.S. Rowntree, *The Labourer and the Land*, London 1914.

Ira D. Sankey, *Sacred Songs and Solos*, n.d. but cheap edition c. 1870.

J.W. Robertson Scott, 'The Farm Labourers' £90,000 Nest Egg', in *The World's Word*, November 1922.

Ernest Selley, *Village Trades Unions in Two Centuries*, London 1919.

E. Selley and George Dallas, *Farm Worker's Fight for a Living Wage*, London, n.d. ? 1920.

A.G. Street, *Farmer's Glory*, London 1932.

A.G. Street, *The Gentleman of the Party*, London 1936.

C. Stubbs, *Village Politics*, London 1878.

C. Stubbs. *The Land and the Labourers*, London 1884.

Rev. William C. Tonks, *Victory in the Villages. The History of the Brinkworth Circuit*, Aberdare 1907.

Christopher Turnor, *Land Problems and National Welfare*, London 1911.

Christopher Turnor, *Our Food Supply. Perils and Remedies*, London 1916.

Christopher Turnor, *The Land and its Problems*, London 1921.

T. Fisher Unwin, *The Hungry Forties. Life Under the Bread Tax*, London 1904.

W. White, *Norfolk Directory*, London 1883.

R. Patrick Wright, *The Standard Cyclopedia of Modern Agriculture and Rural Economy*, 12 vols, London 1908.

4 Biography, autobiography and memoirs

Mosa Anderson, *Noel Buxton: a Life*, London 1952.

William Antliff, *The Life of Hugh Bourne*, new edn, London 1892.

Joseph Arch, *Joseph Arch; The Story of his life, Told by Himself*, London 1898.

George Baldry, *The Rabbitskin Cap*, Ipswich 1974.

Joyce Bellamy and John Saville, *Dictionary of Labour Biography*, London 1972.

M. Blomefield, *Nuts in the Rookery*, London 1946.

J.C. Buckmaster (ed.) *A Village Politician. The Life Story of John Buckly*, London 1897.

H.H. Bullard, *St Harry Bullard*, Norwich 1902.

V.A. De Bunsen, *Charles Rodern Buxton*, London 1948.

Cox' County Who's Who Series. Norfolk, Suffolk and Cambridgeshire 1912, London 1912.

M.L. Davies, *Life as We Have Known It*, London 1931.

Major H.C. Dent, *The Reminiscences of a Cromer Doctor*, Holt, n.d. but 1923.

George Edwards, *From Crow Scaring to Westminster*, London 1922.

Howard Evans, *Radical Fights of Forty Years*, London 1913.

J.R. Fisher, *Clare Sewell Read, 1826–1905*, Hull 1975.

Ernest Gaskell, *Norfolk Leaders Social and Political*, London, n.d. but c. 1910.

H. Rider Haggard, *The Days of My Life*, London 1926.

S. Cozens-Hardy, *Memorials of William Hardy Cozens-Hardy of Letheringsett*, Norwich 1936.

Michael Home, *Autumn Fields*, London 1944.

Michael Home, *Winter Harvest. A Norfolk Boyhood*, London 1969.

Pamela Horn, *Joseph Arch*, Kineton 1971.

O. Jackson, *The Spiritual Hero; or the Life of Mr. William Green Bellman*, London 1858.

Col. Weston Jarvis, *Jottings From an Active Life*, London 1928.

C.R. Jones, *Some Norfolk Worthies*, London 1899.

L.E. Jones, *A Victorian Boyhood*, London 1955.

Robert Key, *The Gospel Among the Masses*, London 1872.

'The King of the Norfolk Poachers', *I Walked by Night*, ed. L. Rider Haggard, Ipswich 1974.

Fred Kitchen, *Brother to the Ox*, London 1940.

Sydney H. Long (ed.), *The Autobiography of Sir Peter Eade M.D., F.R.C.P.*, London 1916.

C. Lucas, *The Fenman's World: Memoirs of a Fenland Physician*, Norwich 1930.

Rev. Cannon W.H. Marcon, *The Reminiscences of a Norfolk Parson*, Holt 1934.

Sybil Marshall, *Fenland Chronicle*, paperback edn, Cambridge 1980.

R.H. Mottram, *Bowler Hat: A Last Glance at the Old Country Banking*, London 1940.

Rev. D. Newton, *True to Principle: The Story of John Kent, An Agricultural Labourer in the County of Norfolk*, London, n.d. but c. 1880.

Norfolk Federation of Women's Institutes, *Within Living Memory*, Ipswich 1972.

W.T. Pike (ed.), *Norfolk and Suffolk in East Anglia: Contemporary Biographies*, Brighton 1911.

Arthur Randell, *Sixty Years a Fenman,,* London 1966.

Arthur Randell, *Fenland Railwaymen*, London 1968.

Arthur Randell, *Fenland Molecatcher*, London 1970.

Robert C. Richardson, *Some Fell on Stony Ground*, Wymondham 1978.

James Ewing Ritchie, *Christopher Crayon's Recollections*, London 1898.

Josiah Sage, *The Memoirs of Josiah Sage*, London 1951.

A.M.W. Stirling, *Coke of Norfolk and his Friends*, new edn, London 1912.

W.R. Ward (ed.), *The Early Correspondence of Jabez Bunting 1820–29*, Camden Fourth Series, vol. 11, London 1972.

Who's Who (1918), London 1918.

Frederick C. Wigby, *Just a Country Boy*, Wymondham 1976.

Henry Williamson, *The Story of a Norfolk Farm*, London 1941.

B. Knyvel Wilson *Norfolk Tales and Memories*, Norwich 1930.

Sir Richard Winfrey, *Great Men and Others I have Met*, Northampton 1943.

Sir Richard Winfrey, *Leaves from My Life*, Kings Lynn 1936.

D   Secondary Sources

1 Published

Peter Ambrose, *The Quiet Revolution: Social Change in a Sussex Village 1871–1971*, London 1974.

Patrick Armstrong, *The Changing Landscape. The History and Ecology of Man's Impact on the Face of East Anglia*, Lavenham 1975.

R. Arnold, 'The "Revolt of the Field" in Kent', *Past and Present*, no. 64.

Roderick Aya, *The Missed Revolution*, Amsterdam 1975.

Michael Barker, *Gladstone and Radicalism*, London 1975.

W.N. Barett, *More Tales from the Fens*, London 1964.

W.H. Barrett and R.P. Garrod, *East Anglian Folklore*, London 1976.

John Bateman, *The Great Landowners of Great Britain and Ireland*, Leicester 1971.

Colin Bell and Howard Newby, 'The Sources of Variation in Agricultural Workers' Images of Society', *Sociological Review*, vol. 21, no. 2, 1973.

J.R. Bellerby, *Agriculture and Industry: Relative Income*, London 1956.

Sir W.H. Beveridge, *British Food Control*, London 1928.

Clyde Binfield, *So Down to Prayers, Studies in English Nonconformity 1780–1820*, London 1977.

Ronald Blythe, *Akenfield*, Harmondsworth 1972.

Harold Bonnett, *Farming with Steam*, Princes Risborough, 1974.

B.J. Briggs, 'The Disciplined Society. Early Victorian Preachers in the Retford Wesleyan Circuit', *Transactions of the Thoroton Society of Nottinghamshire*, vol. LXXV, 1971.

David Butcher, *The Driftermen*, Reading 1979.

David Butcher, *The Trawlermen*, Reading 1980.

J. Bygott, *Eastern England: Some Aspects of its Geography with Special Reference to Economic Significance*, London 1923.

Ian Carter, 'Class and Culture among Farm Servants in the North East, 1840–1914' in A. Allan MacLaren (ed.), *Social Class in Scotland Past and Present*, Edinburgh 1976.

Ian Carter, *Farmlife in Northeast Scotland 1840–1914. The Poor Man's Country*, Edinburgh 1979.

M.J. Carter, *Peasants and Poachers*, Ipswich 1980.

J.D. Chambers and G.E. Mingay, *The Agricultural Revolution 1750–1880*, London 1966.

A. Charlesworth, *Social Protest in Rural Society, the Spatial Diffusion of the Captain Swing Disturbances 1830–31*, Norwich 1979.

E.J.T. Collins, 'Harvest Technology and Labour Supply in Britain 1790–1870', *Economic History Review*, 2nd series, XXII, 1969.

E.J.T. Collins, 'Migrant Labour in British Agriculture in the Nineteenth Century', *Economic History Review*, 2nd Series, vol. XXIX, no. 1, 1976.

Ruth Crichton, *Commuters' Village*, London 1964.

P.A. David, 'Labour Productivity in English Agriculture, 1850–1914:

Some Quantitative Evidence on Regional Differences', *Economic History Review*, 2nd series, XXIII, 1970.

Donald Davie, *A Gathered Church: The Literature of the English Dissenting Interest 1780–1930*, London 1978.

P.E. Dewey, 'Agricultural Labour Supply in England and Wales during the First World War', *Economic History Review*, 2nd series, vol. XXVIII, no. 1, February 1975.

P.E. Dewey, 'Government Provision of Farm Labour in England and Wales, 1914–18', *Agricultural History Review*, vol. 27, pt 2, 1979.

Anne Digby, *Pauper Palaces*, London 1978.

Roy Douglas, *Land, People and Politics: A History of the Land Question in the United Kingdom, 1878–1952*, London 1976.

J.P.D. Dunbabin, 'The Incidence and Organisation of Agricultural Trades Unionism in the 1870's', *Agricultural History Review*, vol. 16, 1968.

J.P.D. Dunbabin, 'The "Revolt of the Field": The Agricultural Labourers' Movement in the 1870s', *Past and Present*, no. 26, 1963.

J.P.D. Dunbabin, *Rural Discontent in Nineteenth Century Britain*, London 1974.

Ginette Dunn, *The Fellowship of Song: Popular Singing Traditions in East Suffolk*, London 1980.

Bertram Edwards, *The Burston School Strike*, London 1974.

J.K. Edwards, 'The Decline of the Norwich Textiles Industry', *Yorkshire Bulletin of Economic and Social Research*, vol. 16, no. 1, 1964.

J.K. Edwards, 'Chartism in Norwich', *Yorkshire Bulletin of Economic and Social Research*, vol. 19, no. 2, 1967.

H.V. Emy, *Liberals, Radicals and Social Politics 1892–1914*, Cambridge 1973.

Martha Winburn England and John Sparrow, *Hymns Unbidden: Donne, Herbert, Blake, Emily Dickinson and the Hymnographers*, New York, 1966.

E.J. Evans, *The Contentious Tithe*, London 1976.

George Ewart Evans, *Ask the Fellows that Cut the Hay*, London 1956.

George Ewart Evans, *The Farm and the Village*, London 1969.

George Ewart Evans, *Where Beards Wag All, The Relevance of the Oral Tradition*, London 1970.

George Ewart Evans, *The Days That We Have Seen*, London 1975.

George Ewart Evans, *From the Mouths of Men*, London 1976.

A.M. Everitt, 'Country Carriers in the Nineteenth Century', *Journal of Transport History*, n.s. III, 3.

A. Everitt, *The Pattern of Rural Dissent: The Nineteenth Century*, Leicester 1972.

Sally Festig, *Fishermen: a Community Living from the Sea*, Newton Abbot 1977.

T.W. Fletcher, 'The Great Depression of English Agriculture, 1873–96', *Economic History Review*, 2nd series, XIII, 1961.

Ronald Frankenberg, *Village on the Border*, London 1957.

Margaret Fuller, *West Country Friendly Societies*, Reading 1964.

G.E. Fussell, *The Farmer's Tools*, new edn, London 1981.

A.D. Gilbert, *Religion and Society in Industrial England*, London 1976.

Mark Girourand, *The Victorian Country House*, Oxford 1971.

John F. Glasier, 'English Nonconformity and the Decline of Liberalism', *American Historical Review*, vol. LXIII(2), 1958.

P.J. Goodrich, *The Story of Trunch*, Cambridge 1939.

E.A. Goodwyn, *Cromer Past*, Beccles, n.d. but 1980?

E.G. Grant and P.G. Bigmore, *Rural Settlement in Norfolk*, London 1974.

D.B. Grigg, 'The World's Agricultural Labour Force 1800–1970', *Geography*, LX, 3.

R. Groves, *Sharpen the Sickle; the History of the Farmworkers' Union*, NUAAW edn, London 1949.

Helen Gurden, 'Primitive Methodism and Agricultural Trade Unionism in Warwickshire, 1872–75', *Bulletin of the Society for the Study of Labour History*, 22, 1976.

J.L. and Barbara Hammond, *The Village Labourer*, paperback edn, London 1966.

Clement Harris, *Hennage, A Social System in Miniature*, New York 1974.

M.A. Havinden, *Estate Villages, A Study of the Berkshire Villages of Ardington and Lockinge*, London 1966.

S. Heiseler, 'The History and Development of Agricultural and Horticultural Co-operatives in East Anglia', *Oxford Agricultural Studies*, VI.

E.J. Hobsbawm, *Primitive Rebels*, Manchester 1959.

E.J. Hobsbawm and George Rude, *Captain Swing*, London 1969.

W.C. Hodgson, *The Herring and its Fishery*, London 1957.

B.A. Holderness, ' "Open" and "Close" Parishes in England in the Eighteenth and Nineteenth Centuries', *Agricultural History Review*, vol. 20, pt II, 1970.

B.A. Holderness, 'Landlords' Capital Formation in East Anglia, 1750–1870', *Economic History Review*, 25, 1972.

Patricia Hollis (ed.), *Pressure from Without*, London 1974.

Pamela Horn, 'Agricultural Trade Unionism and Emigration 1872–1881', *Historical Journal*, XV, 1, 1972.

Pamela Horn, 'Agricultural Trade Unionism in Buckinghamshire 1872–85', *Records of Buckinghamshire*, XIX, 3, 1973.

Pamela Horn, 'Agricultural Trades Unionism in Oxfordshire, 1872–81', *Oxfordshire Records Society*, vol. XLVIII, 1974.

Pamela Horn, *Labouring Life in the Victorian Countryside*, Dublin 1976.

Pamela Horn, *The Rural World. Social Change in the English Countryside 1780–1850*, London 1980.

P.L.R. Horn, 'The Warwickshire Agricultural and General Workers' Union 1893–97', *Midland History*, vol. 1, no. 4, 1975.

George Houston, 'Labour Relations in Scottish Agriculture before 1870', *Agricultural History Review*, VI, 1955.

Janet Howarth, 'The Liberal Revival in Northamptonshire 1880–1895', *Historical Journal*, vol. XII, 1969.

Alun Howkins, 'Economic Crime and Class Law: Poaching and the

Game Laws, 1840–1880' in Sandra E. Burman and Barbara Harrell
Bond (eds), *The Imposition of Law*, New York 1979.

Alun Howkins, 'Television History: Bread or Blood', *History Workshop
Journal*, no. 12, 1981.

Kenneth Hudson, *Patriotism with Profit*, London 1972.

E.H. Hunt, 'Labour Productivity in English Agriculture, 1850–1914',
Economic History Review, 2nd series, XX, 1967.

K.E. Hunt, *Changes in British Agriculture: a Background for a Study of
Present Conditions*, Oxford 1952.

Richard Hyman, *The Workers' Union*, Oxford 1971.

K.S. Inglis, *Churches and the Working Class in Victorian England*, London
1963.

W.P. Jeffock, *Agricultural Politics 1915–1935*, Ipswich 1935.

Inez Jenkins, *A History of the Women's Institute Movement of England and
Wales*, Oxford 1953.

C.B. Jewson, *The Baptists in Norfolk*, London 1957.

C.B. Jewson, *Jacobin City. A Portrait of Norwich 1788–1802*, Glasgow
1975.

Allan Jobson, *Suffolk Yesterdays*, London 1944.

Allan Jobson, *This Suffolk*, London 1948.

Allan Jobson, *An Hour Glass on the Run*, London 1959.

R.S. Joby, *Forgotten Railways of East Anglia*, Newton Abbot 1977.

R.W. Johnson, 'The Nationalisation of English Rural Politics: Norfolk
South West, 1945–1970', *Parliamentary Affairs*, vol. XXVI, no. 1
(Winter 1972–3).

Cyril Jolly, *History of the East Dereham Methodist Circuit*, Wymondham
1955.

Cyril Jolly, *The Spreading Flame. The Coming of Methodism to Norfolk
1751–1811*, Gressenhall, n.d. but 1973.

D.J.V. Jones, 'The Poacher: A Study in Victorian Crime and Protest',
Historical Journal, 22, 4, 1979.

David Jones, 'Thomas Campbell Foster and the Rural Labourer:
Incendiarism in East Anglia in the 1840s', *Social History*, no. 1, 1976.

E.L. Jones, *Agriculture and the Industrial Revolution*, Oxford 1975.

E.L. Jones, 'The Changing Basis of English Agricultural Prosperity
1853–73', *Agricultural History Review*, vol. X, 1962–3.

E.L. Jones and G.E. Mingay (eds), *Land, Labour and Population in the
Industrial Revolution*, London 1967.

Gareth Stedman Jones, *Outcast London*, Oxford 1971.

Gwyn Jones, *Rural Life*, London 1973.

Barbara Kerr, *Bound to the Soil*, London 1968.

R.W. Ketton-Cremer, *Forty Norfolk Essays*, Norwich 1961.

R.W. Ketton-Cremer, *Felbrigg: The Story of a House*, London 1962.

David Lockwood, 'The Sources of Variation in Working-Class Images of
Society', *Sociological Review*, vol. 14, no. 3, 1966.

J. Lovell, *Stevedores and Dockers*, London 1969.

Trevor Lummis, 'The Occupational Community of East Anglian
Fishermen', *British Journal of Sociology*, vol. XXVIII, no. 1, March
1977.

R.W. Malcolmson, *Popular Recreations in English Society 1700–1850*, Cambridge 1973.

R.W. Malcolmson, *Life and Labour in England 1700–1780*, London 1981.

E.W. Martin, *The Shearers and the Shorn*, London 1965.

Susanna Wade Martins, *A Great Estate at Work: the Holkham Estate and its Inhabitants in the Nineteenth Century*, Cambridge 1980.

Karl Marx, *Capital*, 3 vols, Moscow 1957–9 edn.

Karl Marx and Frederick Engels, *The Communist Manifesto*, in *Selected Works*, 1 vol. edn, Moscow 1968.

Joan Maynard (ed.), *A Hundred Years of Farmworkers' Struggle*, Nottingham 1974.

D. Metcalf, 'Labour Productivity in English Agriculture 1850–1914', *Economic History Review*, 2nd series, XXII, 1969.

R.K. Middlemass, *Politics in Industrial Society*, London 1979.

Sir T.H. Middleton, *Food Production in War*, London 1923.

D.R. Mills (ed.), *English Rural Communities: The Impact of a Specialised Economy*, London 1973.

D.R. Mills, *Lord and Peasant in Nineteenth Century Britain*, London 1980.

G.E. Mingay, *Enclosure and the Small Farmer in the Age of the Industrial Revolution*, London 1968.

G.E. Mingay, *The Gentry: The Rise and Fall of a Ruling Class*, London 1976.

G.E. Mingay, *Rural Life in Victorian England*, London 1977.

G.E. Mingay (ed.), *The Victorian Countryside*, 2 vols, London 1981.

Ministry of Agriculture, Fisheries and Food, *A Century of Agricultural Statistics*, London 1968.

B.R. Mitchell and Phyllis Deane, *Abstract of British Historical Statistics*, Cambridge 1962.

David Hoseason Morgan, *Harvesters and Harvesting 1840–1900*, London 1982.

P.B. Munsche, *Gentlemen and Poachers. The English Game Laws 1671–1831*, Cambridge, 1981.

Howard Newby, 'The Low Earnings of the Agricultural Worker: a Sociological Approach', *Journal of Agricultural Economics*, vol. XXIII, no. 1, 1972.

Howard Newby, 'Agricultural Workers and the Class Structure', *Sociological Review*, vol. 20, no. 3, 1975.

Howard Newby, 'Deference and the Agricultural Worker', *Sociological Review*, vol. 23, no. 1, 1978.

Howard Newby, 'The Deferential Dialectic', *Comparative Studies in Society and History*, vol. 17, no. 2, 1975.

Howard Newby, *The Deferential Worker*, Harmondsworth 1979.

Howard Newby, *Green and Pleasant Land? Social Change in Rural England*, Harmondsworth 1979.

Howard Newby, Colin Bell, David Rose and Peter Saunders, *Property, Paternalism and Power*, London 1978.

H. Richard Niebuhr, *The Social Sources of Denominationalism*, Cleveland, Ohio, 1957.

Emmet O'Connor, 'Agrarian Unrest and the Labour Movement in County Waterford, 1917–23', *Saothar*, 6, 1980.

Richard Olney, *Lincolnshire Politics 1832–1885*, Oxford 1973.

R.J. Olney (ed.), *Labouring Life on the Lincolnshire Wolds: A Study of Binbrook in the Mid-Nineteenth Century*, Sleaford 1975.

Christabel S. Orwin and Edith H. Whetham, *History of British Agriculture 1846–1914*, new edn, 1971.

Roy Palmer, *The Painful Plough*, Cambridge 1973.

R.A.C. Parker, 'Coke of Norfolk and the Agricultural Revolution', *Economic History Review*, 2nd series, vol. 8, 1955–6.

R.A.C. Parker, *Coke of Norfolk. A Financial and Agricultural Study*, Oxford 1975.

Luisa Passerini, 'Work, Ideology and Consensus under Italian Fascism', *History Workshop Journal*, no. 8, 1971.

A.J. Peacock, *Bread or Blood*, London 1965.

A.J. Peacock, ' "The Revolt of the Field" in East Anglia' in Lionel M. Munby (ed.), *The Luddites and Other Essays*, London 1971.

Henry Pelling, *The Social Geography of British Elections 1885–1910*, London 1967.

Richard Perren, 'The Landlord and Agricultural Transformation 1870–1900', *Agricultural History Review*, vol. 18, 1970.

P.J. Perry, *British Agriculture 1875–1914*, London 1973.

P.J. Perry, *British Farming in the Great Depression, 1870–1914*, Newton Abbot 1974.

Alessandro Portelli, 'The Peculiarities of Oral History', *History Workshop Journal*, no. 12, 1979.

Enid Porter, *The Folklore of East Anglia*, London 1974.

Roland E. Prothero (Lord Ernle), *English Farming Past and Present*, London 1912.

Arthur Redford, *Labour Migration in England 1800–1850*, new edn rev. and ed. W.H. Chaloner, Manchester 1976.

N. Riches, *The Agricultural Revolution in Norfolk*, London 1936.

Ben Ripper, *Ribbons from the Pedlar's Pack*, Downham Market 1972.

David Roberts, *Paternalism in Early Victorian England*, London 1981.

Jean Robin, *Elmdon; Continuity and Change in a North-West Essex Village 1861–64*, Cambridge 1980.

David Rose, Peter Saunders, Howard Newby, Colin Bell, 'Ideologies of Property: A Case Study', *Sociological Review*, vol. 24, no. 4, 1976.

A.K. Russell, 'Laying the Charges for the Landslide: the Revival of Liberal Party Organisation 1902–4', in A.J.A. Morris (ed.), *Edwardian Radicalism 1900–14*, London 1974.

Rex C. Russell, *The 'Revolt of the Field' in Lincolnshire*, Lincoln n.d. but 1956.

R. Samuel (ed.), *Village Life and Labour*, London 1975.

J. Saville, *Rural Depopulation in England and Wales 1851–1951*, London 1957.

A.C. Savin, *Cromer in the County of Norfolk; a Modern History*, Holt 1937.

N.A.D. Scotland, 'Methodism and the "Revolt of the Field" in East Anglia 1872–96', *Wesley Historical Society Proceedings* 41 (pts 1 and 2), 1981.

Nigel Scotland, 'Zacharias Walker (1843–1900) Norfolk Radical and Agricultural Trade Unionist', *Norfolk Archaeology*, vol. XXXVII, pt II, 1979.

Martin Seabrook, 'Cowmanship', *Farmer's Weekly*, 23 December 1977.

M.F. Seabrook, 'Managing and Motivating the Dairy Worker', unpublished paper given at Scottish Dairy Conference 1977.

Michael Friend Serpell, *A History of the Lophams*, Chichester 1980.

Robert Simper, *Traditions of East Anglia*, Ipswich 1980.

Norman Smedley, *Life and Tradition in Suffolk and North-East Essex*, London 1976.

E. Lorrain Smith, *Go East for a Farm: A Study of Rural Migration*, Oxford 1932.

L. Marion Springhall, *Labouring Life in Norfolk Villages*, London 1936.

G. Stammers, *My Village* (Hempnall), Norwich 1968.

L. Dudley Stamp (ed.), *The Land of Britain: the Report of the Land Utilization Survey of Britain, Pt 70 Norfolk*, by John E. Mosby, London 1938.

Peter J.R. Stibbons, *Crabs and Shannocks*, Cromer, n.d. but 1975?

Marilyn Strathern, *Kinship at the Core*, Cambridge 1981.

E.R. Suffling, *The Annals of an East Coast Village, Hasborou'*, Happisburgh 1910.

Swanton Morely Methodist Chapel 1868–1968, Centenary Booklet, East Dereham 1968.

Joan Thirsk (ed.), *The Agrarian History of England and Wales, IV: 1500–1640*, Cambridge 1967.

Joan Thirsk and Jean Imray, *Suffolk Farming in the Nineteenth Century*, Ipswich 1958.

E.P. Thompson, *The Making of the English Working Class*, Harmondsworth 1968.

E.P. Thompson, 'The Moral Economy of the English Crown in the Eighteenth Century', *Past and Present*, no. 50, 1971.

F.M.L. Thompson, *English Landed Society in the Nineteenth Century*, London 1963.

F.M.L. Thompson, 'The Land Market in the Nineteenth Century' in W.E. Minchinton (ed.), *Essays in Agrarian History*, vol. II, Newton Abbot 1968.

F.M.L. Thompson, 'The Second Agricultural Revolution, 1815–1880', *Economic History Review*, 2nd series, XXI, 1968.

Paul Thompson, *The Voice of the Past: Oral History*, Oxford 1978.

Frank Tice, *The History of Methodism in Cambridge*, London 1966.

Charles Chenevix Trench, *The Poacher and the Squire*, London 1967.

J.A. Venn, 'The Economy of a Norfolk Parish in 1783 and at the Present Time', *Economic History*, 1, 1926–9.

John Walter and Keith Wrightson, 'Dearth and the Social Order in Early Modern England', *Past and Present*, no. 71, 1976.

M.D.G. Wanklyn (ed.), *Landownership and Power in the Regions*, Wolverhampton 1979.

Eugene Weber, *Peasants into Frenchmen*, London 1979.

Max Weber, *The Protestant Ethic and the Spirit of Capitalism*, London 1930.

Roger Wells, 'The Development of the English Rural Proletariat and Social Protest 1700–1850', *Journal of Peasant Studies*, VI, 2, 1980.

P.A. Welsbury, 'Church and People in Victorian Ipswich', *Church Quarterly Review*, CLXIV, 1963.

Edith H. Whetham, *The Agrarian History of England and Wales, Vol. VIII, 1914–39*, Cambridge 1978.

Edith H. Whetham, 'Sectoral Advance in English Agriculture, 1850–1880: a Summary', *Agricultural History Review*, vol. 16, 1968.

Edith H. Whetham, 'The Agriculture Act, 1920 and its Repeal – the "Great Betrayal" ', *Agricultural History Review*, vol. 22, 1974.

Jane White, *Norfolk Child*, London 1978.

Martin J. Wiener, *English Culture and the Decline of the Industrial Spirit*, Cambridge 1981.

Raymond Williams, *The Country and the City*, London 1973.

W.M. Williams, *The Sociology of an English Village: Gosforth*, London 1956.

W.M. Williams, *A West Country Village: Ashworthy*, London 1963.

Bryan R. Wilson (ed.), *Patterns of Sectarianism*, London 1967.

Michael Winstanley, *Life in Kent at the Turn of the Twentieth Century*, Folkestone 1978.

M. Winter, 'Job Satisfaction, Work Motivation and the Need for a New Direction in Agricultural Labour Science', *Journal of Agricultural Labour Science*, vol. 7, 1978.

Eileen and Stephen Yeo (eds), *Popular Culture and Class Conflict, 1590–1914*, Brighton 1981.

Arthur Young, *General View of the Agriculture of Norfolk* (1804), rep. Newton Abbot 1969.

John Young, *Farming in East Anglia*, London 1967.

Kenneth Young, *Chapel*, London 1972.

2 Unpublished

S.W. Amos, 'Social Discontent and Agrarian Disturbances in Essex, 1795–1850', unpublished MA thesis, University of Durham, 1969.

John Archer, 'The Myth and Reality of the Norfolk Incendiary, 1830–1870', unpublished paper given at East Anglian History Workshop, 4 December 1976.

Caroline M. Baker, 'Homedwellers and Foreigners: the Seasonal Labour Force in Kentish Agriculture', unpublished MPhil thesis, University of Kent 1979.

J.C.G. Binfield, 'Nonconformity in the Eastern Counties', unpublished PhD thesis, University of Cambridge 1965.

Felicity B. Carlton, ' "A Substantial and Sterling Friend to the Labouring Man": the Kent and Sussex Labourers' Union', unpublished MPhil thesis, University of Sussex 1978.

L. Caroe, 'Urban Change in East Anglia in the nineteenth century', unpublished PhD thesis, University of Cambridge 1966.

E.J.T. Collins, 'Harvest Technology and Labour Supply in Britain 1790–1870', unpublished PhD thesis, University of Nottingham 1970.

P.E. Dewey, 'Farm Labour in Wartime: The Relationship between Agricultural Labour Supply and Food Production in Great Britain during 1914–18', unpublished PhD thesis, University of Reading 1978.

A. Digby, 'The Operation of the Poor Law in the Social and Economic Life of Nineteenth Century Norfolk', unpublished PhD thesis, University of East Anglia 1972.

Julian Harber, 'Rural Incendiarism in Suffolk 1840–45', unpublished MA thesis, University of Warwick 1972.

Rev. John Penrode Homer, 'The Influence of Methodism on the Social Structure and Culture of Rural Northumberland from 1820 to 1914', unpublished MA thesis, University of Newcastle 1971.

P.L.R. Horn, 'Agricultural Labourers' Trades Unions in Four Midland Counties (1860–1900)', unpublished PhD thesis, University of Leicester 1968.

A.S. Kussmaul, 'Servants in Husbandry in Early-Modern England', unpublished PhD thesis, University of Toronto 1978.

Clifford John Lines, 'The Development and Location of the Specialist Agricultural Engineering Industry with Special Reference to East Anglia', unpublished MSc thesis, University of London 1961.

Michael Madden, 'The National Union of Agricultural Workers 1906–1956 (A Study in the Development of the Policies of Leadership)', unpublished BLitt thesis, University of Oxford 1956.

B. Marsh, 'The Agricultural Labour Force in England and Wales in 1851', unpublished MPhil thesis, University of Kent 1977.

F.D. Mills, 'The National Union of Agricultural Workers', unpublished PhD thesis, Reading 1965.

A.F. Mutch, 'Agricultural Labour in the North-West c. 1870–1920', unpublished PhD thesis, University of Manchester 1980.

James Obelkevich, 'Religion and Rural Society in South Lindsey, 1825–75', unpublished PhD thesis, Columbia University 1971.

Nigel Adrian Scotland, 'The Role of Methodism in the Origin and Development of the Revolt of the Field in Lincolnshire, Norfolk and Suffolk 1872–96', unpublished PhD thesis, University of Aberdeen 1975.

K.D.M. Snell, 'The Standard of Living, Social Relations, the Family and Labour Mobility in South-Eastern and Western Counties c. 1700–1860', unpublished PhD thesis, University of Cambridge 1980.

L. Marion Springhall, 'The Norfolk Agricultural Labourer, 1834–1884. A Study in Social and Economic History', unpublished PhD thesis, University of London 1935.

Rex Stedman, 'Vox Populi:The Norfolk Newspaper Press, 1760–1900', unpublished FLA thesis 1971.

William I. Wilks, 'Jesse Collings and the "Back to the Land" Movement', unpublished MA thesis, University of Birmingham 1971.

Index

This index is designed to take the readers to important references rather than being a list of all names, places, etc. in the book. As the word 'labourer' appears on almost every page there is no reference or entry under that word.

National Agricultural Labourers'
Union (1872–96): general, 57–9,
68–9; East Dereham District, 67–72;
membership, 68–9; politics, 71–3;
strikes, 69–70; Swaffham District, 67
National Agricultural Labourers'
Union (1911–17), 111*ff.*
National Agricultural Party (United
Agriculture Party), 150, 152, 175
National Agricultural Union (Lord
Winchelsea's Union), 145, 151
National Farmers' Union, 130–1, 139,
145, 147, 152, 156, 160, 162–3, 165,
166, 173
National Federation of Discharged and
Demobilised Sailors and Soldiers,
128
National Union of Agricultural and
Allied Workers, 176*ff.*
National Union of Land Workers, 150,
152
National Union of Railwaymen, 111,
119–20, 127, 128, 171
Nicholls, George, 87–8, 89, 95, 100–2,
109
Norfolk and Norwich Amalgamated
Labourers' Union, 76–9; disputes,
77; membership, 76
Norfolk Federal Union, 74–6
Norfolk Small Holdings Syndicate, 81
Norgate, William (St Faiths), 91, 96
Northrepps, 18
North Walsham, 7, 85–6, 87–90, 108,
127, 158, 170
Norwich, 14, 40, 56; labour move-
ment, 99, 110, 112; unemployment,
134

Octagon Chapel, 40
Overman, Henry, 131, 132

Passive resistance campaign, 84–5
Paston, 165
Pearce, Archibald (Hingham), 65
Pearson, De Vere, Dr, 127
Peel, Sam (Wells), 139, 144–7, 148,
149, 150–1, 169, 175
picketing (1923), 163–8
piece work, 25–9
Pightle, John (Erpingham), 87
police, 34, 98, 166–7
Primitive Methodist Connexion:
decline of radicalism, 54–6, 91–2;

East Dereham Circuit, 45–8; and
friendly societies, 51–2; general, 42,
46–7; Norfolk, general, 43–4; North
Walsham, 43; and radicalism, 48–51,
52–4; Reepham, 43–4; and trades
unions, 47–9
pubs, 33–4, 179–80
Purchase, J., 150

Quantrill, Jack, 173

Rayner, Mrs (Swanton Morley), 92, 93
Read, Clare Swell, 2, 83
Reeder, David (Elsing), 64, 67
Reepham, 43
Ringer, E.H., 168
Ringer, Womack William, 16, 140–4,
148–9, 171
Ringland, 33
Ringstead, 174–5
Rix, George (Swanton Morley), 52, 54,
56, 63, 64, 65, 71, 73–4, 75–6, 80,
180
Roberts, G.H., 85, 104, 105, 112,
124–5
Runton, 17

Sadler, Jack (Titchwell), 140–1
Sage, Josiah (Kenninghall), 87, 91
seasonal conflict, 21–30
Sedgeford, 94–5, 143, 174
Selbourne Committee, 121–2
Sewell, Fred (Sedgeford), 141–2, 174
shepherds, 20
Smith, Walter (Cossey), 102, 103, 110,
124, 149
Smith, William (Wymondham), 102
socialism, 105–9
Socialist League, 96, 105
soldiers and agricultural work, 118–19
South Norfolk by-election (1920), 128
Southrepps, 165
Spilling, James, 61–2
Sprowston, 56
Stalham, 112
St Faiths, 77; strike (1910–11), 96–102,
125; RDC, 136, 137
strikes (see also under union names and
villages): harvest, 27–9, 70, 71; piece
work, 25, 27; others, 70, 77, 80–1,
94, 96, 113, 140–4; West Norfolk
(1913–14), 114–16
Sugar beet, 7, 104